Sociology of "Developing Societies"
Central America

Sociology of "Developing Societies"
General Editor: Teodor Shanin

THEMATIC VOLUMES

INTRODUCTION TO THE SOCIOLOGY OF "DEVELOPING SOCIETIES"
Hamza Alavi and Teodor Shanin

SOCIALIST "DEVELOPING SOCIETIES"?
(in preparation)

THEORIES OF SOCIAL TRANSFORMATION
(in preparation)

REGIONAL VOLUMES

SOUTH ASIA
Hamza Alavi and John Harriss

SUB-SAHARAN AFRICA
Chris Allen and Gavin Williams

LATIN AMERICA
Eduardo P. Archetti, Paul Cammack and Bryan R. Roberts

THE MIDDLE EAST
Talal Asad and Roger Owen

CENTRAL AMERICA
Jan L. Flora and Edelberto Torres-Rivas

SOUTHEAST ASIA
John G. Taylor and Andrew Turton

Sociology of "Developing Societies" Central America

edited by Jan L. Flora
and Edelberto Torres-Rivas

Monthly Review Press

Library of Congress Cataloging-in-Publication Data
Central America/edited by Jan L. Flora and Edelberto Torres-Rivas.
    p.   cm.— (Sociology of "developing societies")
    Bibliography: p.
    Includes index.
    ISBN 0—85345—765—4: $27.00.   ISBN 0-85345-766-2 (pbk.):
    $11.00.
    1. Central America — Politics and government.   2. Insurgency —
Central America — History — 20th century.   3. Central America — Social
conditions.   4. Central America — Economic conditions.   I. Flora,
Jan L., 1941—   . II. Torres-Rivas, Edelberto.   III. Series.

f(1436.C45 1989
972.8 — dc19   89—3103
                                                                      CIP

Monthly Review Press
 122 West 27th Street
New York, N.Y. 10001

Printed in Hong Kong

10 9 8 7 6 5 4 3 2 1

To Leonard and Billie Flora

Contents

Series Preface

The question of the so-called "developing societies" lies at the very heart of the political, the economic and the moral crises of the contemporary global society. It is central to the relations of power, diplomacy and war of the world we live in. It is decisive when the material well-being of humanity is concerned: that is, the ways some people make a living and the ways some people hunger. It presents a fundamental dimension of social inequality and of struggles for social justice. During the last generation it has also become a main challenge to scholarship, a field where the perplexity is deeper, the argument sharper and the potential for new illuminations more profound. That challenge reflects the outstanding social relevance of this problem. It reflects, too, an essential ethnocentrism that weighs heavily on the contemporary social sciences. The very terminology which designates "developing" or "underdeveloping" or "emerging" societies is impregnated with teleology which identifies parts of Europe and the USA as "developed". Images of the world at large as a unilinear rise from barbarity to modernity (or vice versa as a descent to hell) have often substituted for the analysis of actuality, as simplistic metaphors often do. To come to grips with a social reality, which is systematically different from that of one's own, and to explain its specific logic and momentum, is a most difficult conceptual and pedagogic task. It is the more so, for the fundamental questions of the "developing societies" are not of difference only but of relationships past and present with the countries of advanced capitalism and industrialization. It is in that light that we encounter as analysts and teachers not only a challenge to "sociology of development", but also a major challenge to radical scholarship itself.

The Sociology of "Developing Societies" series aims to offer a systematically linked set of texts for use as a major teaching aid at university level. It is being produced by a group of teachers and scholars related by common interest, general outlook and commitment sufficient to provide an overall coherence but by no means a single monolithic view. The object is, on the one hand, to bring relevant questions into focus and, on the other hand, to teach through debate. We think that at the current stage "a textbook" would necessarily gloss over the very diversity, contradictions and inadequacies of our thought. On the other hand, collections of articles are often rather accidental in content. The format of a conceptually structured set of readers was chosen, sufficiently open to accommodate variability of views within a coherent system of presentation. They bring together works by sociologists, social anthropologists, historians, political scientists, economists, literary critics and novelists in an intended disregard of the formal disciplinary divisions of the academic enterprise.

Three major alternatives of presentation stand out: first, a comparative discussion of the social structures within the "developing societies", focusing on the generic within them; second, the exploration of the distinct character of the main regions of the "developing societies"; third, consideration of context and content of the theories of social transformation and change. Accordingly, our *Introduction* to the series deals with the general issues of comparative study, other books cover different regions, while a final volume is devoted to an examination of basic paradigms of the theories of social transformation. They therefore represent the three main dimensions of the problem area, leaving it to each teacher and student to choose from them and to compose their own course.

The topic is ideologically charged, relating directly to the outlook and the ideals of everyone. The editors and many of the contributors share a broad sense of common commitment, though there is among them a considerable diversity of political viewpoint and theoretical approach. The common ground may be best indicated as three fundamental negations. First, there is an implacable opposition to every social system of oppression of humans by other humans. That entails also the rejection of scholastic apologia of every such system, be it imperialism, class oppression, elitism, sexism or the like. Second, there is the rejection of "preaching down" each solutions from the comfort of air-conditioned offices and campuses, whether in the "West" or in "developing societies" themselves, and of the tacit assumption of our privileged wisdom that has little to learn from the common people in the "developing societies". Third, there is the rejection of the notion of scholastic detachment from social commitments as a pedagogy and as a way of life. True scholarship is not a propaganda exercise even of the most sacred values. Nor is it without social consequences, however conceived. There are students and teachers alike who think that indifference improves vision. We believe the opposite to be true.

TEODOR SHANIN

Acknowledgements

The editors wish to thank the following people for contributing to the preparation of this book:

Elizabeth L. Hébert Pardo for translating Edelberto Torres-Rivas "Authoritarian Transition to Democracy".

Carol C. Rose for translating Carlos M. Vilas "The Impact of Revolutionary Transition on the Popular Classes: the Working Class in the Sandinista Revolution".

Dr Bradley A. Shaw for translating José Luis Vega Carballo "Parties, Political Development, and Social Conflict in Honduras and Costa Rica: a Comparative Analysis".

Karen Henderson, Tammy Henderson, and Beth Herrmann for typing the manuscript.

Notes on the Contributors

Douglas K. Benson is Associate Professor of Modern Languages at Kansas State University, Manhattan, Kansas, USA.

Cornelia B. Flora is Professor of Sociology at Kansas State University.

Jan L. Flora is Professor of Sociology at Kansas State University.

Professor Jim Handy is in the Department of History at the University of Saskatchewan, Saskatoon, Canada.

Professor Terry Lynn Karl is in the Department of Political Science at Stanford University, Palo Alto, California, USA.

Professor Edelberto Torres-Rivas is Secretary General of the Latin American Faculty of Social Sciences (FLACSO) in San José, Costa Rica.

José Luís Vega-Carballo is Professor in the School of Anthropology and Sociology of the University of Costa Rica.

Carlos M. Vilas is a researcher at the Center of Research and Documentation for the Atlantic Coast (CIDCA) in Nicaragua.

Professor Leon Zamosc is in the Department of Sociology, University of California–San Diego, La Jolla, California, USA.

Introduction

Central America has been a region taken for granted. Because it is a crossroads between continents and oceans, it has also been a geographic bone of contention among outsiders. The 1980s are a time when the pendulum has swung toward the interventionist side. Central America has become a central focus for the Americas and beyond.

This book is a response to that renewed outside interest. Because there are a number of readings books already available on Central America, it was decided not to reprint condensations of already published material as has been done in other books in this series (only one article in this collection has been previously published), but rather to commission essays which would treat important aspects of the sociology of the developing countries of Central America. Essays were tailored to treat particular themes: conflict, social structure and class analysis, and outside influence and intervention.

Conflict

Central to the book is the notion of conflict. Cultural conflict precedes the arrival of the Spaniards as more powerful groups from the North reached into the isthmus. As is suggested in Part I, the conflict between the Spaniards and indigenous peoples was sometimes total, involving disease, war, economic exploitation, and most importantly, sharply contrasting world views. Independence fuzzied the boundaries between different ethnic and racial groups, but in no way reconciled sharply differing perspectives and objectives.

Independence for the states of the Central American Federation was not a critical event. Central Americans did not have to fight for independence, but were granted it along with Mexico in 1823. Weeks suggests that the absence of Central American wars of independence meant that the countries of Central America were slow to develop national identities. This perhaps explains the fact that many Central Americans have identified with the region as a whole as much as with their particular country:

Elsewhere in the New World, wars of independence served to a certain extent to forge alliances among élites, which later provided the basis for national cohesion and identification. But independence came to Central America with virtually no struggle. This allowed the provincialism of the colonial period to carry over largely intact.[1]

Upon independence, the five countries assumed what are approximately their present boundaries. Shortly thereafter, they formed a Central American Federation which lasted nearly fifteen years. The Federation's breakup did not occur because of strong nationalism among the five member-states. The development of cohesive countries was to await the development of coffee as an important export crop in the latter part of the nineteenth century. Honduras, which did not become an important coffee producer, became a cohesive state only after the Second World War.

The Central American Common Market, initiated in the 1960s, and the attempt to create a Central American Parliament in the 1980s, attest to the continued feeling of "Central Americanness". Such efforts at cooperation may be the flip side of internecine conflicts which are an integral part of Central American history, and which are manifested today in the disagreements associated with internal upheavals in three of the countries (El Salvador, Guatemala, and Nicaragua). Conflict within the family may be much more rancorous than that which occurs with outsiders.

Social Structure

Social structure and its relationship to political power is a second theme which is central to this book. The two aspects of social structure which are most emphasized are class and ethnicity. Until the Second World War, both were defined largely by agrarian structure. A major change occurred some years after independence when the traditional landed estate was partially supplanted (depending on the country) by the expansion of export agriculture. While indigo was grown as a cash crop in the eighteenth and into the nineteenth century, particularly in what became El Salvador, coffee was the first region-wide commercial crop, and brought the countries into the world capitalist economy in the nineteenth and early twentieth century.[2] This involved a centralization of political power and a strengthening of the state.

A gradual process of urbanization took place. Unionization began to develop in the 1920s (based more on artisan production than on advanced capitalist proletarianization). Except for Costa Rica, which experienced something resembling the popular front governments of Europe and the more developed countries of South America, the 1930s were a time of personalistic dictatorships – national *caudillos* resembling their locality-based counterparts before the development of coffee production. The Second World War and expanded world commodity demand following it brought winds of change. Middle groups, including professionals, students, industrialists, merchants, and sometimes agrarian capitalists involved in the production of new export crops – cotton, sugar, cattle, cacao – expanded and demanded political participation. Only in the case of Costa Rica did these groups gain "permanent" ascendancy through the "Revolution" of 1948 and the ensuing hegemony of a social democratic political party. For the other countries, except Honduras which had not emerged entirely from its semi-feudal past, the postwar period involved conflict between the conservative coffee élites and these new middle groups, and when the former were in the ascendency (in alliance with elements of the military) workers, peasants, students, and others were repressed.

Another theme which underlies much that is in this book is the importance of great power politics in Central America. In colonial times, Britain was, after Spain, the chief power in the isthmus. Britain provided an outlet for trade in raw materials and manufactured goods produced in Central America whose production was prohibited by the Spanish Crown. Britain became the major trading partner after independence. The Monroe Doctrine of 1923 announced US intent to become the dominant power in the region, which occurred with the Clayton–Bulwer Treaty of 1850.[3] Britain continued to have a secondary role through its influence along the Atlantic (really the Caribbean) coast. The presence of British troops today in recently independent Belize serves as a reminder of the past power of Britain in the isthmus.

Weeks divides the international relations of post-colonial Central America into two periods, with the initiation of the second decade of the twentieth century as the dividing point:

> During the first period . . . the great powers – Great Britain and the United States – were content to let the political stability or instability of Central America be determined by regional strongmen. In this period various Guatemalan dictators dominated the entire region, and at the turn of the century José Santos Zelaya of Nicaragua briefly continued this tradition. Then, with the coming of the banana companies and the building of the interoceanic canal, this period of

the relative autonomy of Central American rulers came to an end. Coinciding with the fall of Zelaya in 1909, Washington established a de facto protectorate over the region, and subsequent governments would wax or wane to the extent that Washington nurtured them, with a few notable exceptions. This would be the golden age of North American influence in the area.[4]

Direct military intervention was not necessary most of the time, though the USA did intervene militarily in Nicaragua (1912–25, 1927–33), in Costa Rica (1917), Honduras (1924, 1981–present), and through surrogate forces in Guatemala (1954) and Nicaragua (1982–present). Pro-US governments generally maintained themselves in power without direct US military assistance. These governments were usually military dictatorships. In the 1930s and into the 1940s, all but Costa Rica were ruled by personalistic dictators. Following brief attempts at democratic rule after the Second World War in all but Nicaragua where the Somoza dictatorship remained, El Salvador, Guatemala, and Honduras settled into more or less continuous institutionally-based military rule, until the 1980s when all three have experimented with electoral politics with civilians nominally in control.

Belize and Panama are not included in this volume. Belize is a mini-state with a population of 160 000. Previously called British Honduras, it received its independence in 1981. Its culture and history are quite distinct from the rest of the isthmus, though as just indicated it has been linked through trade with the rest of Central America, serving as a commercial link between Great Britain and the rest of Central America.[5]

Panama has a number of similarities with the other countries of Central America, having received its independence from Colombia in 1903 without having fought for it. The USA engineered a declaration of independence and insured the success of Panama's separation through a naval blockade of its ports so that Colombian ships could not get through to contest this loss of territory.[6] Construction of the Panama Canal began shortly thereafter.

Panama has some geopolitical similarities to Nicaragua because both were candidates for the transisthmian canal. However, Panama became a virtual protectorate of the USA, and had no promise of sovereignty over the Canal Zone until that was negotiated in 1978. The extreme political and economic dependence of Panama on the USA – even in comparison with Nicaragua during the Somoza era – resulted in its having a very different history from the five countries which were in the Central American Federation. Thus, when page constraints became an issue, we reluctantly omitted Panama from the book.

This book is about five small countries with similar politico-historical origins. They are all so small that the capital city tends to be the clearly dominant city.[7] Regionalism is not of major importance. (The autonomy statute approved by the Nicaraguan government for the Atlantic Coast belies that statement, but it is essentially true.) Small agriculturally based countries such as those in Central America tend to be affected more profoundly by swings in world commodities prices than are larger countries with distinct regional variations. The similarities and differences among the Central American countries allow us to draw at least tentative conclusions regarding cause and effect, which might be more difficult in the comparison of countries which are more regionally complex.

The book includes works by Central Americans and other Latin Americans. Three are works translated from Spanish. Certain important features have been underemphasized, including the importance and complexity of religion in contemporary social change, the role of women in revolutionary change, and the ideology and political alliances of the insurgents of this decade. The bibliography offers readings for those who desire to fill in these and other gaps.

Notes

NB In these and all subsequent notes at the ends of chapters, details of publication are included only for those works which are not detailed in the Bibliography.

1. John Weeks, *The Economics of Central America* (New York and London: Holmes & Meier, 1985) pp. 9–10.
2. The exception was Honduras, whose main export was bananas. It thus became part of the international export economy in a very different way.
3. See Weeks, *Economies*, p. 20.
4. Ibid, p. 17. See also Walter LaFeber, *Inevitable Revolutions: the United States in Central America.*
5. Weeks, *Economies*, p. 5.
6. Ibid, pp. 29–31.
7. Honduras is an exception. The existence of two principal cities is in part due to the peculiar character of export agriculture in that country – the dominance of the banana enclave. See Flora and Torres-Rivas in Part I of this volume for more detail.

Part I

Historical Origins of Social Structure and Class Formation

Introduction

This introduction to Part I briefly summarizes major economic and political changes in Central America from pre-Columbian times to the Second World War. We rely heavily on the works of Miles Wortman and Ralph Lee Wordward and on the introduction in the volume on Latin America in this series.[1]

Sociology of "Developing Societies": Latin America, edited by Archetti, Cammack and Roberts provides an excellent background for understanding the region. A central theme of that introduction is that (except for the first fifty years) colonial and post-independence Latin America was and is an export-oriented region. The development of Latin America and of Central America in the late nineteenth and early twentieth century can only be understood in the context of the development of industrial capitalism, led first by Great Britain, and after the First World War, by the USA:

> It is as foolish to asume that the nations of Latin America have been following independently, if belatedly, the same path to industrial maturity as had been traced out by the first industrial nations (as some of the simpler exponents of modernisation theory would have us believe) as it is to claim that the role of primary producers is one forced upon an unwilling sub-continent by scheming European power, and bound to endure for as long as the sub-continent remains within their commercial and political orbit (as the prudent dependency theorists would seem to believe). The truth is that Latin American development has been complementary to that of the most advanced industrial nations and is hence incomprehensible except within that broader global picture, but that at the same time it has had its own complex internal dynamic, varying from region to region, arising primarily out of the secular struggle between the different class forces spawned by that complementary pattern of development.[2]

Colonial Central America differed from the region as a whole in the following ways: the Kingdom of Guatemala (Central America) was less export-oriented than the central parts of the empire – Peru,

Mexico, and north-east Brazil. Increasingly since Liberalism became the dominant force in Central America in the latter part of the nineteenth century, the isthmus has become *more* dependent on the international economy than have other parts of Latin America, except perhaps the Caribbean.

For Latin America in general the disruptions caused by the wars of independence resulted in fifty years of languishing before the region was once again integrated into the world economy.[3] The same was true of Central America, except that the disruptions were caused not by the war for independence (there was no war), but by the internecine conflicts within and among the "city-states" which in 1840 formally separated from one another to become "independent" countries after fifteen years of formal federation.

The élites of the Liberal period were natural collaborators with foreign merchant capital both in terms of Latin American exports and the import of cheap manufactured goods. Hence there was little impetus for the development of industry in Latin America,[4] nor did a significant industrial working class develop until the 1930s and 1940s (later in Central America). The rural proletariat which developed tended to be a semi-proletariat, for its members maintained their peasant plots. The banana workers of Central America, who migrated to the sparsely-settled, inhospitable lowlands to engage in full-time salaried labour formed a partial exception. In general, due to the form taken by the international division of labour, "Latin America's insertion into the capitalist world economy thus did not mean the inevitable spread of wage labor throughout its national economies".[5] This observation is especially applicable to Central America, even today.

Regarding the dominant class, during the Liberal period in Latin America:

> the counterpart of industrial development in Europe was export-led development, based upon the land, or upon the exploitation of mineral resources. This meant that throughout Latin America the landed class played the role played in many parts of Europe by the urban bourgeoisie. Whereas in Europe, then, the industrial revolution often meant the displacement of the landed élite from political power, in Latin America it meant that the hold of this class on power and on the state was strengthened.[6]

While in other parts of Latin America the agricultural bourgeoisie became subordinated to the growing industrial and financial bourgeoisie in the period immediately after the Second World War, the agrarian élite of Central America, although much transformed, remains a major force in the Central American countries. In the countries where insurgency has arisen in recent years, it forms the core of the opposition of reforms which might have undercut support for the insurgent groups. As will be seen in the introduction to Part II of this volume, the Central American Common Market was an attempt to bring import-substitution industrialization to Central America, but its effects were not lasting.

A more detailed treatment of changes in Central America from the time Columbus reached Costa Rica until the end of the Second World War follows.

Indigenous Political Economy

In pre-Columbian times, Central America was influenced by cultures from the north – before the birth of Christ by the Olmecs of what are today Tabasco and Veracruz and by the Toltecs and Nahuatls of central Mexico after the decline of the Mayan civilization. Around 500 BC an agrarian civilization developed in the Guatemalan highlands. Knowledge of this civilization is limited, because excavations for an expanding Guatemala City destroyed many of the mounds before they could be examined by archaeologists. That civilization was the basis for continuous agriculture and dense population to the present day. The Olmecs had influenced it as well as the Mayan civilization, which reached its apogee in the period AD 600 to 900 in the lowlands of the Yucatan peninsula, and had spent itself, except for isolated enclaves, well before the Spaniards arrived.[7]

Important for understanding the development of the Spanish Kingdom of Guatemala (which reached from Chiapas, now in Southern Mexico, to Costa Rica) is the fact that the bulk of pre-Columbian populations were agriculturalists (except for those in the sparsely settled Caribbean lowlands) and carried on an active trade within the region:

> The Indian men tended the maize and other crops. The women ran their households and manufactured utensils, clothing, and housewares. A high degree of specialization evolved as each village developed a particular skill. Some engaged in cotton spinning and weaving, or pottery-making; others manufactured jewelry or basketry, or musical instruments, or toys, or tools, or furniture. Merchants carried these

objects far and wide to the village market-places, a practice which still continues in Guatemala. They raised and traded indigo, cochineal, and a wide assortment of dyewoods to give their clothing and bodies bright colors. Financing of this activity was at a primitive level. Barter was common, but semiprecious stones and cacao beans provided a kind of currency . . . The cornfields, or *milpas*, were and are the key to life in the Indian villages, and around their ownership or use revolved the social and economic status of the individual Indian. Private ownership *per se* seems to have been evolving by the time of the Conquest. Communally-owned land was important and such land ownership persisted into modern times. But the Spanish emphasis on privately owned land challenged and altered Indian landholding patterns.[8]

The agricultural experience of the indigenous population readily allowed for the Spaniards to exploit their labour, particularly once it became clear that the basis of the Central American colonial economy was to be agriculture, not the mining of precious metals.

A related characteristic of pre-Columbian Central America – in spite of the lively trading which took place – was a strong orientation to the local community. Woodward says that the Central American Indian "holds a view of the world which is oriented toward his own family and community, not toward the nation, which is alien to him".[9] As we will see, this local orientation was compatible with the political system developed by the Spaniards. It was only in the latter half of the nineteenth century, when Liberal reforms were instituted, that indigenous locality-orientation became a major problem for the governments in Central America – though the Bourbon colonial rulers of the eighteenth century tried unsuccessfully to change it also. Thus, the Maya city-states (which differed from the centralized empires of the Aztecs and Incas) were replaced by politically *and* culturally diverse agricultural groups, which were conquered by Spaniards who formed what might be described as Spanish colonial city-states. Only in the last half century of Bourbon reign were inroads made in centralizing control within the Guatemalan kingdom.

The Conquest and the Rule of Hapsburg Spain

The conquest of Central America, while less dramatic than the conquest of Mexico and Peru, was quite devastating for the indigenous population. The *conquistadores* used a divide-and-conquer approach, making alliances with certain indigenous groups to conquer others, and then cruelly subduing their former allies when they rebelled.[10] Indians from what is now northern Nicaragua and southern Honduras were captured and enslaved for labour in Hispaniola, resulting in substantial depopulation of the zone of origin. Hernán Cortés, the conqueror of Mexico, made an expedition to Central America in 1524, preceded by an epidemic of smallpox. It was not until around 1600 that the Indian population of the region stabilized and slowly began to climb to its previous levels.

The conquerors fought one another as well. For instance, Balboa, who discovered the Pacific Ocean in 1513 and established the first permanent settlement on the isthmus in Panama, was beheaded by Pedrarias, one of the more cruel of the conquistadores. Wortman states succinctly, "The search for immediate wealth was the prime concern of these conquerors, the first generation of colonists."[11] It was not until after 1550 that a stable Spanish government was established for the region. The silver in Honduras, which in the early 1540s had briefly represented the largest production in the Americas, had by then petered out. Agriculture seemed to be the only alternative.

While the New Laws were promulgated at the behest of Father Bartolomé de las Casas in 1542, the *encomienda*, prohibited under those laws, continued in limited form in Central America until 1720. The *encomiendas* were "licenses to collect tribute for the crown that were, in reality, permissions to compel Amerindian labor in personal service".[12] Under the New Laws, the *encomienda* was largely superseded by the *repartimiento*, which became the principal form of labour supply until the end of the eighteenth century:

> Each week every Indian *alcalde* was legally compelled to furnish a labor force equal to one-fourth of the *pueblo*'s male population. Theoretically that labor force was to work from eight in the morning until five in the afternoon from Monday to Friday with a two-hour rest at noon and were paid a *real* for each day's work.[13]

The reality of the *repartimiento* was quite different:

> Indigenous populations were forced to travel away from their *milpas* during harvest time, paid five *reales* for a week's work that began Monday morning at six and ended Saturday evening at six, allowing them no time to go to and from their homes. Indians who arrived late or left early lost a day's pay. Many times Indians received only a half *real* for a week's work after they paid the high prices for food and other goods. Indians were made to purchase their tools or allowed only two

or three weeks a year to rest and farm their own fields in violation of the law that stipulated only three months of labor. When a man could not report for work because of illness, or if he had fled the town, his wife, son, or daughter had to take his place.[14]

In the Valley of Mexico and in Peru, because of the need for labour in the mines, the shortage of indigenous labour drove Indians to the protection of the *hacienda* and into debt peonage. The relatively abundant population in Central America (Guatemala in particular) meant that Indians continued to live in their villages. Village leaders were obliged to make sure that the labourers were available. Failure to organize the villagers could result in corporal punishment or death to the Indian *alcalde*. Still, the retention of indigenous villages with some autonomy (at least until the late 1970s), has provided the Indians in modern day Guatemala with some bargaining power with outsiders.

It was acknowledged by all that Indian tribute was the economic base of the colony:

> Every healthy male Indian between the ages of eighteen and fifty was obliged to pay commodities worth two pesos in annual tribute to a king. The levy supported defense, government, and church expenses as well as remissions to Spain – 80 to 90 per cent of all income to the royal coffers. Unlike Peru or New Spain, where merchants and mineral and agricultural producers contributed sizeable revenues to the crown, the non-Indian populations in Central America administered and profited from the fruits of the Indian tribute to the extent that they barely paid taxes.[15]

This unwillingness of the élites in Central America to pay taxes persists to this day; the issue of business taxation currently provides an element of instability in the Christian Democratic governments of El Salvador and Guatemala.

The crown did not have sufficient resources to pay good salaries to its agents in the New World. This encouraged corruption. Tax-farming, whereby merchants were given a specific region in which to collect tribute and assigned a quota, was the rule in the Kingdom of Guatemala; anything they collected above that amount was theirs. Government officials and merchants sometimes engaged in illegal trade with other European powers. For instance, Martin de Mencos, president of the *Audiencia* of Guatemala from 1659 to 1668, was involved in illegal trade in silver (from Peru) and indigo with Holland, but was never punished because he substantially increased sales-tax collections from merchants in Guatemala.[16]

The church generally played an ameliorative role in Spanish treatment of the Indians, though its role *vis-à-vis* indigenous peoples was complicated. Some clerics served the creoles (Spaniards born in the New World) and others, the Indians. Those prelates who served Indian *pueblos* gained a significant part of their livelihood from emoluments provided by the indigenous people: only baptisms were free. Perhaps the most interesting ecclesiastical institution to develop among the Indians was the *cofradía*, the sodality or lay fraternity. Controlled by the clerics, it "was established to finance the celebration of the town's saint, the Virgin, Jesus, and the sacrament".[17] But the *cofradías* became powerful economic institutions of agricultural production and processing, often rivalling those controlled by creole businessmen. Sometimes creole clerics took much of the wealth of the *cofradías*, but more commonly, the *cofradías* served as an economic buffer between the Indian and the government, providing employment and in emergencies paying tribute on behalf of their indigenous members. *Cofradía* rituals often incorporated pagan practices overlaid by a thin veneer of Catholicism. The clerics attempted to control such practices to no avail. Thus these lay fraternities served as both economic and cultural defence for their indigenous members.[18]

During the Hapsburg period, the Church possessed many mechanisms of obtaining wealth – through productive enterprises operated by the *cofradías*; via the *capellanía*, funds obtained from property willed to the church by well-to-do creoles for the purpose of having mass said on their behalf "in perpetuity"; from dowries from creole families to enable a family-member to become a nun; as well as through other emoluments and donations from creoles, *peninsulares* (Spaniards), and Indians. The church was controlled by the Spanish crown, which named bishops and other ecclesiastical authorities, rather than their being named by Rome. The church did not pay any taxes; in fact, the government financed the imported wine and oil used in religious services. "This eccesiastical arm thus reinforced local economies as compared with the secular state, which withdrew capital to the metropolis."[19]

The Bourbon monarchs, who gained control of Spain in 1700, were products of the Enlightenment, while the Spanish Hapsburgs were of a pre-counter-reformation ilk. When the Bourbons gained the Spanish throne, they implemented anti-clerical policies, which included invalidating the substantial loans which the various orders and *cofradías* had made to the state (some 200 000 pesos in total by 1700).[20]

In 1700, there was no Hapsburg heir to the Spanish throne. Spain had been substantially weakened. The decentralized systems which it had developed in the New World involved a delicate balance among various local interests, and in the case of Central America, was based principally on tribute and tax-farming. The resilience of this system contributed to the downfall of the Hapsburgs, for it was not a system from which additional resources could be extracted in order to fight its European wars. The Spanish Hapsburg dynasty died both economically and militarily and because it had no heir.

Bourbon Rule

Bourbon rule was strikingly different from that of the Hapsburgs in two major respects. Bourbon government was (i) absolutist; it involved transfer of power from the *cabildo* (municipal government, controlled by the traditionalist creole élite) to the *audiencia*, the body representing the crown; and (ii) developmentalist, rather than extractive; the Bourbons invested in the colonies, rather than simply sending tribute to Spain.[21] This developmentalist perspective required a sharp reduction in the power of the church.

Wortman makes it clear that the church's economic role was inimical to the commercial perspective:

> If the Bourbon state were to stimulate private economic development with ties to the metropolis, the church's control of labor and capital had to be broken. If taxation to develop state power were to be increased, the ecclesiastical credit institutions had to be destroyed and replaced by private individuals whose primary aim was profit from an increase in commerce.[22]

By the eighteenth century, the proportion of the population which defined itself as Indian had declined substantially. A substantial middle group of *mestizos* or *Ladinos* had come into being. Neither they nor the creole and Spanish élites were taxed substantially, and the declining proportion of Indians meant a stagnating tax base. Furthermore, the Hapsburgs allowed tribute to be paid in kind, rather than in specie. In 1747, legislation ordered that tribute be paid in coin.[23] Although not strictly enforced, it discouraged the subsistence economy which was a key to the maintenance of indigenous separateness.

The Bourbons, influenced by their French mercantilist brethren, envisioned a more commercially-oriented system. Thus, beginning in the 1720s through economic incentives, they stimulated the rejuvenation of silver production in Honduras. The stimulation of silver production established a pattern for other industries:

> Bourbon fiscal and labor intervention stimulated an underexploited industry; as the industry developed, Guatemalan merchants, by virtue of their strategic position at the center of the legal trade and their control of capital, siphoned off the greatest profits. Amerindian populations were either compelled or induced to labor, their numbers were reduced and their cultures weakened.[24]

The Bourbons also proposed that the fastest growing sector – trade – be taxed, not simply with a view to extracting wealth, but rather to stimulating commerce, not only between Spain and the colonies but also among the colonies, including the Philippines. Through the Peace of Utrecht, Spain was forced to allow limited legal trade between Central America and Britain.[25]

Growth in the British textile industry stimulated indigo production and commerce. In the second half of the eighteenth century, indigo became the principal export of Central America, and remained so until after independence. Merchants replaced clerics as the principal economic force alongside the crown. Aggressive merchants from Spain, attracted particularly by the indigo trade, married into prestigious creole families; those creole families which refused the entreaties of the Spanish merchants quickly fell into oblivion.[26]

Wortman indicates two phases in the relationship between the state and merchants during the Bourbon period:

> First, the state allied itself with the new merchant families, using their force to eliminate Hapsburg institutions, the *encomenderos*, the church, and "old families" whose wealth and productivity had dissipated. Second, after weakening the power of the Hapsburg sectors the government turned its assault against the new merchants who had developed power during the first two-thirds of the eighteeenth century ... The government began to institute reforms in the 1760s that changed the tax structure dramatically, altering the centuries-old reliance upon the Indian for fiscal support and providing the state with sufficient funds to expand its power. The measures precipitated tension and minor violence, and created the antagonism between merchant and government official that continued until, and created one of the basic underlying causes of, the movement for independence.[27]

Central America did not have to fight for independence. The Napoleonic wars were necessary for the colonies to rebel, but

Bourbon mercantilism, which had strengthened Spain was also its weakness. So long as the Spanish monarchy was strong and commerce was expanding, the merchants grudgingly accepted taxation of their commercial activities:

> The basis of the Bourbon state . . . was the fiscal system, and it was here that the state was weakest. The crown required a large bureaucracy to maintain direct control over all regions and a large army to fight its wars. Fiscal reform had led to the growth of the bureaucracy and the army. But military expenses rose constantly, caused by the series of wars between 1790 and 1815. When the state had to sacrifice colonial military power for the metropolis it began to lose control of the colony itself. Raising taxes to support larger armies led to even greater defections.[28]

Central America followed Mexico in declaring independence on 15 September 1823.

Independence, the Central American Federation, and Subsequent Conservative Dominance

Central America briefly cast its lot with Mexico, but soon became a Federation, at least nominally. During the period of formal federation (1825–40) the country was never fully integrated. Conflict between Liberals and Conservatives was almost continuous:

> The Conservatives pleaded for moderation, order and the stability of traditional, familiar institutions. The Liberals argued for a continuation of the reforms already begun under the Spanish Bourbons . . . Often idealistic, they sought to make Central America a modern, progressive state, casting off the burden of Iberian heritage and to absorb eagerly republican innovations from France, England, and the United States. This meant . . . that Liberals stood for restrictions of clerical power and privilege, abolition of slavery, abolition of burdensome taxes on commerce; elimination of privileged and exclusive *fueros* and guilds; more egalitarian political and judicial institutions; public education and economic development, especially road, port, and immigration projects.[29]

While both parties contained members of the aristocracy (white creoles), the Liberals came to represent the interests of professional-level *Ladinos* or *mestizos*, who had been on the outside under Spanish rule.[30] The lower socio-economic levels of the *mestizo* population, after many years of turmoil, took a position contrary to professional-level *mestizos*:

> As regional families fought over disputes the crown had mediated, heretofore peaceful castes and classes, who had recognized Creole and Spanish authority, resorted to violence and rebellion to improve their position. The order of the colony dissolved into the disorder of the nation, until the Indian, *mestizo*, and mulatto "bandits" and rebels coalesced around regional leaders at the end of the 1830s to create a semblance of stability . . . Thus, in many ways, the true revolution occurred, not in 1821, but from 1838 to 1840.[31]

In the end, an alliance was made between conservative castes (Indians and *mestizos*), who opposed the liberal anticlerical measures and other cultural changes; Conservative merchants, who opposed commercial taxation; and traditional agrarian interests, who favoured local autonomy. The leader of the guerrilla army which wore down and eventually defeated the Liberals was Rafael Carrera, a Guatemalan *Ladino* (*mestizo*) with no formal education. He led a peasant army which opposed (a) the head tax reinstated in 1829 because there was little international commerce to tax; (b) Liberals' promotion of individual land-ownership at the expense of communal control; (c) their stepped-up assault on the church and its property, and (d) their effort to reform the judicial system by instituting a US-style system which included trial by jury.[32] Prominent Conservatives established an alliance of convenience with Carrera, and many colonial structures were restored. But as Woodward points out, "The hold of the white élite over government was clearly broken, even if their social dominance had been restored in the State of Guatemala."[33] Carrera ruled Guatemala until 1865 and had considerable influence over the governments of the other states, where Conservatives predominated in office until 1870.

The newly independent Central American "countries" had more in common with Hapsburg, than with Bourbon, colonial Central America: each country was one or more city-states; the countryside was dominated by agrarian *caudillos*; Indians returned to subsistence agriculture and their communities were strengthened, though forced Indian labour was again legislated for there was no other way to obtain their labour; the church, while not regaining its former splendour, became ascendent through its shaping of dominant values, though "enlightened" thought continued to be shared by many in the urban areas. What had been communal and church lands were in large part returned to their former holders.[34]

The Liberals Return to Power

It was not until after the development of coffee production and export in Central America in the 1860s and the death of Carrera that the tide began to turn toward the Liberals. In fact, only with the coming to power of the Liberals in Guatemala in 1871 were Liberal regimes in the adjacent states safe, for Guatemala was still the dominant state in the region. The new Liberal leaders were less idealistic than their predecessors of the Central America Federation period. Their primary concern was with economic development; democratic ideals were secondary. In fact, Conservative *caudillos* were replaced by Liberal *caudillos*; except in Costa Rica, political democracy remained only an ideal. The Liberals, given their free-trade orientation, were open to foreign investment. While, except in Nicaragua and to a lesser degree in Guatemala, ownership of coffee production was overwhelmingly in the hands of Central Americans, there was substantial foreign investment in railroads, ports, roads, and banking – all necessary for coffee exportation.[35]

The power of the Church was curtailed again. Education was removed from its domination, and communal lands, whether belonging to the Church or to peasant communities, were declared to be private property to be bought and sold.[36] In typical understatement Woodward says:

> The Indians and rural peasants gained little from the new Liberals . . . Through forced labor, vagrancy laws, and legalized debt peonage the poor were put to work on the plantations or roads. In Guatemala, where the *mandamiento* virtually restored the colonial *repartimiento*, Indian villages provided labor for both private and public works. Much Indian land was alienated when residents could not produce legal title documents. Such land became available at low cost for planters, while its inhabitants were forced to seek wage employment on the *fincas*. The Guatemalan *mandamiento* formally ended with the Labor code of 1894 . . . In essence the system created a new class of landholders who lived off the exploited labor of serfs. It remained in force until the overthrow of Jorge Ubico in 1944.[37]

The second major export crop of the Liberal era was bananas, which were first exported in commercial quantities in the 1880s. The United Fruit Company (UFCO) was formally established in

1899 and Standard Fruit grew out of several smaller companies in 1924. In Costa Rica, the concessions of land for banana production resulted from an agreement with persons later affiliated with UFCO to build a railroad from Limón to San José. In the cases of Honduras and Guatemala, the other two major banana-producers, the railroads established by the banana companies led only from the port city to the banana lands, thus not contributing to the integration of the country. More important than the railroads was the shipping monopoly established by United Fruit, in which rates from the USA to Central America were higher than those from Central America to the USA. Though connections with the USA were good, there was little seaborne (or any) commerce among the Central American countries. Only El Salvador and Guatemala came to be linked by rail.[38] Woodward summarizes the early impact of the banana companies:

> The banana industry accomplished many of the Liberals' objectives, albeit at the price of national sovereignty and economic independence. Among the benefits were development of transportation and ports; valuable foreign exchange, which financed further (if modest) economic development; substantial tax revenues; exploitation of lowland regions; and eradication of deadly diseases endemic to the tropics.[39]

Following the First World War, US investment in Central America expanded rapidly and Britain fell to third behind the USA and Germany. By the 1920s over half of Central American commerce was with the USA.[40] This also brought a larger political and military role for the USA in Central America. While there were brief interventions in Honduras, Costa Rica, and El Salvador, the most significant US military intervention was in Nicaragua. The intervention of the US Marines began in 1912. They remained almost continuously until 1933. Nicaragua became a US protectorate. US financial officers handled collection of Nicaraguan customs duties and took over the National Bank and the railways. Of great significance were the agreements which culminated in the Bryan–Chamorro treaty of 1916 which gave the USA exclusive and permanent rights to build a transisthmian canal and established a 99-year lease on the Corn Islands in the Caribbean and on a naval base in the Gulf of Fonseca on the Pacific. The Central American Court of Justice, established with the collaboration of the USA in 1907, ruled in 1916 and 1917 that the treaty violated Nicaraguan sovereignty, but the US and the Nicaraguan puppet government refused to accept the ruling. Nicaragua withdrew from the Central American court and the Court collapsed.[41]

The 1920s marked the beginning of a significant labour movement in Central America. This occurred as a response to the growing commercialism in all the countries but Honduras, where the banana industry was an enclave isolated from the rest of the country and economy. Unionism grew chiefly among two groups: workers in the agroindustrial export industries, and artisans whose livelihood began to be threatened by the increase in imported consumer goods.[42] Communist Parties with their base in organized labour were established in the 1920s or early 1930s in all countries except Honduras. The organizational strength of the labouring groups was short-lived:

> The crash of 1929 was a serious blow to these [foreign-dominated] oligarchies, and in all but Costa Rica the response was a rise of strong dictatorships which could reestablish "order and progress" and restrain the rising demand for reform from the working classes. The governments of Ubico, Hernández Martínez, Carías, and Somoza reaffirmed their faith in foreign capital, and they clamped an iron rule over the isthmus from Guatemala through Nicaragua.[43]

Beginning in 1940, Costa Rica pursued a mild version of the "Popular Front" governments. For the other nations, the above-mentioned dictators represented the last of the *caudillos* in Central America. They generally lasted through the Second World War and, except in the case of Nicaragua, were overwhelmed by the development of new middle sectors, which initially led the countries toward more pluralistic government. Subsequently, institution-based (rather than personalistic) military governments, in alliance with the traditional oligarchies, suppressed those pluralistic trends, often with the encouragement of the USA.

The period following the Second World War is the subject of Part II of this book.

Notes

1. Miles L. Wortman, *Government and Society in Central America, 1680–1840*; Ralph Lee Woodward, Jr, *Central America: a Nation Divided*, 2nd ed.; Eduardo P. Archetti, Paul Cammack and Bryan Roberts (eds) *Sociology of "Developing Societies": Latin America* (London: Macmillan, 1987).
2. Archetti, *et al.*, *Sociology of "Developing Societies"*, p. xvi.
3. Ibid, p. xv.
4. Ibid, p. xv.

5. Ibid, p. xviii.
6. Ibid, p. xvi–xvii.
7. Woodward, Jr, *Central America*, pp. 10–20.
8. Ibid, pp. 17 and 20.
9. Ibid, p. 22.
10. Ibid, pp. 26–34.
11. Wortman, *Government and Society*, p. 5.
12. Ibid, p. 5.
13. Ibid, p. 13; note: the *alcalde* is the mayor or headman of the community.
14. Ibid, p. 29; note: a *real* was one-eighth of a peso; pesos were silver coins, and hence were worth considerably more than is a British pound or US dollar today.
15. Ibid, pp. 25–6.
16. Ibid, p. 34; note: The *audiencia* was the chief administrative and legislative body of the Kingdom; the president of the *audiencia* was the representative of the Crown.
17. Ibid, p. 43.
18. Ibid, pp. 43–6.
19. Ibid, pp. 52–4 and 58; quotation is from p. 54.
20. Ibid, p. 100.
21. Ibid, p. 105.
22. Ibid, p. 133.
23. Ibid, pp. 103 and 174.
24. Ibid, p. 116.
25. Ibid, pp. 117–18.
26. Ibid, pp. 120–6.
27. Ibid, pp. 130–1.
28. Ibid, p. 196.
29. Woodward, Jr, *Central America*, pp. 92–3.
30. Ibid, p. 93.
31. Wortman, *Government and Society*, p. 247.
32. Woodward, Jr, *Central America*, pp. 99–105.
33. Ibid, p. 113.
34. Wortman, *Government and Society*, pp. 268–77. Note: a *caudillo* is an authoritarian figure who governs by the use of traditional (clientelistic) authority, often with a dash of charismatic authority manifested in *macho* behaviour. *Caudillos* were originally regional agrarian overlords who formed their own "state within a state", with their own armies and "laws". In the nineteenth century, a modified form of *caudillismo* became the form of governance by many national leaders. Juan Peron of Argentina was perhaps the last of the *caudillo* of the twentieth century.
35. Woodward, Jr, *Central America*, pp. 160–72.
36. See Zamosc, pp. 59–60, in this volume, for a description of the violent impact of the Liberal abolition of Indian communal lands in El Salvador.
37. Woodward, Jr, *Central America*, pp. 174–5.
38. Ibid, pp. 177–82.

39. Ibid, p. 182.
40. Ibid, p. 184.
41. Ibid, pp. 197–8.
42. See Zamosc, pp. 66–7 and 71 in this volume for a discussion of the role of artisans in the labour movement of the 1920s and the uprising in 1932.
43. Woodward, Jr, *Central America*, p. 186.

Central America: Cultures in Conflict

Jan L. Flora, Douglas K. Benson, and Cornelia B. Flora

Even before the coming of Balboa and Pedro de Alvarado, the first Spanish *conquistadores* in Central America, cultural differences between Indian peoples had created rivalries and conflict. For example, the Mexican-influenced Pipiles of El Salvador had imposed new ideas of social and religious organization, new deities and artistic concepts, on the villages around them.[1] The Quichés of highland Guatemala, drawing on a variety of Mayan and Mexican sources, were able to organize themselves militarily and become resoundingly victorious over the native people of the area, which came to be called the Quiché after these outsiders who conquered it.[2] Most Central American Indians, however, were sedentary agriculturalists who were similar to one another in the broad cultural values and attitudes they expressed. It was these groups that entered into the most direct and long-term conflict with the Spanish culture from the earliest moments of contact, and that most directly felt the impact of an entirely new way of looking at people's role in society and nature.

Once it was clear that Central America offered little in the way of precious minerals, Spanish settlement developed in areas where there were large concentrations of indigenous peoples, for they served as a readily available labour force for what came to be landed estates (*haciendas*). Those were precisely the indigenous sedentary agriculturalists, who conveniently had skills which were essential for the development of the landed estates. Few black slaves were brought to Central America, and today's black population along the Atlantic (Caribbean) Coast consists largely of descendants of runaway slaves from the Caribbean islands; those coastal regions did not and do not represent the central areas of Spanish or creole influence (creoles, in colonial times, were those of Spanish descent born in the New World). In fact, until the beginning of this century much of the Atlantic Coastal region was under the suzerainty of Great Britain. Belize remains so to this day.

In general terms, we can speak of a dominant landed patriarchal Spanish culture, and various cultures of resistance – indigenous cultures, cultures of various non-élite social classes, various female

17

cultures. "Culture of resistance" is used here in the broad sense of being different from and having to interact with the dominant culture, and resisting it at least to the degree of consciously or unconsciously seeking to maintain a separate cultural identity. Subordinate cultures – particularly élite female culture – often accommodated themselves to the patriarchal culture based on the landed estate, but also developed subtle ways of exercising control over, and hence shaping, that dominant culture. The interaction of the various and often cross-cutting cultures is quite complex.

Relationship to Nature

Spanish culture, drawing upon both European and Middle Eastern roots, saw the New World as a hostile place, needing conquering, whose fruits were there for the picking. The version of Spanish culture transferred to and modified in the New World, then, was one bent on exploiting and taming nature. Land was to be awarded, bought and sold as just compensation for duty to one's king or as a tangible reward of one's nobility, Spanish birth or social status. In contrast, indigenous culture stressed human beings' apprenticeship to nature rather than their dominion over it (as the Judeo-Christian Old Testament teaches). In the indigenous view, the universe is already in a state of harmony which only humans can disrupt:

> All things were alive and capable of acting upon all other things. The belief in an animating essence common to people, animals, plants, and physical objects resulted in a world in which these elements were interrelated. The natural elements were personified, and people and gods were closely tied to animals, plants, and natural forces.[3]

By studying the signs of nature (plants, animals, stars), indigenous people learned to live in and with its vast system of interconnecting causes and effects, its mutually compensating forces, and its consequences for those who did not follow the way. This apprenticeship was an integral part of becoming an adult member of the community.

In indigenous cultures, individuals did not own land; they could only be given the right to use it through community allocation mechanisms.[4] They took only what they needed, and often performed rituals requesting the earth's permission to do so. If the earth's equilibrium was put out of kilter by human error, it could be brought back through ritual, ceremony, accommodation and (in a few societies only) sacrifice. Only the priests could read the signs and interpret the will of the gods for the good of the community, but all had to work together to ensure that no calamity would befall the community because of the consequences of an individual act.[5]

In the creation story of the Mayan *Popol Vuh*, on their third attempt, the gods created men made of wood. But these men refused to honour their makers, and so they were annihilated by a flood as well as by the very animals, pots and pans, and trees that they had mistreated in their arrogant strutting upon the earth. When the gods did finally discover a material from which men and women could be fashioned (white and yellow corn), it was only with the help of all the animals that they were able to find it. These lessons, by contrast with the Christian version in *Genesis*, show us that, in nature as in society, all beings depend upon each other. There are no accidents, only consequences. The indigenous relationship to nature can thus be described as one emphasizing sustainability and mutual interdependence, while the Spanish/European relationship was one of domination, exploitation and extraction. Even today, for many indigenous groups, land is seen as a sacred trust. To be without land is to be torn from one's connection to nature. To work on the land for another who "owns" it is a repulsive, and perhaps sacrilegious, act. Most Indian uprisings in the Americas have been over the appropriation of their lands; the 1932 *machetazo* and consequent *matanza* in El Salvador is but one example. And yet as a result of Spanish and North American institutions, the changeover to private ownership and cash crops is inexorably changing this relationship with nature as well as with the tribal elders who previously assured community adherence to the old ways.[6] Even today, though, "wealthy" members of Indian communities work the land with their own hands; a measure of their wealth is access to enough land to work. In *ladino* society, of course, a measure of wealth is one's distance from manual labour.[7]

Relationship of People to One Another

In examining the dominant culture and various cultures of resistance, we will emphasize three ways of assigning people to groups. These are (a) ethnicity; (b) class, and (c) gender. Obviously there are important interactions among these three group determinants.

Ethnicity   Perhaps the most important difference between indigenous and Spanish approaches to interpersonal relationships is
that the cultures rest on two quite different forms of collective
orientation. Indigenous groups place great importance on the
geographic and social community (the clan or the tribe) as a moral
community, while the dominant social and moral unit for Spanish
and *mestizo* society is the family – what Lomnitz and Pérez-Lizaur
call the "grand-family", the three-generation family headed by the
grandparents, and including all their descendants and spouses.[8]

The Indian community of today evolved directly from the Spanish-
imposed Indian commune of the seventeenth century, and formed
the basis for indigenous cultural survival from the colonial period
until the period after the Second World War.[9] Lewald notes that in
the three most widely studied indigenous civilizations (Aztec, Maya,
Inca) – all highly centralized and stratified at least in terms of the
city-state – land was distributed through community structures and
was never considered private property. In some societies, the right
to work a private plot came with birth, but if an adult did not work
the allotted land, producing for the clan, the land reverted to the
community and the person could be enslaved or exiled. Labour as
well as ceremony tended to be collective. In this communal style of
life, crops were cooperatively planted, harvested, divided and
distributed in a manner consistent with the wellbeing of the
community. Crimes against the community, such as theft of commun-
ally-stored food, were considered more serious than those against
an individual.[10] Of course, if the crime affected the efficient operation
of the community, as did marital discord, it would be dealt with
through counselling or separation. Indeed, "trial marriages" were
quite common and matrimonial ties were rather flexible. Among the
Maya, the community considered a couple married only when it
had produced a child.[11]

There were, of course, differences between regional groups in
Central America. In addition to the Maya and Quiché of Guatemala,
Helms describes three different types of social pattern in the sixteenth
century: (a) the rank or chiefdom societies of Panama and Costa
Rica (chiefdoms in Costa Rica were less stratified); (b) the much
more stratified Mesoamerican-influenced peoples of Pacific Nicaragua and Nicoya, and (c) the tribal societies of the extensive
Caribbean lowlands of eastern Nicaragua and Honduras, with their
egalitarian family groups living semi-nomadically along the coasts
and rivers.[12] Nevertheless, they all held similar views of society and
nature; even in the most stratified, all classes shared a common
culture.

These cultural patterns differed radically from the European individualistic-familistic tendencies, based on a money economy, which the Spaniards brought with them. Some indigenous societies were obliterated during the conquest. In Central America over the next four centuries, the majority lost land and independence to the landed estates. The corporate Indian community, a version of the communal village structure with roots in the seventeenth century, continued to resist *mestizo* inroads into the middle of the twentieth century through its self-sufficiency, its strict hierarchy dominated by village elders, and its levelling of economic inequality through the required financing of festivals. But the common views of pre-Colombian society had been shattered. New values had developed which were both an accommodation and resistance to those of their rulers, whose values were in sharp contrast to pre-Colombian indigenous perspectives.

Class While people under the colonial system were initially assigned to a particular socially-relevant group based on their ethnicity, boundaries were permeable and mechanisms developed to legitimize persons born out of wedlock of mixed parentage. Persons of a "lower" ethnic group could be defined as being in a more powerful group if they occupied a position of prestige and power within the subordinate group, or if they were extremely talented. While permeable class barriers existed for uncommon individuals, on a macro level such mechanisms served to strengthen and perpetuate the class system.

The central institution for determining class position until the Second World War was the landed estate or *hacienda*.[13] The *hacienda* and associated labour relations went through various transformations throughout its nearly 400-year history, but certain elements are common to all periods. The landed estate was preceded by the *encomienda*, which gave the *encomendero* control over vast expanses of land and the labour of indigenous people living on it, but ownership of neither. In contrast, the *hacienda* involved ownership of land by the *hacendado* and control of labour successively through the *repartimiento* (a system whereby persons living in indigenous villages were required to give a certain number of days labour per month to the *hacienda*, supposedly in exchange for a modest fixed amount of money), debt peonage, and more recently (following Liberal reforms of the nineteenth century) through vagrancy laws and other coercive methods of insuring the availability of "free" labour to the estate.

During the colonial period, the upper-class Spanish or creole family was most influenced by its counterpart in Spain, but was shaped by the landed estate as it developed in the Americas. Primogeniture and political marriages, a favourable legal structure, and the distance of the crown and its unwillingness to give up authority to the *audiencia* (based in Guatemala City), all contributed to the landed estate becoming a unit unto itself, with its own police force and legal system. Hence the extended family was the principal social unit, with no effective or regularly present higher authority available to adjudicate disputes.[14] With the growing commercialism of the Bourbon period (eighteenth century), commercially-oriented Spaniards married daughters of *criollo* notables. This was the case in the marriage of the Basque immigrant Juan Fermín Aycinena with Ana Carillo y Gálvez, a descendant of notable Guatemalan families who could trace lineage in America back to the sixteenth, seventeenth, and eighteenth centuries. As Wortman indicates, "The union cemented peninsular dynamism with local privilege."[15]

The landed estate and the political and economic system which surrounded it created a flexible system of clearly defined social classes, with modestly permeable boundaries and vertical relations which enhanced the stability of the system. The *hacienda* historically has been the principal means of status validation for the aristocracy/oligarchy through conspicuous consumption. The landed estate was not technologically advanced, for technology is incompatible with the gentlemanly leisure which was the cultural analogue to such an economic institution. Manual labour on the part of the landowner, of course, was out of the question.

Indigenous persons initially formed the core of tied labour which worked the landed estates. As the colonial period progressed, the number of *mestizos* grew and they also became tied labourers on the estates. Unlike Mexico, where the *peones* usually lived on the estate, in Central America the tardy demise of the *repartimiento* meant that politically autonomous indigenous communities continued to exist outside the boundaries of the *hacienda*.[16] Such communities were a vehicle for maintaining a strong indigenous culture of resistance even after independence, especially in Guatemala until the regime of Ubico (1931–44). While significantly weakened, indigenous communities continued to have some autonomy until the culturally genocidal policies of the Ríos Montt regime (1982–3).[17]

In the colonial period, *mestizos* and Indians were called *castas*. They were assigned outcast status supposedly because of their vices, shiftlessness, and promiscuity – which we now recognize as results, rather than causes, of their status as pariahs. Such classification originated in medieval Spain, where the concepts of *limpieza de sangre* (purity of blood) and *linaje* (lineage) were used against persons of

Moorish and Jewish ancestry. But in the New World where there was such a shortage of Spaniards, and particularly of Spanish women, the system was practised with considerable flexibility. Specifically, *linaje* could override *limpieza de sangre*, particularly when the system was greased with money paid to make a bastard son legitimate. Precise fees were charged for legitimizing bastard sons; it was more expensive if the father was a cleric or a nobleman in a military order than if the child was the offspring of another married man and an unmarried woman. Another mechanism was the *cédula de gracias al sacar*, literally a "document of thanksgiving for being pulled up". According to King, cited in Willems, its purpose was "to compensate individual merits among the subjects of color, to drain the possible leader force from the colored masses by creating . . . partisans grateful to the Crown who added to the white minority and undermined the pretensions of the *criollo* aristocracy". This mechanism, which defused much dissent, was used widely in the eighteenth century.[18]

In colonial times, *mestizos* became small merchants, artisans, and independent peasants or medium-sized farmers, as well as peons. Indigenous people were relegated to tied labour on the estates and/or to their peasant holdings. With independence, the formal mechanisms for defining the classes disappeared, but the distinctions between groups remained. The distinction between *mestizo* and Indian was that of cultural practices and dress. By changing one's dress and language, an indigenous person could become a *mestizo* or *ladino*.

Patriarchy and Gender   Patriarchy was closely associated with the landed estate. Variations in kinship and family structure were primarily functions of social class. The landholding aristocratic family was characterized by its large size, stability over time, structural complexity, high degree of solidarity and multiplicity of functions. In colonial times, *patria potestas*, which derived from the legal norms of *Las Siete Partidas* promulgated in Spain under Alfonso X, was practised in the New World and shaped the culture of the landed aristocracy. *Patria potestas* is the authority of fathers "over their children and grandchildren and all others descended from them in direct line *who were born in lawful wedlock*". Unmarried women were under the control of their fathers; married women, under their husbands. Not surprisingly, adultery was an offence only if committed by a woman. According to Spanish law, a woman who had committed adultery was to be turned over with her lover to the offended husband in order that he might satiate his thirst for revenge on the guilty. The only limitation on the insulted husband's action was that he could not kill one of the adulterers without killing the other also.[19] Allowing a family member to execute the law dovetailed nicely with the legal and *de facto* autonomy of the American landed estate, which was often isolated geographically within a weak system of central authority. The sole central authority which supposedly reached directly to each estate and *ayuntamiento* (municipal government) was the Spanish crown, which was so far away that it exercised only sporadic control.[20] This system was at issue in the nineteenth century (after independence) when Liberal commercially-oriented merchants and export-oriented landowners attempted (successfully, by and large) to strengthen the power of the state so that it might serve their interests better. Holders of traditional landed estates, of course, preferred a weaker state that would allow them to maintain their own local autonomy.

Under *Las Siete Partidas*, no Spaniard (which included creoles – Spaniards born in the New World) could marry without paternal consent. Such a requirement was closely linked to the need to preserve the landed estate. Consent was rarely given if it did not conform to family interest. Romantic love only occasionally conflicted with such a system, since for males there was no legal or cultural prohibition on extramarital affairs. In fact, such extramarital activities were encouraged; the virility complex was (and is) a central feature of *machismo*. Prostitution and the *casa chica* (having a second non-legally sanctioned family) are natural outcomes of such a system.[21]

On the other hand, daughters and wives were carefully watched through chaperonage, sex segregation, and extreme punishment for extramarital transgressions. Implicit in this system is the belief that women (especially those in the aristocracy, who are closest to the male-defined Spanish ideal) are unable to resist sexual temptations on their own. According to Octavio Paz, the Spanish attitude toward women is as follows:

> Woman is a domesticated wild animal, lecherous and sinful from birth, who must be subdued with a stick and guided by the "reins of religion". Therefore Spaniards consider other women – especially those of a race or religion different from their own – to be easy game.[22]

The Catholicism brought to the New World was that of Inquisition Spain. Spanish religious practice demanded the unquestioning acceptance of doctrine, at least for women. Males, in their sexual behaviour, were exempt from following the relevant moral precepts, because such actions were not their fault. Women, of whatever social class, were defined as sexual beings. Males, being *macho*, simply had no means of warding off such sexual temptations.

Stevens describes *machismo* as "the cult of virility" and gives the corresponding (male-defined) female ideal the name of *marianismo*, characterized by "semi-divinity, moral superiority, and spiritual strength".[23] While the dual *machismo–marianismo* stereotype affects all social classes in modern Latin America, the degree to which it is practised varies by social class. It is particularly entrenched among the bourgeoisie and petty bourgeoisie because, as we saw in the colonial period, it is important in the defence and institutionalization of property. The degrees of acceptance in indigenous communities varies widely, depending on the extent to which *ladinoization* has occurred.

The sexual repression of women by aristocratic moral and legal norms placed them in a vulnerable position. The assumed higher moral nature of women as they got older and less attractive sexually, the perceived willingness of women to suffer (after all, their husbands frequently engage in sexual exploits with other women, over which they have no power), and the sole responsibility of women for child-rearing and for the household, all contribute to women gaining power within the realm of the household. The mother–son link is particularly important, even after the son marries. His mother is the only woman with whom he can have a relationship in which sexuality is not the sole or principal driving force. His wife serves other functions; she cements economic relationships between families, first through marriage and then through procreation. She is not often a companion and close confidante – and is generally expected not to enjoy sex with her husband.[24] On the other hand, the mother has her greatest possibility of influence and control outside the household through her sons, more so than through her husband. In addition, since in a patriarchal society men tend to marry younger women, the sons are likely to be the new patriarchs while the mother is still relatively young. She gains even greater social stature after her husband's death, though until recently she has had no legal claim to property.

In colonial times, the *castas* were not bound by these patriarchal rules of marital consent. Though the *patria potestas* was modified following independence, the cultural patterns represented by the aristocracy expanded to the *mestizo* sector of society. In contrast, indigenous marital and sexual practices remained dominant in the corporate Indian communities. While fidelity was more often honoured in the breach than the observance, the relationships between men and women differed greatly from Spanish-derived practices, as can be seen by Wolf's contemporary description:

> The Indian man seeks a woman to bear his children and to keep up his home: there is little romantic love. Ideally, people conform to strict standards of marital fidelity. In practice, however, there is considerable latitude for sexual adventure outside marriage, and philandering does not usually endanger the bonds of the union. Nor do Indians engage in sexual conquest as a validation of their masculinity; sexual conquest does not add luster to the reputation of the individual. Exploitation of one sex by the other encounters little sympathy, just as political or economic exploitation of one man by another is not countenanced within the boundaries of the community.[25]

Three Modern Manifestations

Today aspects of Central American indigenous cultures survive through intermarriage and cross-cultural contact in *mestizo* culture, even in those areas where there are no longer significant Indian populations. The profound desire to have land on which to grow crops, and thus to have a connection to the world of natural beings, the communal religious rituals, the art forms, foods, and even ways of looking at nature and society have become an integral part of *campesino* culture.[26] A telling example of how ingrained – and how misunderstood – this is can be seen in Nicaraguan writer Omar Cabezas's memoir of his rural and urban training for the Sandinista revolution, *Fire from the Mountain*. Many of the methods of surviving in the jungle which he learns as a guerrilla are clearly Indian in origin (such as walking in each other's footprints). Coming from the urban petty bourgeoisie, however, he is unaware of this. The most revealing chapter of the book is "The Mountain Mourns a Son". Heavily imbued with an animistic vision of the mountain as Mother Earth, with a strong feeling of sentient communicability with the natural environment, and with a heightened sensorial awareness of that environment, Cabezas's prose takes on a lyrical quality very similar to that of the indigenous world view (and very out of keeping with the style of the rest of the book). He could only have learned it from the *campesinos* who taught him to see this way.[27] Yet nowhere does he demonstrate any knowledge of the cultural roots of this vision in indigenous perspective nor, in all probability, would the *campesinos* from whom he learned it. Cabezas can understand the perspective now, but does not tie it to the Indians of Nicaragua for whom he ostensibly fought the revolution.

The expansion of international capitalism into all sectors of Central American economies since the Second World War, and especially since the creation of the Central American Common Market, has contributed to the growth of the middle sectors, but also in some ways has contributed to the conflict between city and country and between male and female.

Brintnall documents the recent breakup of the corporate Indian community in Guatemala, but sees new hope: the conversion to cash crops, the weakening of the authority of the elders and their control over land inheritance, the greater access to education, and the lessening fear of *ladino* control over their labour may have caused the much more visible political activity of Guatemalan Indians in the late 1970s.[28] In the short run, the price of that political activity has been high, as the Guatemalan military, in addition to forcing indigenous people into civil patrols and restructuring the countryside through the strategy of development poles, seeks to suppress Maya religious festivals, discourage the growing of the sacred crop (corn) by indigenous peoples, and replace the use of indigenous languages with Spanish. That the military seeks cultural genocide for the most rebellious indigenous groups is indicated in this quote from the Guatemalan army's *Revista Militar* regarding the Ixil of Northern Quiché, which proposes:

> the *ladinoization* of the Ixil population in such a way that it ceases to exist as a cultural subgroup. What is meant by *ladinoization*, is that they become Spanish speakers, that their distinctive clothing and all other external features that differentiate them as a group be suppressed. Without these differentiating characteristics, they will cease to think of themselves as such (Ixiles) and accept the abstract concepts of nationality and homeland.[29]

The consumption ethic which accompanies capitalist social patterns has also contributed to the need for women in all urban classes, except the bourgeoisie, to enter the labour force. Labour-force participation often becomes an absolute imperative for women of working-class and marginally-employed families. Such patterns have an impact on women's culture.

While male domination was historically linked to the preservation and expansion of the landed estate, today the disintegration of family structure at the lower end of the social scale is also consistent with the interests of capital accumulation.[30] New cultural forces, such as television programmes from the USA, presented individualistic alternatives to the collective orientation of the indigenous cultures and the family orientation of the *criollo* culture. Particularly in the shanty towns around Guatemala City and San Salvador, where industry and a growing informal economy provided new relations to the means of production, the need for a highly mobile and interchangeable labour force was reflected in forms of mass culture, particularly comics and photonovels. In these inexpensive and widely distributed publications, the focus was on the individual, not the collective. The theme tended to be romance (by its very nature individualistic, and not necessarily part of courtship and marriage in either indigenous or *criollo* culture). Subthemes, particularly of the Mexican-produced photonovels, include the linking of sex and death, the just individual in an unjust society, and the repressive nature of class relationships (with no collective options for resolution presented).

Photonovel themes evolved dramatically in the three decades from the mid-1950s to the 1980s. The 1950s saw the development of stories of poor but pure virgins attracting, then marrying, cynical but handsome millionaires – implying that class boundaries, as any others, could be overcome by the power of love. The photonovel of the 1980s was much more explicit in its portrayal of sex and violence – and in the limited options present for the poor in a harsh urban environment. Emphasis changed from chastity to necessity. The wife forced into prostitution to keep her family alive replaced the heroine who would not allow even a kiss from men driven frantic by passion. If the nature of the Latin male did not change from colonial times to photonovel representation, the nature of women did. No longer was a woman either Eve or the Virgin Mary. Characters, especially lower-middle- and working-class female characters, were increasingly forced by economic necessity into situations that denied their human dignity – an important subtheme that emerged in the 1970s.[31] Photonovels increasingly pointed out the difference between outward sexual degradation and inward purity and integrity. But the inward state of grace was known only to the characters portrayed and to the readers. The contradictions of the plots could only be resolved through the death of the major characters – usually death caused directly by the misunderstanding of those who should have loved and protected them the most. The "new" photonovel repeated the individualistic theme of the *fotonovelas rosas* (Cinderella photonovels) of the 1950s, but by the 1980s even these denied the possibility of two people uniting to find happiness.[32]

Conclusion

Clearly, in order to understand the complexities of modern Central American nations, there is a need to consider cultural/historical elements as well as contemporary political, economic and military spheres of influence. In addition, urban centres of political power are not the only contexts in which political and social change can be initiated. Indeed, the consequences of centralized attempts to change a cultural reality may be quite different from those which were originally envisioned by the developers of policy. Thus, a lack of awareness of the "cultures of resistance" can lead the ruling classes to consequences for which they are unprepared and for which they have no explanation nor appropriate response. The Omar Cabezas example offers one possible reason why the Sandinistas have had problems in reaching accommodation with the Miskito Indians of the Atlantic coast, and why the *contras* have had no better luck in trying to convert them politically to their cause. Other factors, such as the Miskitos' historical relationship with English traders and smugglers, add further layers of complexity. The case of the politicization of Guatemalan Indian groups is a development which must horrify the Guatemalan military and to which they have responded with brutal tactics which, in turn, can only deepen potential for revolution in that country. New developments in the *fotonovela* suggest that social/sexual awareness, rather than escapism, is becoming an increasingly common mode of thought among female shanty-town readers. We can, of course, only guess at the directions this awareness might take.

Cultural conflict has been at the root of misunderstandings in Central America since the time of the Spanish conquest. Today it stands between us and our own understanding of the forces which define the area and its people. It is our hope, then, that this book presents fresh perspectives on a region whose complexity appears only to increase with the passage of time.

Notes

1. Ralph Lee Woodward, Jr, *Central America: A Nation Divided*, pp. 10–15.
2. Robert M. Carmack, *The Quiché Mayas of Utatlán: The Evolution of a Highland Guatemalan Kingdom* (Norman: University of Oklahoma Press, 1981) pp. 369–70.
3. Carmack, *Quiché Mayas*, pp. 82–3 (quote is from p. 82), describes an

important example of this type of animistic world in his study of the Quiché of Utatlán. See also H. Ernest Lewald, *Latinoamérica: sus Culturas y Sociededes* (New York: McGraw-Hill, 1973) pp. 41–2.

4. Woodward, *Central America*, pp. 18–20; Emilio Willems, *Latin American Culture: An Anthropological Synthesis*, p. 132; Lewald, *Latinoamerica*, pp. 38–9.
5. Douglas E. Brintnall, *Revolt Against the Dead: The Modernization of a Mayan Community in the Highlands of Guatemala*, pp. 90–4; Lewald, *Latinoamerica*, p. 42.
6. Brintnall, *Revolt*, pp. 1–31. Brintnall believes that it is this very opening up of the corporate Indian community that has given the Guatemalan Indian population the tools it needs to join political organizations, which he sees occurring in the late 1970s. The article by Handy in this volume appears to lend support to his thesis.
7. Woodward, *Central America*, pp. 14–17.
8. Larissa A. Lomnitz and Marisol Pérez-Lizaur, "Dynastic Growth and Survival Strategies: the Solidarity of Mexican Grand-Families", in Raymond T. Smith, ed., *Kinship Ideology and Practice in Latin America* (Chapel Hill: University of North Carolina Press, 1984) pp. 183–95. Lomnitz and Pérez-Lizaur studied middle- and upper-class grand-families which are descendants of a nineteenth-century scion, and compared them with the inhabitants of a Mexico City shanty town. They find that the grand-family ideal is more readily realized by the middle- and upper-class families because of their greater economic resources than is true for shanty-town residents. But the ideal in terms of seeking to maintaining solidarity of the grand-family through frequent contact and contiguous residence, is just as important to the shanty-town dwellers.
9. Eric Wolf, *Sons of the Shaking Earth*, pp. 33–4; Mary W. Helms, *Middle America: a Cultural History of Heartland and Frontiers*, pp. 196–200; Willems, *Latin American Culture*, p. 131.
10. In a short story by the Peruvian writer Enrique López Albújar entitled "Ushanan-Jampi" ("The Last Resort"), one member of the community has committed a theft against another member despite two previous warnings by the elders. So all members (including children) congregate under the direction of the elders to hear the case. The elders serve essentially as takers of testimony, and it is only when the entire community has seen that the protagonist cannot be rehabilitated (and therefore cannot become useful in the community) that he is forever banished. When he returns for the fourth time, and then tries to shoot his way back out of the village, he is killed in a horrible fashion by all the members. Since all members depend on each other, such exaggerated acts of individualism cannot be condoned, for they endanger the survival of the entire clan. Yet, except in extreme cases, slavery was the preferred punishment because the person could still contribute labour, and thus function as a productive member of the community. The translated story is found in Harriet de Onis (ed. and trans.) *The Golden Land: An Anthology of Latin American Folklore in Literature* (New York: Alfred A. Knopf, 1948) pp. 238–47.

11. Lewald, *Latinoamerica*, pp. 38–42; Wolf, *Sons*, p. 36. A well-known story in which the conflicting ideas of marriage in Latin and indigenous cultures result in a heartrending tragedy is "Barranca Grande" ("Big Precipice") by Ecuadorian novelist Jorge Icaza, translated in Pat McNees Mancini (ed.) *Contemporary Latin American Stories* (Greenwich, Connecticut: Fawcett, 1974) pp. 79–99.
12. Helms, *Middle America*, pp. 114–19.
13. Willems, *Latin American Culture*, pp. 27–34.
14. Ibid, pp. 31–2. See also Miles Wortman, "Central America", in Diana Balmori, Stuart F. Voss, and Miles Wortman, *Notable Family Networks in Latin America* (Chicago: University of Chicago Press, 1984) p. 71, for a description of the Zelayas of Olancho, Honduras, who paid no taxes, occupied all important provincial posts, and dispensed patrimonial favours and punishment well after Central American independence in the nineteenth century.
15. Wortman in *Notable Family Networks*, pp. 61–7 (quotation is from p. 61).
16. Woodward, *Central America*, p. 44.
17. See Handy, this volume, for a description of the Rios Montt and subsequent policies toward indigenous people in Guatemala.
18. Willems, *Latin American Culture*, pp. 41–2.
19. Ibid, pp. 55–6. Quotation is directly from *Las Siete Partidas* (our italics).
20. Ibid, pp. 91–3.
21. Ibid, pp. 56–62.
22. Octavio Paz, *The Labyrinth of Solitude: Idea and Thought in Mexico* (New York: Grove Press, 1961) p. 36.
23. Evelyn P. Stevens, "Marianismo: the Other Face of Machismo in Latin America", in Ann Pescatello (ed.) *Female and Male in Latin America: Essays* (Pittsburgh, Pennsylvania: University of Pittsburgh Press, 1973) pp. 89–101.
24. Shoshona B. Tancer, "La Quisqueyana: the Dominican Woman, 1940–1970", in Pescatello, *Female and Male*, pp. 216–17.
25. Wolf, *Sons*, p. 37.
26. Eugenio Chang Rodriguez, *Latinoamerica: su Civilizacion y su Cultura* (Rowley, Massachusetts: Newbury House, 1983) pp. 41–3.
27. Omar Cabezas, *Fire From the Mountain*, pp. 54–62, 101–2, 115–28.
28. Brintnall, *Revolt*, pp. 170–9.
29. Quoted in Patricia K. Hall, "Military Rule Threatens Guatemala's Highland Maya Indians", *Cultural Survival Quarterly*, 10, 2 (1986) p. 48.
30. Cornelia Butler Flora and Jan L. Flora, "The Fotonovela as a Tool for Class and Culture Domination", *Latin American Perspectives*, vol. 5 (Winter 1978) p. 142.
31. Cornelia B. Flora, "Domestic Service in the Mexican Photonovel", *Studies in Latin American Popular Culture*, 4 (1985) pp. 79–84.
32. For more detail, see Cornelia B. Flora, "The Fotonovela in Latin America", Studies in *Latin American Popular Culture*, vol. 1 (1982) pp. 15–26; and Cornelia B. Flora, "Women in Latin American Fotonovelas: from Cinderella to Mata Hari", *Women's Studies: An International Quarterly*, 3, 1 (1980) pp. 95–104.

Sociology of Developing Societies: Historical Bases of Insurgency in Central America

Jan L. Flora and Edelberto Torres-Rivas

Introduction

Paige, espousing an agrarian base for revolution, focuses on the development of export agriculture. He bases his theory on a shift from land to capital and wages as principal sources of wealth, arguing that a system in which the principal source of wealth for agricultural non-cultivators in which land is inherently unstable, since it requires direct political control of labour rather than the exercise of economic control through the market-place. Such systems are economically weak (technologically backward). Therefore those in control perceive a zero-sum political and economic game; hence the need for political control over the cultivating classes, either in a manorial system (*hacienda*), sharecropping or migratory labour estate (plantation).[1]

Paige's emphasis on export agriculture as a conditioning factor for agrarian rebellion or revolution is useful but limited. His clear distinction between economic and political factors in explaining agrarian revolution is also useful, but needs modification in its application. The growth in importance of export agriculture and the type of export agriculture have an impact not only on the cultivator classes, but also on the society as a whole, particularly on the kind of state structure which develops. Specifically, if control of production and export are in the hands of a domestic élite, a stronger state will develop than if export agriculture is controlled by foreign firms. In states in which domestically-controlled export agriculture is important, and particularly in which one such export crop is the dominant export (export monoculture), the relatively strong state will reflect the view of the dominant élite (the export oligarchy) that there is a zero-sum economic situation; hence that oligarchy will seek to maintain absolute political control. Such efforts are likely to lead to repression. Such repression can lead to rebellion or insurgency, particularly in times when the economic *reality* approaches a zero-sum situation (e.g. in times of shrinking export values) and/or when, with diversification of agricultural exports and growth of industrialization, shifting alliances develop among peasants, artisans and workers, and new urban élites who have not been allowed a share of political power. Countries in which foreign-owned enclave agriculture or traditional domestically-oriented manorial agriculture develop are not likely to experience insurgencies, (a) because the poor classes are sufficiently isolated one from another as to manage at most sporadic rebellions, and (b) because the state is not strong enough to suppress "legitimate" attempts at organization by the lower classes. Countries where the peasantry is a major export-crop producer will not develop insurgencies, as the peasantry will at least perceive that it has some influence over decision-making by the state, due in part to that group's belief in the possibility of social mobility.

We have chosen the five countries which once formed the Central American Federation, and operationally define a revolutionary situation as one in which a significant armed insurgency has arisen. These five countries have a similar political history, having received independence from Spain in 1821. They formed the Central American Federation, which broke up by 1840 and each of the five provinces became a politically independent country.² However, the five countries have evolved differently economically, and hence politically.

The objective of this chapter is to explain why insurgency has arisen in three of the countries (Guatemala, El Salvador, and Nicaragua) and why it has not arisen in the other two (Honduras and Costa Rica). The Central American Republics are a particularly propitious locale in which to test the perspective outlined above, because each state is small, thus minimizing the impact of regionalism. Each state is unitary: none has a federal system. Thus, the entire society is affected similarly by export agriculture or by any particular government policy. Also, there is little mineral wealth of importance; since independence, all countries have relied on agricultural commodities as their dominant exports.

The body of this chapter is in two parts – an economic and a political section. The economic section will examine the different ways in which each country became part of the international economic system and the effect that had on the role of the state. The political section will examine the degree to which all social classes – especially the poor majority – have been allowed to participate in political affairs and to feel they had some influence over the allocation of resources through the political system.

Incorporation into the International
Economic System and Role of the State

Liberal reforms, growth of the coffee oligarchy, and establishment of the banana enclaves From the second half of the last century until after the Second World War, coffee and bananas were the dominant exports of Central America. Coffee growing expanded in the Central American Republics in the second half of the nineteenth century (earlier in Costa Rica). Except in Honduras, a coffee bourgeoisie became the dominant domestic political force. Somewhat later, foreign enclaves of banana production became important in Honduras, Costa Rica, and Guatemala (in that order of importance), and to a lesser extent in Nicaragua.[3]

The impacts of coffee and banana production on Central American domestic economies differed from each other in that capital invested in coffee cultivation, whether domestic or foreign, stimulated the national economy. Foreign capital used by the banana industry, on the other hand, created enclave economies that were rather independent of the national economy.[4] Coffee production was in domestic hands (with some foreign investment), but export banana production was foreign-owned and controlled, principally by the United and Standard Fruit companies.

Politically, the growth of coffee production meant the growth of a dominant or hegemonic social group – the coffee oligarchy. In El Salvador and Guatemala, those oligarchies gained power after Liberal "reforms" in the second half of the nineteenth century. Nicaragua experienced a tardy and less pronounced Liberal reform. The reforms involved (a) making land into a commodity by virtually eliminating communal and church lands so they could be acquired by coffee-growing entrepreneurs, (b) insuring an adequate labour force by variously "freeing" or coercing workers to work in coffee, and (c) strengthening the state to ensure orderly and profitable marketing of the new export crop.[5]

A coffee oligarchy did not dominate Honduras. Traditional large land-holders were important in the political power configuration in Honduras, but they tended to be livestock producers *who were not tied to the international market.*[6]

Costa Rica (having neither mineral wealth nor Indian labour) "the least populated and the poorest" of the independent Central American provinces, was gradually settled by peasant farmers. Coffee production began to expand within ten years after independence, partly because there were no entrenched interests to resist it; Costa Rica had no important existent export crop.[7] Land inequalities grew somewhat as processing machinery required increased investment per unit of production and as exporters accumulated capital. But most rural people remained land-owning farmers, so there was a continuing labour shortage,[8] and constant upward pressure on wages,[9] discouraging the growth of large estates.

By the 1920s the Costa Rican state was "fully representative of powerful coffee interests",[10] and the coffee sector consisted of a mix of yeoman family farmers and *latifundistas*. Labour relations on the coffee *haciendas* tended to be capitalist; workers were salaried, not peons.[11]

Coffee export agriculture became important in all the Central American countries but Honduras. Only in El Salvador did this lead to fully capitalist productive relations. Coffee production gave rise to specific productive structures: notable concentration of land in large land-holdings (Costa Rica was a partial exception), low investment in productive techniques other than those used to process the crop, and relations of production ranging from semi-servile to semi-proletarian.

Absolute political control was of primordial concern to the coffee oligarchy, since control of land – rather than investment of capital – was central to their acquisition of wealth, for coffee production was technologically rather stagnant: the best way to increase one's wealth was to acquire more coffee land. On the other hand, marketing and export of coffee required considerable infrastructural investment (roads, port facilities, banking and related financial establishments). By gaining control of and subsequently strengthening the state, the coffee oligarchy could accomplish both ends – infrastructural costs could be socialized and the poor rural classes could be controlled politically, and hence economically.

Banana production *was* fully capitalist. The level of technological advance was considerable, if not initially in the field, certainly in the transport system. Approximately 80 per cent of the labour force consisted of wage workers, but at the height of employment in banana production in the 1950s, Central America had only about 100 000 banana workers.[12] Because of the importance of timing in the harvesting and marketing of this perishable product and because of the great investment which port facilities and ships represented, commercial banana production has been controlled by outside firms.

Honduras epitomizes the geographic isolation of fruit company operations from the rest of the country's economic activity. Although bananas were the principal export, there was no paved road from Tegucigalpa to the north coast, the centre of banana production, until after the Second World War. Honduras was the least developed of the Central American Republics, lacking even a Central Bank until 1950.[13]

In summary, strong coffee oligarchies developed late in the nineteenth century in Guatemala and El Salvador as part of a thorough-going Liberal transformation and alienation of collective forms of land-holding. The coffee oligarchy was most dominant in El Salvador because of the virtual absense of competing exports or of foreign investment. Costa Rica's coffee oligarchy gained hegemony after 1880 and even then had to accommodate the peasant coffee producers; Nicaragua's coffee oligarchy was less important and subordinated to foreign interests related to that country's strategic location for potential transisthmian traffic.

Honduras continued to have a traditional cattle oligarchy, with pre-capitalist labour relations. Because that oligarchy produced only for the domestic market and many of the productive relationships were non-monetary, little investment capital was accumulated. The *hacendado* saw little need for a strong Honduran state, and espoused a philosophy of a weak central government. Capitalist production in Honduras was represented by foreign-owned banana firms. The state was so weak it could not impose taxes on the banana companies, so until 1950 "enclave" was an apt description of the export banana industry in that country.

Export Expansion after the Second World War With the growing demand for primary products by the developed countries after the Second World War, commercial agriculture expanded and diversified in all Central American republics. Export crops, now grown on the best land, displaced peasants and removed fertile lowland areas from potential colonization or reception of human overflows from densely settled, upland areas. New export crops gained prominence: cotton,[14] sugar, and livestock for export.[15]

Expansion of capitalist export agriculture in the post-war period seems to have been consistently at the expense of food production. Since export crops are grown on large holdings and basic grains and other wage foods are grown predominantly by peasants, per capita production of wage foods declined, while imports of foodstuffs, semi-proletarianization, and landlessness increased.[16] At least in the case of El Salvador, there was increased immiseration of peasants and the rural landless population.[17] Production, even in the coffee sector, became more fully capitalist. As seasonal labour requirements increased in the export sector, more poor peasants and rural landless people became temporary or permanent migrants, often crossing national borders in response to seasonal labour requirements.

Variations in these patterns occurred chiefly in Costa Rica and Honduras. Costa Rica, as a colonial backwater with peculiar expansion of coffee production, is the only country with a majority of land dedicated to a primary export crop (coffee) in the hands of peasants.[18] Peasants' tenure is more secure in Costa Rica than in any other Central American Republic, although rural landlessness is a severe problem.[19]

Honduras was half a decade behind the other countries in diversifying its export agriculture, and pre-capitalist labour relations continued to be strong in the non-export sector. In 1974, Honduras exported a lower percentage of its agricultural production than any other Central American country.[20] Although its rural population is the poorest of all Central America,[21] because of the late insertion of capitalist relations in the countryside, Honduras did not develop peasant movements until quite recently.

"Import Substitution" Industrialization   Industrialization, which occurred earlier in the rest of Latin America, reached Central America in the 1960s with the establishment of the Central American Common Market (CACM). Industrialization *should* have decreased the necessity for foreign exchange. Instead, even though the imported part of Central American industrial output declined from 57 per cent to 44 per cent after the CACM was established (1963 to 1969), rapid industrial growth increased the absolute demand for imports, including the raw or partially finished materials that went into consumer goods and machinery used to produce the goods.[22]

The industrial output of all the Central American countries – except for Honduras – grew between 7 and 9 per cent annually from 1960 to 1976; Honduras's annual rate was 4.6 per cent for the period. Guatemala and El Salvador, with the earliest starts and larger internal markets, remained the most industrialized. Growth in industrial activity, along with the growing need to import food, increased the need for agricultural exports, because more foreign exchange was needed for agricultural and industrial investments.

The growth of agricultural export activities had negative impacts on rural people. The rapid increase in industrialization and commercial agriculture increased total per capita income, but the income of people lowest on the income scale declined. That undesirable situation resulted from the rapid increase in population, the capital-intensive nature of growing industrial activity, and the fact that people were being pushed off the land by large-scale commercial agriculture, which employed fewer workers than the peasant agriculture it replaced.

Torres-Rivas suggests that although the CACM was designed to deal with insufficient demand within each Central American country, the result was increased emphasis on low wages by employers in each country rather than on increasing demand through improved standards of living – for that would have meant power shifts and reduction of income inequalities. He concludes that "the final logic of repression is not the danger of guerrillas but the containment of salaries".[23] It is no coincidence that in the late 1970s increasing repression in all Central American countries except Costa Rica paralleled the decline in profits in the export sector, which resulted from the world economic slowdown.

Inclusion or Exclusion of Poor Classes and New Elites in the Political Dialogue

Equally important as the question, "Why has insurgency arisen in El Salvador, Guatemala, and Nicaragua?" is the question "Why has it not arisen in Honduras and Costa Rica?" In addition to the objective economic circumstances prevailing in the five Central American countries, political events in the first three countries involved repression of peasants, workers, and marginal urban classes who attempted to organize to defend their collective interests. We will first examine the relevant political events in the countries with insurgency which indicated a pattern of repression of popular movements, especially those in the countryside. This will be followed by a discussion of how a degree of legitimation of participation of non-bourgeois classes in the national dialogue occurred in the other two countries.

Countries with Insurgency

El Salvador   Following the Liberal reforms of the 1880s, consolidation of the coffee oligarchy was so complete that Liberal and Conservative parties did not exist as such. *Ad hoc* parties were organized when needed, and members of the coffee oligarchy rotated in power through coups and elections which ratified the hand-picked choice of the existing president.[24] Many landless persons moved to the towns where some became artisans, a group periodically threatened by the manufactured products brought into the country during periods of good coffee prices.[25]

In 1924, artisans, employees and workers formed the National Federation of Salvadoran Workers (FNTS), in spite of repression of peasants and of the small labour movement.[26] The decline in demand for coffee during the Great Depression led to a wave of peasant land dispossessions with accompanying political repression.[27] Worker organization reached into the countryside, particularly in western El Salvador where Indians still remembered the loss of their lands from the Liberal reforms. The Communist-organized rebellion of 1932 and the genocidal reprisals of the military (*la matanza*) consolidated military rule which lasted fifty years.[28] For the oligarchy, acquiescence in military rule was more acceptable than the spectre of peasant rebellion. All worker and peasant organizations were prohibited, and none emerged again until the 1950s.

General Maximiliano Hernández Martínez (1931–44) was overthrown by a popular uprising, organized by junior army officers, professional and university elements, with participation of segments of the urban middle class.[29] After a brief liberalization the coffee bourgeoisie reasserted control. In 1948, another military coup brought a systematic attempt at modernization. In 1949, the first party representing the military as an institution was formed, later becoming the PCN (National Conciliation Party). This representative of the "modernizing" bourgeoisie (both agrarian and industrial) and of the dominant sector of the military favours minimal reforms coupled with repressive measures when these are deemed necessary to maintain control. The PCN "won" presidential elections in 1962, 1967, 1972, and 1977 with massive and well-documented fraud.

In October 1979, a coup, led by young progressive officers, occurred under the shadow of a nascent home-group Marxist guerrilla movement. A civilian–military junta was installed, but it was soon clear that the military establishment continued to hold power. The Popular (People's) Forces – a group of organizations consisting of the poorer classes – demanded major reforms and effective participation in decision-making.[30]

In March 1980, Archbishop Romero, a supporter of the Popular Forces, was killed while saying mass. In November, the six principal leaders of the Popular Forces alliance, now called the Democratic Revolutionary Front (FDR), were kidnapped by uniformed forces, tortured and killed. The FDR, having been given no other alternative, went underground and became the political wing of the unified guerrilla movement, the Farabundo Martí National Liberation Front.[31] The middle ground had for the time being disappeared; the poor classes were excluded from participation in the "legitimate" political dialogue.

Guatemala   The event in recent Guatemalan history that contributed most to closing off peasant and worker participation in the political process was the overthrow of the elected reformist government in 1954 by a CIA-supported force of Guatemalans.

The growth of commercial agriculture during the Second World War brought about a new class of artisans, professionals, businessmen, university students, and a few industrial workers. These groups saw coffee monoculture as a straitjacket inhibiting their continued growth.[32] The downfall of General Ubico, who ruled from 1931 to 1944, was engineered by these new groups in alliance with middle-level military officers. The reform governments of Arévalo and Arbenz (1944–54) represented an attempt to deal with the growing contradictions in the Guatemalan system. Arévalo maintained a base of support through a broad coalition of middle-class political parties, though opposition of the large landowners grew throughout his presidency.

In the early days of Arbenz's government, large landowners, led by United Fruit, reacted against application of a mild Arévalo law requiring them to rent unused land to peasants at reasonable prices. In response to lockouts on the large plantations, Arbenz concluded that the only option consistent with his concern for reform was to deprive the conservative landowners of their power base – the land itself. He proposed a sweeping agrarian reform similar to the Mexican one. The multi-class coalition build by Arévalo unravelled following Arbenz's reform proposals. Though Arbenz had support from the embryonic labour movement, the top–down character of the reform did not generate enough grassroots support in the countryside to resist the invasion of Colonel Castillo Armas, chosen by the CIA to implement a coup supported by United Fruit against Arbenz in 1954.[33]

Torres-Rivas estimates that 8000 peasants were killed in the first two months of the Castillo Armas regime.[34] The aim was more to suppress agrarian organization than to eliminate urban unions, although the latter were persecuted as well.[35]

Concurrent with repression in the countryside, rural cooperatives were first promoted by Catholic missionaries in the late 1950s. They were given financial help in the late 1960s and early 1970s by the US Agency for International Development, so that by 1976, there were 132 000 members organized in eight large federations. Most of the cooperatives were in the Indian highlands.[36]

As the cooperatives grew in the countryside, the industrial labour force grew in the urban areas. In 1976, eight of Guatemala's largest unions formed a coordinating committee. One of its priorities was establishing contact with rural organizations, especially cooperatives. A Peasant Unity Committee (CUC) was organized in 1978, the first labour organization to link poor Ladino workers with Indian peasants effectively.[37]

The third period of heavy repression in the era of diversified exports (after those of 1954–5, described above, and 1965–7, when a guerrilla movement arose and was exterminated) began in the early 1970s and culminated under the regime of General Ríos Montt (March 1982–August 1983). General Lucas García (1978–82) who preceded Ríos Montt, was rather ineffective in combating the guerrillas. Under Lucas, death squads associated with the armed and security forces ran rampant. The leaders of the two principal non-Marxist left-of-centre parties were assassinated, along with many of their followers.[38] This third period was clearly the time of greatest official terror.

General Ríos Montt largely put an end to the military death-squad activity in the cities. He unleashed a systematic and cruel counterinsurgency campaign in the countryside.[39] The back of the guerrilla movement was broken by Ríos Montt, though not completely destroyed. Under Ríos's successor, General Mejía Víctores, elections were held in November and December 1985 because of a declining economy and a desire on the part of the military for US economic and military aid. They were won by the Christian Democrats. The machinery of repression is still intact and slayings and disappearances have continued under the Cerezo government,[40] in direct contradiction of the clearly-stated desires of the president. The installation of a civilian government appears to have had no impact on the military's campaign of repression. Aside from the guerrillas, autonomous collective action by the peasantry today is nil, although urban workers continue to struggle to participate in the "legitimate" political system.

Nicaragua A somewhat weak Nicaraguan state, more like that in Honduras than those in Guatemala, El Salvador, or Costa Rica, resulted from the interaction of two phenomena:

(a) Nicaragua was a colonial backwater with neither a substantial indigenous labour force (the Indian population of the Pacific part of Nicaragua was rapidly decimated, especially through disease) nor important mineral wealth.

(b) US geopolitical concerns stunted the political development of Liberalism. It was first discredited by associating with the William Walker interregnum in 1854 and then severely hampered from gaining hegemony through direct US support of Conservatives in 1911. The distorted Liberalism of the Somoza dictatorship was at heart a personal (family) dictatorship that outlived its counterparts in the other countries because of Nicaragua's historic geopolitical importance to the USA.

The USA supported the overthrow of the Liberal government of Zelaya in 1909, for he championed Central American unity and sovereignty. Specifically, he refused to grant the USA rights to build a canal through Nicaragua which would have involved surrendering sovereignty over some Nicaraguan territory.[41] From 1912 to 1933, US Marines occupied Nicaragua almost continuously in an attempt to maintain US interests. In 1926, when a Liberal uprising was crushed, one of the Liberal commanders – Augusto César Sandino – refused to accept continued American occupation, and began a six-year guerrilla war. During Sandino's insurgency, the Liberals won one of the few "clean" elections in Nicaraguan history. The USA switched its support to the Liberal Party. They won partly because the Conservatives had compromised Nicaraguan sovereignty by signing the Brian–Chamorro treaty in 1914, guaranteeing the USA rights in perpetuity to build a transisthmian canal across Nicaragua. The Sandino insurgency against the Yankees (now allied with Sandino's own party) culminated in the US Marines leaving Nicaragua and turning the military reins to the US-trained National Guard, headed by Anastasio Somoza García, a Liberal.

The National Guard effectively eliminated peasant organization and sharply circumscribed labour unions for most of the Somoza era. From 1933 to 1979, the Guard served as the principal vehicle for establishing and maintaining the Somoza dictatorship.

The rule of Anastasio Somoza García, killed in 1956, and that of his son, Luís, who died in 1967, was characterized by strengthening of the Guard, cultivating the Americans, and co-opting important domestic power contenders.[42]

The Somozas learned to participate in – and control – the fruits of modernization. The Somocista state sought to neutralize bourgeois opposition through a series of pacts with the Conservative political opposition. The trade-off was to allow members of the élite outside the Somoza coterie to have relatively free access to economic power in exchange for a junior partnership in politics.[43]

When his brother died, Anastasio Jr (nicknamed *Tachito*), who had been head of the National Guard since his father's death, took over the government. Luís had attempted to build a strong civilian power base in a rejuvenated Liberal party; Tachito relied simply on military power. Luís had felt that, for the sake of image, the family should consolidate rather than expand its already vast fortune. Tachito exercised no restraints in using public office for personal enrichment, so by the early 1970s, his legitimacy and civilian power-base were evaporating rapidly.[44] Corruption became overt as he siphoned off relief after the 1972 Managua earthquake.

The lack of subtlety of Tachito's rule, his complete abandonment of the state's economic neutrality among bourgeois factions, and his failure to ensure the state's legitimacy among Nicaraguans of all social classes ultimately spelled his downfall. The bourgeoisie found itself in a profound contradiction: its heretofore reliable power base – the Somoza dynasty – was cutting back the bourgeoisie's potential for expansion. Both the main parties split, and bourgeois groups began to seek alternative political formations such as the Democratic Liberation Union (UDEL), a coalition which was held together by the popular Conservative politician and editor of *La Prensa*, Pedro Joaquín Chamorro.[45]

The FSLN (the Sandinista Front for National Liberation, founded in 1961) grew in importance against the background of a generally weak labour and peasant movement, though those movements grew in militancy in the mid-1970s. The Nicaraguan labour movement, before the insurrection led by the FSLN, was the least organized of all labour movements in the Central American Republics. The Association of Rural Workers (ATC), the rural labour union and peasant movement of the Sandinistas, was formally founded only in March 1978. And the Sandinista Workers' Federation (CST) was not formally organized until *after* the Sandinista victory, although Workers Fighting Committees (CLTs) or workers councils had been organized in the factories earlier.[46]

Thus worker and peasant organizations were derived from, rather than contributed to, the emergence of insurgency – a situation attesting to the smallness of the proletariat, the economic instability of enclave agriculture and extractive activities, and to the effectiveness of the Somoza regime in suppressing popular organizations, particularly those in the countryside.

Countries Without Significant Insurgencies   That repressive governments did not develop in Costa Rica or Honduras does not mean that conflict did not occur there. Rather, the context for such conflict differed markedly from responses in Nicaragua, Guatemala, and El Salvador. Though Costa Rica and Honduras developed quite differently politically, they are similar in one regard: armed opposition groups have been largely absent in both countries in the contemporary period.

Costa Rica   In 1940, Rafael Ángel Calderón Guardia was elected president representing the National Republican Party. His and his protégé's (Picado's) administrations were moderate reform governments. To capture the impetus for reform from the *criollo* Communists whose base was organized labour, Calderón Guardia accelerated official reform, which caused him to lose his right-wing support. Two years into Calderón Guardia's administration, he and the Communist party made an agreement. Communist support was important in passing a series of reforms.[47] While *Vanguardia Popular* (the Costa Rican Communist party) had a rather small electoral base, it was large enough to provide Calderón Guardia's party with an operating majority in Congress and it ensured a popular support base for his policies.[48]

Calderón Guardia's opposition consisted of two widely divergent groups: the conservative oligarchy whose wealth was based principally on coffee, and a group of middle-class persons of social democratic tendency, led by José Figueres, a young intellectual *hacendado*, who sought many of the reforms enacted by Calderón Guardia, but opposed them tactically.[49] The one element Figueres and his social democrats had in common with their conservative allies – aside from their common opposition to Calderón Guardia – was an élitist approach to leadership.

The 1948 election pitted Calderón Guardia against Otilio Ulate, a conservative candidate from the united opposition. Both candidates unknowingly played into Figueres's plans for an insurrection to implement the "Second Republic". When the ballots were counted, Ulate had apparently won. The Calderonistas alleged fraud, and, since they controlled Congress, certified the election of Calderón. Calderón, not realizing that Figueres had obtained military assistance from the Caribbean "legion" through the good offices of President Arévalo of Guatemala, saw no danger in having Congress declare him President, rather than requesting a new election.

After forty days of fighting with the poorly trained Costa Rican army and police on one side, and Figueres's Caribbean-exile-assisted middle-class rebels on the other, President Picado, rather than risk a full-scale civil war, gave up San José. One of the first acts of the Figuerista junta was to jail *Vanguardia Popular* leaders and outlaw their party.[50] Ulate was allowed to take over eighteen months later, suggesting that Figueres was comfortable with a democracy limited to élites, but could not brook autonomous participation by the working class.

Several elements were important in the 1948 revolution, which reinforced formal democracy, eliminated the army, and did not lead to repression:

(a) The power of the coffee oligarchy was broken by setting the stage for the growth of élites based on industrial activities and diversified agricultural exports (particularly livestock). The first step taken was nationalizing both the banking system and coffee exporting under the junta in 1948, wresting these functions from the oligarchy. While the old and the new élites have rotated in power through electoral determination since 1949, the impetus for structural change has been with the National Liberation Party (PLN), the party of the new élites.[51]

(b) Workers and peasants have effectively been kept from power, not through repression, but by the PLN economic programme supporting a greater role for the state by creating favourable conditions for industrialization. Such conditions included strong support for the CACM, and agricultural export expansion along with heavier export taxes on coffee and bananas, the two traditional exports. Welfare state policies neutralized serious opposition from organized workers and peasants.[52] By the mid-1970s the contradiction between subsidizing economic expansion by the new industrial and agrarian élites and in maintaining the welfare state and decent salary levels was evident. Following the world economic downturn, Costa Rica came to have the largest foreign debt per capita in Latin America.[53]

(c) Reform movements of the 1920s, 1930s, and 1940s, coupled with the small, ill-prepared Costa Rican army in 1948, all showed that the coffee bourgeoisie in Costa Rica was much weaker than in Guatemala and El Salvador. The rich coffee peasantry was an important buffer to the development of autonomous peasant organizations and their linking to urban industrial or rural agro-industrial unions.[54]

The recent pressures on Costa Rica to abandon its traditional position of neutrality and the push from the USA to strengthen the Civil Guard in return for US economic aid place the only consistently democratic country in Central America in a difficult political situation.

Honduras Honduras was the most "backward" of the Central American Republics.[55] Honduras's social forces were not well enough developed for a confrontation between revolution and counter-revolution. Neither was Honduras's bourgeoisie developed enough to confront international capital. Honduras's élites could only set relatively low taxes and receive "clientelistic" privileges for themselves.[56]

After the Second World War, an agrarian bourgeoisie began to emerge from the expansion of cattle and cotton production for export, and to form around an expanding coffee industry.[57]

The United Fruit Company after 1929 had a monopoly on marketing Honduran bananas. The first important strike in the country was among United Fruit banana workers in 1954. The weakness of what Posas called class-based unionism allowed the Fruit Company, the government, and the American Federation of Labor (which pressured United Fruit for a settlement) to arrest the more militant members of the strike committee and to negotiate a settlement with few official recriminations.[58]

The labour movement came to be dominated by pro-US "bread and butter" unions.[59] Growth of the labour movement under Liberal President Villeda Morales (1957–63) was rapid – first along the north coast, and then in Tegucigalpa among agro-industrial workers, then other urban workers, and finally peasants. The unions could not make or unmake presidents, but unions became part of the power-mix, along with the landed oligarchy, the army, the middle class, and the fruit companies.[60]

Particularly after the 1969 war with El Salvador, the Honduran agrarian sector became the principal focus of class struggle.[61] Peasant organizations were spawned by labour unions and by rejuvenation of the Catholic church. The ORIT-oriented peasant organization, the National Association of Honduran Peasants (ANACH), became strongest along the north coast and adjacent valleys. The Christian peasant movement developed in the south. Both areas were zones of growing commercialized agriculture.

The Honduran church was quite underdeveloped until the 1960s. From 1921 until 1962 there were serious problems of vacant sees and incompetent bishops.[62] The weakness, and indeed irrelevancy, of the formal church hierarchy meant that there were no strong links between the church and the bourgeoisie on the local, regional, or national levels.

Partly because of the historic weakness of the Honduran Church, it readily became a lay-oriented organization. Beginning in 1969, after the Latin American Bishops Conference (CELAM) in Medellín, Colombia, a lay ministry was established. Called the Celebration of the Word of God, it spread to other Central American countries. In

1971, there were some 5000 lay ministers, or Delegates of the Word, nearly all of them rural.

In 1963, fear that the National Party (the historic conservative party) would not win the forthcoming elections resulted in a military coup led by Air Force Colonel Oswaldo López Arellano and supported by the traditional agrarian bourgeoisie. López Arellano played an important role in Honduras the next twelve years. He was the loyal implementer of National party policies from 1963 to at least 1967, the year in which peasant pressure moved him closer to the progressive bourgeoisie and young military officers in sporadic support of agrarian reform that would help modernize the countryside.

Under the threat from ANACH of a hunger march on the capital in 1967, López Arellano agreed to institutional changes which allowed for land reform to proceed. The National Agrarian Institute (INA) began intervening on the side of peasant squatters by purchasing the land and distributing it to them. That was the mechanism that was to be the principal means of land reform for the next eight years.[63]

The agrarian reform law provided that only Honduran citizens could receive title to land. In April 1969 INA's director declared that he would immediately order Salvadoran peasants without proper title to leave the country.[64] The resultant 100-hour war between El Salvador and Honduras in June 1969 tipped the balance in favour of reform. Defeat of the Honduran troops during the short conflict revealed an inefficient, backward, corrupt command structure, paving the way for the increasing influence of a group of younger officers who drew their inspiration from the military reformers in Peru and Panama.[65]

In April 1975 President López Arellano fell from power as a result of the bribery scandal in which United Brands paid Honduran officials to undercut the Union of Banana Exporting Countries (UPEB), the banana equivalent of OPEC. The government's resolve to continue the agrarian reform weakened. Wariness by the church hierarchy toward the agrarian reform movement grew, stemming from pressures and violence from landowners.[66] Two priests were killed by landowners in Olancho in June 1975.

Posas puts the end of reform at early 1977, when conservatives, with some assistance from United Brands, blocked INA's proposed expropriations.[67] Simultaneously, the government of General Melgar Castro developed "a clear policy of wage limitations and repression of the leadership of the popular class-based organizations".[68] Thus concluded the period of agrarian reform.

In 1981, there was a return to civilian government. Two successive Liberal presidents have been elected, and have held nominal power, but real power has been in the hands of the military and increasingly in the hands of the USA, as Honduras, because of its strategic location in the isthmus, has become the centre of the US military presence in Central America. Though electoral support for the two traditional parties remains strong, acquisition of massive resources by the Honduran military from the USA, the disquiet caused by the presence of the Nicaraguan counter-revolutionaries on Honduran soil, and the attendant repression (although sporadic) by the Honduran military against its people, all indicate the potential for serious domestic strife in years to come unless reform policies are again implemented.

Conclusions

Following are the generalizations on the roots of insurgency which link economic and political events in each of the five Central American Republics:

(1) *Grassroots insurgency is more likely to develop in countries where productive forces of capitalism have developed to the degree that there is a significant agrarian working class, a growing industrial working class, and perhaps a threatened artisanry.*

The country with the most capitalistic labour relations is El Salvador, followed by Guatemala. Since the 1920s, the proportion of their economies devoted to industrial activity has been higher than for any of the other countries. Honduras's industrial sector is the smallest. El Salvador developed capitalist labour relations in the countryside in the 1880s, earlier than any other Central American Republic. That fact helps to explain why coffee workers attempted an insurrection which culminated in the *matanza*, where no such event occurred in any of the other four countries, either because of the cushioning effect of pre-capitalist labour relations (Guatemala, Nicaragua, and Honduras), lack of participation in the international market (Honduras), or the existence of a significant independent peasantry in the most important export sector (Costa Rica). Artisans played an important role in the 1932 insurrection in El Salvador and in the Nicaraguan insurrection of 1977–9.[69]

(2) *Grassroots insurgency is more likely to develop in societies where social*

differentiation, which is a product of a modern capitalist economy, does not find full political expression.

Such political expression in Central America in the period after the Second World War took the form of socially-based struggles for democracy, political participation, and social organization. Often such efforts were frustrated through official violence. In Guatemala, El Salvador and Nicaragua, political expression by all sectors was blocked, something which never occurred in Costa Rica, except perhaps for a brief time in 1948. Such blocked political systems encouraged development of consciousness of the inevitability of violent response and of the need for revolutionary change. In Honduras, the two traditional political parties continued to have legitimacy even during periods of military rule thereby channelling the interests of diverse sectors of the society (most critically, rural sectors) in very traditional and even primitive directions.

(3) *The development of an export-oriented agrarian oligarchy results in the strengthening of the role of the state, increasing its capacity for repressive action and for exclusion of the poorer classes from the political dialogue.*

A strong state apparatus is in the interests of the domestic export oligarchy, (a) because it allows its members to socialize some of the costs of marketing their crop through the development of infrastructure, and may even allow them to develop policies which subsidize inputs or prices of their product, (b) because it aids their access to and control of agricultural land, and (c) because the state can be used to enforce a low-wage regime.

The Liberal reforms of the 1870s and 1880s in Guatemala and El Salvador were important in ensuring the emergent coffee bourgeoisie access to adequate amounts of land for their rapidly expanding plantations. In the period following the Second World War that control – though increasingly encroached upon by other groups – has been used to prevent their loss of land through land reform. Either land reform was not put on the agenda (Somocista Nicaragua); or it was rescinded through an alliance of the domestic oligarchy, a foreign firm which perceived itself threatened by land reform, and the CIA, which imagined international communism to be behind the reform effort (Guatemala, 1954); or it was limited so that coffee lands were not included in land reform as implemented (El Salvador: 1980s).

Aside from the agrarian reform in revolutionary Nicaragua, Central America's most extensive land reform, although modest in absolute magnitude, was carried out in Honduras. Honduras did not go through a liberal period; the traditional domestically oriented *terratenientes* maintained hegemony until 1950. The postwar diversification of export agriculture, growth of the rural population, and the attendant conflict over land set the pattern for a major confrontation, between landowners and the banana companies on one side, and peasants and the rural proletariat on the other.

The Honduran confrontation thus far has been much less bloody than were those in El Salvador, Guatemala, and Nicaragua, largely because of the failure of the landed oligarchy to develop a strong state. The weakness of the state was also reflected in a very underdeveloped Catholic Church. The absence of links between landed and small town élites and the Church allowed the rejuvenated Church to establish close ties with the peasantry. When worker and peasant organizations gained strength, the military was not strong enough to suppress them. Corruption and poor organization of the Honduran military was exposed in the 1969 war with El Salvador, bringing young reform-minded officers into the military power structure.

Land laws passed in Costa Rica in the 1940s encouraged colonization and allowed peasant farmers to gain title to land they already farmed. Although land is quite unequally distributed in that country, there has been no significant pressure for further reform, because of the security of title and the strategic location in the export sector of an important segment of the peasantry, and because the welfare state has defused any strategic alliance between urban labour and the rural proletariat and semi-proletariat by reducing the appeal of class-based unionism.

Another objective of the strong oligarchical state is to keep labour's share of income low. That can best be accomplished by limiting class-based organization of the rural proletariat and seasonal agricultural workers. While the oligarchy may also repress urban workers, that is not as critical, since labour is a smaller component of total production costs than is true in plantation agriculture. (It is also easier to repress peasant than labour movements.)

As Paige points out,[70] lack of mobility of capital and inefficient production techniques which are characteristic of pre-capitalist relations invite strong political controls. Estate expansion occurs not through capital intensification, but through expanding control over land and labour. The requisite political controls for such expansion and labour force control imply repression, which, since the state is strong and controlled by the oligarchy, is carried out by the state. In the traditional *hacienda*-based oligarchical state, the oligarchy is also accustomed to ruling with unchallenged authority, but only on the local level; by mutual agreement of the agrarian oligarchy, the national state is kept too weak to engage in effective repression of popular movements (the case of Honduras). Where the export oligarchy had to share economic, and hence, political power with the peasantry – where yeoman export agriculture was important – repression is neither possible or needed (Costa Rica).

In the countries where the export oligarchy has dominated, it seeks unchallenged control. Hence, groups which would challenge such control must be prevented from organizing. Thus, repression at the level of the plantation necessitates repression at the national level. Hence, it is "natural" to exclude the poorer classes – and sometimes other social groups also – from the legitimate political dialogue. The scene is set for the development of insurgency. All that is needed is a precipitating factor.

(4) *As the economy diversifies (particularly the export portion of the economy) interests of different class fractions of the bourgeoisie diverge. In the face of organized activity by the popular classes, those differences are generally put aside* (e.g., Guatemala in 1954; Honduras in 1978). *However, when a zero-sum situation arises among the bourgeois groups, the newer and more progressive elements, if crowded out both politically and economically by the oligarchy, may seek alliances with the popular classes.*

In Nicaragua, the turning-point in the coalescence of the opposition was the unwillingness of Tachito Somoza to share economic power with other sectors of the bourgeoisie, illustrated most vividly by his keeping the "spoils" of the 1972 Managua earthquake for himself and his associates. In El Salvador, the world economic downturn was a critical point. In Guatemala, the world economy also had an impact, but the Guatemalan economy remained relatively strong until 1984. A critical factor for the development of the guerrilla movement at the beginning of this decade included increasing organizational capacity of rural – and particularly indigenous – groups. The guerrillas suffered critical setbacks before economic conditions might have pushed some bourgeois groups into an alliance with them. Honduras was less immersed in the international economy, received increasing amounts of US aid, and did not have to fight an insurgency. Thus, it was not as affected as the other countries by the world recession. It lacked the other requisites for growth of insurgency. Costa Rica was hard hit by the international economic recession, but had none of the other requisites for the development of insurgency.

In summary, the current Central American crisis suggests the failure of a legal, gradualist, and peaceful approach to the modernization of oligarchical élites. The incomplete modernization of the oligarchy occurred because of the development within this class of tensions created by economic and technological modernization, juxtaposed with the use of power and social control resources which are traditional and backwards.

Notes

1. Jeffery M. Paige, *Agrarian Revolution: Social Movements and Export Agriculture in the Underdeveloped World.* (New York: The Free Press, 1975) p. 11.
2. Miles L. Wortman, *Government and Society in Central America, 1680–1840.*
3. Blas Real and Mario Lungo, "Costa Rica, economía y estado: notas sobre su evolución reciente y el momento actual", *Estudios Sociales Centroamericanos*, no 26 (1980) p. 14.
4. Mitchell A. Seligson, *Peasants of Costa Rica and the Development of Agrarian Capitalism,* p. 56.
5. E. Bradford Burns, "The Modernization of Underdevelopment: El Salvador, 1858–1931"; Ciro Flamarion and C. Santana, "Historia económica del café en Centroamérica (Siglo XIX), estudio comparativo", *Estudios Sociales Centroamericanos*, vol. 10 (Enero–Abril 1975) pp. 9–55.
6. Rafael del Cid V., "Las clases sociales y su Dinámica en el Agro Hondureño".
7. Santana, "Historia economica", p. 11.
8. J. Edward Taylor, "Peripheral Capitalism and Rural–Urban Migration: A Study of Population Movements in Costa Rica", *Latin America Perspectives*, vol. 7, no 2 (Spring 1980) p. 80.
9. Santana, "Historia economica", p. 24.
10. Taylor, "Peripheral Capitalism", p. 80.
11. Santana, "Historia economica", p. 27.
12. Anthony Winston, "Class Structure and Agrarian Transition in Central America", *Latin American Perspectives*, vol. 5, no 4 (Fall 1978) pp. 29 and 34.
13. James A. Morris and Marta F. Sánchez Soler, "Factores de poder en la evolución política del campesinado Hondureño", *Estudios Sociales Centroamericanos*, no 16 (1977) p. 87.
14. Winston, "Class Structure", p. 40; Real and Lungo, "Costa Rica", p. 19.
15. Shelton H. Davis, "State Violence and Agrarian Crisis in Guatemala", in Martin Diskin (ed.) *Trouble in our Backyard: Central America and the United States in the Eighties*, pp. 155–71; del Cid, "Las Clases Sociales", p. 124; Morris and Sánchez, "Factores de Poder"; Naciones Unidas, CEPAL, FAO, OIT *Tenencia de la Tierra y Desarrollo Rural en Centroamerica* (San José, Costa Rica: EDUCA, 1973); Taylor, "Peripheral Capitalism".

16. Davis, "State Violence".
17. Phillip Berryman, *The Religious Roots of Rebellion: Christians in Central American Revolutions*, New York, p. 103; Carlos Samaniego, "Movimiento Campesino: Lucha del Proletariado Rural en El Salvador?" *Estudios Sociales Centroamericanos*, no 25 (Enero–Abril 1980) pp. 137–9.
18. Naciones Unidas, *Tenencia de la Tierra*.
19. Winston, "Class Structure".
20. William R. Cline and Enrique Delgado (eds), *Economic Integration in Central America* (Washington, DC: The Brookings Institution, 1978) p. 321.
21. Edelberto Torres-Rivas, "La integración económica centroamericana: resumen crítico", p. 19.
22. Edelberto Torres-Rivas, "The Central American Model of Growth: Crisis for Whom?" *Latin American Perspectives*, vol. 7, no 2 (Spring 1980) p. 30.
23. Torres-Rivas, "The Central American Model", p. 36.
24. Thomas P. Anderson, *Matanza: El Salvador's Communist Revolt of 1932* (University of Nebraska Press, 1971).
25. Leon Zamosc, "Class Conflict in an Export Economy: The Social Roots of the Salvadoran Insurrection of 1932", in this volume.
26. Anderson, *Matanza*, p. 7.
27. Liisa North, *Bitter Grounds: Roots of Revolt in El Salvador*, p. 29.
28. Zamosc, "Class Conflict".
29. Berryman, *Religious Roots*, pp. 145–8; Rafael Menjivar, "El Salvador: The Smallest Link." *Contemporary Marxism* #1: Strategies for the Class Struggle in Latin America (San Francisco: Synthesis Publications, 1979) pp. 19–28.
30. Thomas P. Anderson, *Politics in Central America: Guatemala, El Salvador, Honduras, and Nicaragua*, pp. 79–84.
31. Anderson, *Politics in Central America*, pp. 85–7, 91–2.
32. Robert Wasserstrom, "Revolution in Guatemala: Peasants and Politics Under the Arbenz Government", *Comparative Studies in Society and History*, vol. 17, no 4 (1975) pp. 448–9.
33. Ibid, pp. 456–8.
34. Edelberto Torres-Rivas, "Guatemala: Crisis and Political Violence", *NACLA Report on the Americas* (January–February 1980) p. 24.
35. Richard Newbold Adams, *Crucifixion by Power: Essays on Guatemalan National Social Structure, 1944–1966*, p. 450.
36. Davis, "State Violence", p. 11.
37. Ibid, p. 16.
38. Anderson, *Politics in Central America*, pp. 38–41.
39. Americas Watch, "Guatemala: A Nation of Prisoners", an Americas Watch Report (New York: Americas Watch Committee, 1984); Americas Watch, "Extermination in Guatemala" (condensation from Americas Watch Report, "Creating a Desolation and Calling it Peace") *New York Review of Books*, vol. 30 (2 June 1983) pp. 13–16.
40. Nairn, Allan and Simon, Jean-Marie, "Bureaucracy of Death", *New*

Republic (30 June 1986) pp. 13–17; for a fuller discussion of the period from Lucas to Cerezo, see Jim Handy, "Insurgency and Counter-insurgency in Guatemala", in this volume.

41. Charles L. Stansifer, "José Santos Zelaya: A New Look at Nicaragua's Liberal Dictator", *Revista/Review Interamericana*, vol. 7, no 3 (Fall 1977) pp. 468–75.
42. Thomas W. Walker, *Nicaragua: The Land of Sandino*, p. 27.
43. Edelberto Torres-Rivas, "El estado contra la sociedad: las raíces de la revolución Nicaragüense", *Estudios Sociales Centroamericanos*, no 27, p. 88.
44. Walker, *Nicaragua*, p. 30.
45. George Black, *Triumph of the People: The Sandinista Revolution in Nicaragua* (London: Zed Press, 1981) p. 63.
46. Ibid, pp. 275–7; for discussion of the smallness of the working class and its pre-insurrectionary organizational weakness, see Carlos M. Vilas, "The Impact of Revolutionary Transition on the Popular Classes: The Working Class in the Sandinasta Revolution", in this volume.
47. John Patrick Bell, *Crisis in Costa Rica: The 1948 Revolution*, p. 29.
48. Ibid, pp. 42–4.
49. Ibid, pp. 33–4.
50. Ibid, Chapter 7.
51. Jorge Rovira Mas, "Costa Rica, economía y estado: notas sobre su evolución reciente y el momento actual", *Estudios Centroamericanos*, no 26 (May–August 1980) p. 39.
52. Ibid, pp. 40–6, 57.
53. Torres-Rivas, "The Central American Model", p. 33.
54. Francisco Barahona, "Reforma agraria y organizatión campesina", *Estudios Sociales Centroamericanos*, no 22 (Enero–Abril 1979) pp. 220–1, 224.
55. Thomas P. Anderson, *The War of the Dispossessed: Honduras and El Salvador, 1969*, p. 53; William H. Durham, *Scarcity and Survival in Central America: Ecological Origins of the Soccer War*, p. 115.
56. Mario Posas, "Honduras at the Crossroads", *Latin American Perspectives*, 7, 2 (Spring 1980) pp. 4–6.
57. Ibid, p. 47.
58. Mario Posas, "Lucha ideológica y organización sindical en Honduras (1954–65)" (Tegucigalpa, Honduras: Editorial Guaymuras, 1980); Anderson, *The War of the Dispossessed*.
59. Steven Volk, "Honduras: On the Border of War", p. 8.
60. Anderson, *The War of the Dispossessed*, p. 58.
61. Mario Posas, "Política estatal y estructura agraria en Honduras (1950–1978)", *Economía Política*, Instituto de Investigaciones Económicas y Sociales, Universidad Nacional Autónoma de Honduras, vol. 17 (Abril–Noviembre 1979) p. 62.
62. Robert Anthony White, "Structural Factors in Rural Development: the Church and the Peasant in Honduras", p. 190.
63. Posas, "Política Estatal y Estructura Agraria", pp. 49–50.
64. Anderson, *The War of the Dispossessed*, pp. 91–2.

65. Volk, "Honduras", p. 16.
66. White, "Structural Factors", pp. 296–7.
67. Posas, "Política estatal y estructura agraria", pp. 83–4.
68. Posas, "Lucha ideológica y organización sindical", p. 74.
69. See Zamosc, "Class Conflict", and Vilas, "The Impact of Revolutionary Transition", in this volume.
70. Ibid, Chapter 1.

Class Conflict in an Export Economy:
The Social Roots of the Salvadoran Insurrection of 1932[1]

Leon Zamosc

The Salvadoran uprising of 1932 was one of the main episodes in the cycle of popular unrest that shook Central America during the great world depression. In form and content, the insurrection had little in common with the guerrilla war waged by Sandino in Nicaragua, or with the great strikes staged in American banana plantations throughout the region. What it did share with these other struggles was the same background of unprecedented crisis as the collapse of the international markets sharpened the social contradictions of the Central American export economies to an intolerable degree. A further correspondence had to do with the similar outcomes of these expressions of popular protest: their successful repression marked the beginnings of a new period in Central America, a period in which "peace and stability" were forcibly maintained by some of the longest and most ruthless dictatorships ever known in the continent.

For decades, the Salvadoran élites have explained the events of 1932 in terms of a "Communist conspiracy", manipulating the memory of the episode as an ideological deterrent to social protest. However, with the publication of new research and detailed testimonies of the period, the real story of the insurrection and its repression has been emerging since the 1970s.[2] El Salvador, a "coffee republic", was the smallest and most densely populated of the Central American countries. In 1931 the Salvadorans had democratically elected a self-proclaimed reformist, Arturo Araujo, for the Presidency. But the deteriorating economic situation prevented Araujo from carrying out any of his promised reforms. There was widespread discontent, and the situation worsened when the army ousted Araujo and appointed a well-known hard-liner, General Maximiliano Hernández Martínez, as president. On account of intense organizational work in the rural areas, the newly created Salvadoran Communist Party commanded substantial support among the agricultural workers. In January 1932, the army cancelled the municipal elections, in which the Communists were participating. Evaluating the situation as ripe for a revolution, the Communist Party started to prepare an armed uprising, organizing popular commands in the countryside and trying to recruit support within the army. Although the government discovered the plot and captured the main leaders, large crowds of agricultural workers occupied many towns in the central and western parts of the country. The response of the army was swift and brutal: the towns were recaptured, the rebels crushed, and systematic killings began in the rural areas. There were mass executions of presumed "Communists", and it has been estimated that 30 000 people were butchered in the aftermath of the insurrection. Hernández Martínez remained in power until 1944.

This chapter examines the situation that led to the uprising, its repression, and the establishment of a dictatorship in the country. Seeking the roots of class conflict at the level of the productive base, the analysis focuses upon the Salvadoran socioeconomic structure of the 1920s. This structure is particularly interesting because it appears as a pristine example of the export economy that prevailed in Latin America before industrialization. It can be speculated that the insurrection of 1932, as one of the most dramatic Latin American political upheavals resulting from the world crisis, was an expression of the special characteristics of El Salvador as an archetypal case of the export economy. Starting from a brief sketch of the socioeconomic historical background, the chapter considers the expansion of coffee in the country and examines the structure of the export economy in order to define the social classes and mark the roots of their antagonisms. It then proceeds to discuss the political processes, emphasizing the patterns of class domination and charting the evolution of class conflict during the 1920s.

Before Coffee: The Socioeconomic Background

As in other regions of the Americas, the community was the basic unit of Indian social organization in what today is El Salvador. Communal lands were periodically redistributed according to family needs, and surpluses were provided for the maintenance of clergymen, warriors and craftsmen.[3] But the Spanish made rapid contact with the local peoples and smashed their political and religious institutions. New forms of social organization emerged, according to the ways in which the land was appropriated and the labour of the Indians exploited. In the more populated western part of the country, Spanish merchants and *encomenderos* established an export business, making the Indians specialize in cacao cultivation by imposing a tributary system upon the existing communities.[4] Eventually, the cacao boom came to an end as a result of extreme exploitation, population decline, soil exhaustion, and other factors. Still, the pattern of organization of this colonial enterprise proved crucial for the preservation of the Indian communal form in western El Salvador.[5]

In other regions, the Crown allocated land to Spanish settlers, who also received *repartimiento* rights over the labour of Indians from neighbouring communities. Stock raising was central from the beginning, but indigo production quickly became the most important activity in many Salvadoran *haciendas*.[6] Indigo required a large input of labour, which could not be efficiently obtained under the *repartimiento* system. The landowners followed a strategy of land monopolization, encroaching on the communities in order to force the Indians to become tenants within the *haciendas*. This led to the rapid territorial expansion of the estates and new relations of production by which subsistence plots were given to the Indians in exchange for their labour in the production of indigo.[7] Thus, while tribute in kind had helped to preserve the Indian community in western El Salvador, in the rest of the country labour tribute led to a rapid decline of the communal form and to the predominance of servile relations based upon land monopolization.

The continuing expansion of the *haciendas* provoked permanent conflicts between landowners and communities. A third party was the growing group of *Ladinos*, the offspring of Indian–white miscegenation. Since the *Ladinos* did not belong to the communities, they could either become tenants within *haciendas* or try to establish new settlements of their own, which always led to land disputes with the Indians.[8] The Spanish Crown had addressed the problems by concentrating the Indians in new communities with recognized titles over smaller tracts of land.[9] The policy of *congregación* benefited the landlords, because it facilitated monopolization of land in the less populated areas. But it also accommodated part of the land demands of the *Ladino* peasants and gave some protection to the Indians in their reserved areas. The reformed Indian communities kept the old patterns of production and communal property, and the Crown-imposed hereditary chiefdom as a system of political control and brokerage. The Church influence was exerted through *cofradías*, local religious societies devoted to the worship of a single saint or person of the Trinity.[10]

By the end of the Colonial period, then, the Salvadoran productive structure included three main sectors: (a) the *haciendas* were characterized by servile relations and produced subsistence crops, indigo for export, and some sugar, tobacco and cattle for local and regional markets;[11] (b) the *Ladino* settlements were composed of free peasant smallholders who used their own family labour; they produced to meet their own needs and sold surpluses in the local markets;[12] (c) family production was imbedded in the structure of communal property within the Indian communities, which emphasized subsistence production.[13]

After independence, the opening of new foreign markets stimulated indigo exports and the towns developed as administrative and artisan centres. But these changes did not alter the existing patterns of production. The *haciendas*, free peasants and Indian communities remained basically self-sufficient, supplying marginal surpluses for a still very restricted internal market. Clear proof of the low level of internal economic integration was provided by the rapid decline of indigo exports. When the dye was displaced by chemical substitutes during the 1860s, the Salvadorans did not experience a total economic collapse.[14] The crisis was mainly felt within the *haciendas*, where the landowners had suddenly lost their main source of wealth. There were many experiments with new crops, in a frantic search for anything that would command a good market abroad. The new panacea was coffee, whose introduction would lead to rapid transformations in the country.

Coffee and Primitive Accumulation in the Highlands

In 1928 coffee accounted for 93 per cent of all Salvadoran exports.[15] It was mostly produced by wage labour in large plantations that dominated the landscape of the highlands. Since the expansion of coffee in other situations occurred on peasant holdings, it is relevant to ask why it was that capitalist plantations came to prevail in El Salvador. Part of the answer lies in the specificities of coffee cultivation and the characteristics of the Salvadoran setting. The coffee tree tolerates only limited climatic variations, demands intensive care throughout the year, and requires a great deal of additional work for collection and processing during harvest time. In El Salvador, the areas suitable for coffee were limited in extent and concentrated in the valleys and on the slopes of the highlands.[16] One consequence of this scarcity of suitable land was that the servile systems of the *haciendas* were inadequate for large-scale cultivation, because it would have been unprofitable to use land for the subsistence crops of tenants.[17] All the available space had to be devoted to coffee, which necessarily implied that large-scale production had to be based on wage labour. This helps explain why and how the expansion of coffee led to capitalist relations of production in El Salvador: *haciendas* with suitable land for coffee were redefined as plantations, their tenants were replaced by wage labourers, and some traditional landowners became capitalist planters.

However, this is only part of the story. Before the expansion of coffee it was the Indian communities, and not the *haciendas*, that predominated in the highlands.[18] The dispossession of the Salvadoran Indian communities was, by all accounts, a classic case of primitive accumulation.[19] The anticipated returns of coffee cultivation placed two imperatives on the agenda of the landowners and other would-be entrepreneurs: access to suitable land and control of labour power. The 1882 law of *Abolición de Ejidos* denounced the communal system as an "obstacle to modernization" and, with the abolition of communal property, created the conditions for the achievement of both goals. Against the will of the communities, communal lands were distributed among the families, individual property titles were given over the plots, and the way was paved for dispossession through forced sales backed by sheer violence. Resistance was quelled by the army, most of the families were left landless, and even those who kept some land came to depend upon seasonal wage labour in order to subsist. Thus, the coffee plantations that emerged in the highlands found themselves with a plentiful labour supply. In fact, there were so many prospective workers that they could not all be employed on a permanent basis.

This introduces a very important characteristic of the development of export capitalism in El Salvador. Since part of the displaced labour power was not absorbed by the new plantations, a central consequence of the process of primitive accumulation was the reinforcement of the non-capitalist sectors. The remnants of the Indian communities were reorganized as a new subsistence sector of *minifundistas* and marginal squatters who depended upon temporary work in the coffee harvests.[20] Some of the landless moved to the towns, where they contributed to the expansion of an artisan sector that included foundries, tanneries and many workshops producing textiles, shoes, candles and furniture.[21] Others went to the lowlands, where the landowners took them on as tenants and sharecroppers in *haciendas* that had been languishing since the end of the indigo boom.[22] But it was not only through the reallocation of labour power that the expansion of the coffee plantations strengthened the non-capitalist sectors. A further crucial element was the creation of a sizeable internal market. Analysing data from the 1930 census, which reported 309 000 agricultural wage-labourers out of a total population of approximately 1.5 million, an American demographer observed that "during the dry season almost every laboring family in the nation is employed to assist in gathering the coffee crop".[23] The fact that most Salvadoran families came to depend totally or partially on plantation wages implied a thorough monetization of the economy and created an ample demand for articles of consumption. This demand, in turn, stimulated commercial production by the *haciendas,* free peasants and artisans. The state-built infrastructure of roads and railways, originally intended to facilitate the transport of coffee to the ports, greatly assisted the commercialization of the economy.[24] Thus, coffee capitalism not only reshaped the other productive sectors, but also involved them in the dynamics of its own reproduction. Tight integration became a central feature of the Salvadoran export economy.

The Export Economy and its Class Contradictions

For the sake of brevity, the analytical scheme presented in Figure 1 can be used to review the most salient features of the Salvadoran productive structure, define the main social classes, and identify the basic sources of class antagonisms. The export sector is the most convenient starting-point. As previously explained, this sector was characterized by capitalist relations of production in which the coffee planters appeared as the dominant class. But this class was not homogeneous. There were bigger planters who owned the coffee mills and export firms.[25] Such command of strategic resources allowed for faster accumulation and the eventual formation of finance capital. The three banks that printed money and regulated the rates of exchange during the 1920s were owned by the main families of coffee planters.[26] Thus, although the planter class as a whole was the main focus of accumulation, there was within this class a dominant fraction that controlled the export economy and derived the greatest benefits from its operation. The subordinate classes in the plantations were the permanent workers and the seasonal labourers who were taken on during harvest time. The latter came from the subsistence sector which, as seen before, included the semi-

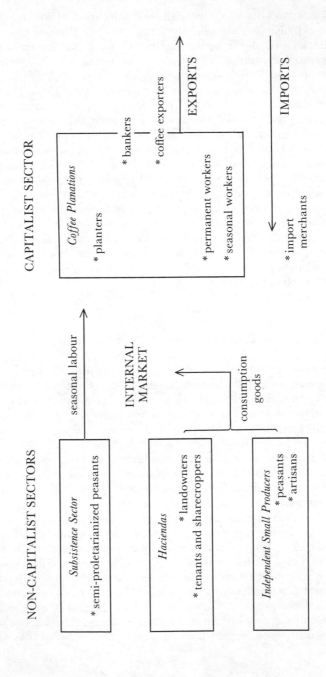

Figure 1 *Productive sectors and social classes in the Salvadoran export economy of the 1920s*

proletarianized remnants of the Indian communities.

Most of the consumption goods required by the plantation workers came from the sectors of non-capitalist commodity production. The main classes in these sectors were the free peasants, the urban artisans, and the landowners, tenants and sharecroppers of the *haciendas*. Peasants and artisans specialized in foodstuffs and other articles which they sold in the market in order to buy the other commodities they needed. Since they used family labour and their output was small, these petty producers could not accumulate significant surpluses. Only the *hacienda* landowners, who exploited many sharecroppers and tenants, were able to accumulate wealth in the non-capitalist sectors.

Although internal production supplied basic foodstuffs and some manufactures, the Salvadoran productive system depended heavily upon imported goods.[27] Without foreign machinery, tools, fertilizers and raw materials, the coffee plantations and the other sectors could not sustain production. Manufactured consumer goods and luxury goods for the wealthy classes were also imported. The import merchants represent the last relevant class sector. This was a small group of businessmen with good commercial contacts in Europe and the USA.[28] Most of them were immigrants of German, Dutch and English extraction. Control of the import trade secured handsome profits for this commercial fraction of the capitalist class.

The analysis of the Salvadoran productive system clearly shows that the capitalist sector represented the dominant pole of the economy. The dynamics of the export sector conditioned the operation of the system as a whole, because the reproduction of the other sectors hinged on the requirements of the coffee plantations. There was, however, a weak link in the chain: at such levels of internal integration any crisis in the export sector would rapidly engulf the entire economy. This raises another general issue; namely, that the Salvadoran productive system was not an autonomous system. It was incorporated into the world system as a supplier of a single tropical commodity. European and American demand shaped the coffee market, whose fluctuations ultimately determined the fortunes of the Salvadoran economic cycle. Thus, while the plantation sector was the dominant pole within the national system, it was in turn subordinated to the dynamism of the metropolitan hubs of the world economy. It is easy to see that, given the dependent nature of the Salvadoran system, the most threatening sources of crisis were those related to possible recessions in the metropolitan economies.

Having identified the main social classes and fractions, it is possible to pinpoint various roots of antagonism in the Salvadoran social formation. Among the dominant classes, there were conflicting interests regarding the distribution of surpluses. The *hacienda* land-owners and the import merchants, for example, would always try to raise the prices of their commodities, which was against the interests of the coffee planters, who wanted to keep wages low. On the other hand, control of the mills, banks, and export trade enabled the large planter fraction to capture the main share of the coffee profits, which was of course at the expense of the rest of the planter class. However, these frictions were diminished by the fact that the dominant groups had a common stake in the system. The really relevant cleavages for prospective unrest were those that affected the social classes that had nothing to gain from the existing arrangements. The artisans were under threat of ruin because the free-trade policy, which served the interests of the dominant classes in an export economy, was flooding the country with cheap imported manufactures.[29] In the countryside, the main class contradictions involved exploiters and exploited within the most important produc-tive sectors: landowners *vs* sharecroppers and tenants in the *haciendas*, and planters *vs* permanent and seasonal workers in the coffee plantations. Taking into account that the capitalist coffee sector was the dominant pole of the economy and included a substantial part of the working population, it can be concluded that the contradiction between capital and wage labour was the principal structural contradiction in Salvadoran society.

The key potential initiators of class struggle in El Salvador, then, were the proletarians and semi-proletarians of the coffee plantations. This potential was enhanced by the conditions of extreme exploit-ation and misery that prevailed in the plantations. A Canadian officer reported what he called "insignificant" wages for ten-hour working days. He described appalling working and living conditions, and estimated that labour costs in the plantations represented less than 10 per cent of the total value of production.[30] In the same vein, the British consul in San Salvador observed that:

> The planters have done nothing to improve the condition of their laborers, who live in miserable huts for which they have to pay rent. Sometimes the laborers are obliged to spend their small earnings at a shop belonging to the planter, and I have heard of wages being paid in token checks which could only be exchanged for goods at the plantation shop. Further, some planters adopt an arrogant and insulting demeanour towards their employees and commit various offences against them and their families.[31]

Given the fact that my analysis has identified the relations of exploitation in the plantations as the principal class contradiction, these descriptions suggest that the edifice of the Salvadoran export economy rested on a veritable social time-bomb. It is not difficult to see that a serious slump like the world recession of the late 1920s could easily trigger the explosion. However, the concrete form assumed by a social upheaval would not only depend upon economic factors, but also upon other determinants operating at the political level.

The Political Regime and the Class Struggles of the 1920s

Despite their skirmishes on the distribution of surpluses, coffee-planters, import merchants, and *hacienda* landowners had a common interest in the maintenance of the export structure in El Salvador. This shared interest was the basis of a tight alliance against the subordinate, exploited classes. As could be expected, the bigger planters represented the hegemonic fraction within this alliance of the dominant classes. In fact, since the overthrow of the Conservatives in 1871, all the successive presidents had come from the main planter families and the Liberal political tradition.[32] Intra-élite competition had been initially marked by the frequent use of violence. The stakes were high, because control of the state entailed the possibility of getting the lion's share of resources freed in the process of Indian dispossession that was paving the way for expansion of the planta-tions. However, with the consolidation of the most powerful fraction of the planter class, a period of relative stability began at the turn of the century, a period in which the political hegemony of this fraction was accepted by the other dominant groups.

What were the characteristics of the state and the political regime erected by the Salvadoran dominant classes? It has been argued that the common interests of these classes were rooted in the specific features of the export economy. These same features also defined the conditions of state action and, therefore, the nature of the state. In the Salvadoran case, the capitalist export economy required the operation of a liberal state; that is, a state devoted to the creation of the necessary framework for the development of capitalism within the country and, at the same time committed to the maintenance of a specific form of insertion into the world market through the principle of free-trade. However, the liberal state that emerged in El Salvador did not generate a political regime of the bourgeois-democratic type that came to prevail in Europe and America. In

order to establish the premises of capitalist production for export, the
state had to destroy some of the previous principles of socioeconomic
organization. This implied the ruthless enforcement of policies that,
as in the case of the abolition of the Indian communes, paid
little attention to "democratic" rights. On the other hand, heavy
dependency meant that the dominant classes lacked effective influence over the ultimate causes of eventual crisis. Unable to anticipate
the political conjunctures, the Salvadoran élites needed a system of
tight social control. In these conditions, and given the absence of
any significant previous democratic tradition, it is not difficult to
understand why the dominant classes preferred repressive domination to democratic hegemony.[33]

Thus, the political regime that came to prevail in El Salvador
was formally republican, but authoritarian, exclusionary and personalistic in its real content. The political scene was shaped by the
interaction of small cliques and the formation of transient parties
that supported particular personalities at election time.[34] Once
the dominant groups informally agreed on a suitable presidential
candidate, the outgoing administration secured his election by
manipulating the polls and repressing any opposition.[35] This system,
which also regulated the "election" of legislators and local authorities, provided the basis for the remarkable political stability of the
first quarter of the century. Still, with the consolidation of the export
economy, a new phase began in the mid-1920s, a phase in which
the growing pressure of the subordinate classes would force important
changes in the strategy of domination of the Salvadoran élites.

To understand these significant transformations, one must start
with the development of popular organization. Despite the fact that
the formation of unions was extremely difficult in the countryside,
demands for better wages and improvements in working conditions
were frequent in the coffee plantations. In the western part of the
country, where the Indians kept a fresh memory of their dispossession
by the coffee planters, this agitation provoked continuous outbreaks
of violence and rioting. The *Guardia Nacional*, a paramilitary police
that operated at local levels, was reinforced by the planters in order
to deal with the growing protests.[36] In the towns, discontent was
also increasing in the artisan workshops, encouraged by the already-
mentioned threat posed by cheap imported manufactures. Politically,
the artisans were strategically placed as a more educated urban
group that could follow public affairs, try to organize the defence of
its interests, and develop an active interest in participation. The
guild associations, which started assuming mutual help, welfare and
cultural functions, rapidly became a vehicle for the expression of

the artisans' demands.[37] They also provided a transmission channel for revolutionary ideas: books and pamphlets came from European working-class parties and Latin American labour organizations; there were lively discussions on international events like the Russian Revolution, and the debate began about the possibility of struggling for reforms in El Salvador.[38]

Agitation gained momentum in the towns. Between 1919 and 1922 there were strikes of shoemakers, teachers and railway employees.[39] In 1923, when artisans and market women picketed in the capital to protest against fraud in the presidential election, the army fired on the crowd and killed many demonstrators.[40] The elected president, Alfonso Quiñónez, described by an historian as one of those "through-going dictators who ruled with an iron hand on behalf of the aristocracy", reinforced the police and the army.[41] But despite the increasing repression, the process of organization went on. In the capital, unions were organized in different trades, while in the smaller towns a single association of various trades embraced all the local artisans, employees and workers. In 1924, all these unions came together under a National Federation of Salvadoran Workers.[42] The Federation organized cadres of young activists and for the first time in the history of the country elevated demands on behalf of the plebeian classes. Although reformism and anarchism were the prevailing initial attitudes, the ideological spectrum changed with affiliation to the Latin American Labor Confederation. There were visits of veteran labour organizers from Mexico and South America, many Salvadoran activists gained experience abroad, and a Marxist current took shape within the Federation.[43] Under the leadership of Agustín Farabundo Martí, the Marxists extended their activity to the countryside. By the end of the Quiñónez administration, they were working with remarkable success in the coffee areas.

Pío Romero Bosque, who was in his seventies and had served as vice-president under Quiñónez, took over as the new president in 1927. Romero Bosque is frequently presented as the father of democracy in El Salvador. His administration was indeed very different from the previous ones: he lifted the state of siege, criticized the repressive style of his predecessors, took measures that for the first time addressed some popular grievances, and closed his period allowing the first truly free and fair elections in the history of the country.[44] But interpretations that see in Romero Bosque's initiative the main cause of these changes are very naive, because they take at face value that personalistic form of the regime and disregard its class content. After all, Romero Bosque came from a planter family and had faithfully served the dominant groups during the four previous administrations. This suggests that his innovations must have been motivated by much deeper reasons than personal good will.

To understand their significance, one must submit Romero Bosque's policies to closer scrutiny.[45] It is true that economic concessions were made to some subordinate classes: peasant producers of basic foodstuffs were exempted from taxes, tariffs were imposed to protect some artisan manufactures from foreign competition, and labour legislation was passed with benefits for workers and employees. It is also true that a new political climate of popular participation was created by the abolition of the state of siege, the granting of organization rights for labour unions, and the provision for free elections. Still, Romero Bosque's measures were not inconsistent with his firm commitment to the coffee interests. In fact, none of the economic and political concessions applied to the agricultural proletariat: the eight-hour working-day and the other benefits for workers were effective for all branches of production except agriculture, and a decree was issued actually banning the formation of unions of agricultural workers. Furthermore, it was under Romero Bosque that the Coffee Planters' Association was granted semi-official status and assumed formal control of the export economy.

What the Romero Bosque administration expressed, then, was a change in the strategy of domination. It was an attempt to modify the political regime while at the same time maintaining the basic principles of the liberal state that served the interests of the dominant classes. The exclusionary regime had worked when the subordinate classes were weak, but it had proved unable to deal with the new scenario of popular mobilization. The dominant classes hoped that well-timed economic and political concessions would gain support at popular level. More important still, they expected that the selective nature of these concessions (giving something to the other sectors and nothing to the rural workers) would prevent the radicalization of the urban left and thus contain the spread of revolutionary ferment among the rural masses. The main issue now was to ensure that the future president would really suit the new strategy of domination: the candidate had to appear reformist enough to command popular support, but he had to be reliable in his commitment to the basic interests of the dominant classes.[46]

The belief that tactical concessions would check the revolutionary tide showed that the Salvadoran élites failed to grasp the real dimensions of the process of popular mobilization. Decisive changes were taking place in the Workers' Federation. Strengthened by their

organizational success in the coffee areas, Martí and his followers
were arguing that the economic struggle had to be transcended by
political demands. Despite intense repression by the *Guardia Civil*,
the activity of the cadres of the Federation was by now almost
entirely devoted to the permanent workers of the plantations and
the semi-proletarianized peasants who provided the temporary
labour. In ethnic terms, these two classes were basically Indian
classes, and the activists were particularly successful in recruiting
the support of the Indian chiefs and using the religious sects, the
cofradías, as channels for political agitation.[47] The Marxist wing
became strong enough to expel the anarchist and reformist leaders
from the Workers' Federation in 1929. Once in control of the trade
union federation, the leftist militants created the Communist Party
as a separate political organization.[48] The Party denounced Romero
Bosque's reforms as phoney concessions and decided not to take
part in the forthcoming presidential elections.

By this time, the dominant classes had found a suitable future
president. Arturo Araujo, the son of a wealthy family of coffee
planters, had thrown in his hat as a candidate. He had admired
social democracy while studying in Europe and, back in El Salvador,
he earned a "good planter" reputation by giving fair treatment to
his workers. In 1929 Araujo founded the Salvadoran Labor Party
with the support of students, intellectuals, and some of the trade
unionists who had been expelled from the Workers' Federation.[49]
The activists conducted a lively campaign, boosting Araujo's image
as a reformist and making big promises on his behalf. However,
when he felt that enough had been done to secure popular support,
Araujo publicly repudiated his radical followers and struck an
electoral deal with a conservative list of planters.

Although Araujo was an adequate candidate for the dominant
classes, the situation turned out to be much more complex than
anticipated. The effects of the world depression were beginning to
be felt in El Salvador. Coffee prices started to go down and wages
in the plantations were automatically affected.[50] The Communists
were rapidly capitalizing on the increasing unrest. A youth chapter
of the party was created with the explicit task of organizing young
workers and penetrating the university and the army.[51] On May
Day 1930, the Communists organized a massive parade in the
capital: 80 000 agricultural workers demanded guaranteed labour
contracts and minimum wages in the plantations.[52] Thus, the world
economic slump reached El Salvador when the class struggles
were approaching their climax. Araujo's electoral appeal was now
becoming a source of deep concern for the Salvadoran élites: since

the hopes of the masses were not going to be fulfilled, they feared that disappointment and embitterment would facilitate the work of the Communist agitators. With an economic and political crisis of frightful proportions looming on the horizon, second thoughts about the wisdom of the democratic experiment started to haunt the dominant classes.

Final Remarks

The rest of the story has been succinctly told in the opening paragraphs of this chapter. Araujo won the election with great popular support and took over in February 1931.[53] During the first months of his administration the country felt the full impact of the world recession. In July, the prices of coffee plummeted and many planters preferred to let the harvest rot in the fields. Wages went down to 40 per cent of what they had been in 1928, and lack of work in the plantations brought a disaster for the majority of the population. Rural protest, led by the Communists, swelled into a movement of incredible proportions. Araujo's government vacillated between open repression and demagogic measures. But given the total dependency of the system upon the foreign market, nothing substantial could really be done to solve the problem. Alarmed, the dominant classes decided that these were no conditions under which to go on with democratic strategies of domination. The army was mobilized and Araujo was deposed in December. To appease popular unrest the new president, General Hernández Martínez, decided to allow the municipal elections due in early January 1932. But this time the Communists had registered their candidates, and when it became clear that they could actually carry the polls in many parts of the country, the elections were cancelled. The Communist leadership formed a Revolutionary Military Command and set 22 January as the date for the uprising. Detailed plans for the insurrection were prepared, including contacts within the army. But all the preparations collapsed when Martí and the other main leaders were caught. Instructions were issued calling off the uprising, but the government had imposed a total curfew and communications were very difficult. On top of everything, unexpected volcanic eruptions in the western part of the country contributed to the ominous atmosphere that made the revolt inevitable. When the dust settled, the landscape included the fresh graves of Martí, his followers, and the thousands who had been massacred by the army of General Hernández Martínez.

The uprising was clearly rooted in the contradictions of the export economy. In two generations, the development of coffee capitalism destroyed a world of economic self-sufficiency, proletarianized the bulk of the Salvadorans, and created a society in which a few made rapid fortunes at the expense of the misery of the majority. It was this social exploitation that prepared the ground for an upheaval. Creating a situation in which the very survival of the people appeared to be threatened, the world depression acted as a detonator. But the social dynamite had been already there, first in the objective class antagonisms of the export economy, and then in the popular movement that rose to give expression to a broad alliance of the subordinate classes. The permanent and temporary workers of the plantations provided the main base of the movement. In the absence of an urban proletariat or a middle-class *intelligentsia*, political and ideological inspiration came from the ranks of the artisans, who represented the strategic group from the point of view of plebeian leadership in El Salvador. Some authors have considered Martí and his followers as simple adventurers, leaders with an artisan mentality in a pre-capitalist society.[54] Was that the case? It is true that there were peasants, artisans, and servile *haciendas* in the country. It is also true that El Salvador was not a fully developed industrial nation. Still, the principal contradiction in Salvadoran society was to be found in the coffee plantations, and that was a capitalist contradiction: it was capital facing wage-labour. On the other hand, although the Communist leaders came from the artisan class, they were by no means "primitive rebels". It is quite clear from all the evidence that they assumed a proletarian perspective and tried to define a socialist strategy of revolution. They may also have been right in their diagnosis of the existence of a revolutionary conjuncture in El Salvador. But did their insurrection have any real chance of military success? Should their plans be seen as an expression of "childish leftism"? What type of socialism could they have built in a coffee republic like El Salvador? These questions are – and most probably will remain – very difficult to answer.

This chapter has shown that the causes of the 1932 insurrection can be traced back to the class contradictions of the export economy and the expression of these contradictions in the political process. But no analytical approach can grasp all the determinations that shape complex social events like the Salvadoran uprising. In this sense, and taking into account the central role played by the Indian peasants, chiefs, and *cofradías*, class analysis must come to terms with the accumulated effects of centuries of racial oppression in the country. The social roots of the insurrection will not be completely understood without a thorough inquiry into the ways in which the Indian rebellious consciousness was articulated into a social movement that assumed a proletarian content.

Finally, what was the historical significance of the dictatorship that came after the insurrection? This chapter has shown that the export economy had originally developed on the basis of an authoritarian pattern of political domination. But coffee capitalism created and reshaped social classes that raised their own demands for economic improvements and political participation. Facing the organization of these classes, the Salvadoran élites tried to develop a new, more participatory strategy of domination. Similar democratic openings took place elsewhere in Latin America during the 1920s. However, countries like Argentina, Brazil, and Colombia had been able to develop incipient urban industry alongside their export sectors. In these countries the world depression actually stimulated growth, because the flow of imported manufactures was interrupted and local industry had a chance to expand into new branches of production. Industrialization helped to placate the social unrest provoked by the crisis of the export economy, creating new employment and consolidating the political opening towards popular participation. This was not the case in El Salvador and the other Central American countries, where the restricted scale of the markets had prevented industrial development and the interests of the dominant sectors had remained totally committed to the export economy. Since popular mobilization was posing a threat to the basic structures of this export economy, democracy led to a *cul-de-sac*. The Salvadoran élites resorted to total repression in order to save their privileges and inflict an exemplary punishment on the people. Once the crisis was over, they saw the establishment of a strong dictatorial regime as necessary to keep the export economy on its feet. Only after the changes produced by industrial development within the framework of the Central American Common Market, would the subordinate classes return to the political arena. Their struggles for participation and social justice are the ones we are witnessing today.

Notes

1. For useful comments on earlier versions of the paper I am grateful to

Bob Antonio, Jan Flora, Héctor Lindo Fuentes, Bill Richardson and Stu Shafer.

2. T. P. Anderson, *Matanza: El Salvador's Communist Revolt of 1932*; R. Dalton, *Miguel Mármol: Los Sucesos de 1932 en El Salvador* (San José: Editorial Universitaria Centroamericana, 1972); R. Guidos Véjar, *El Ascenso del Militarismo en El Salvador* (San Salvador: Universidad Centroamericana Editores, 1980); M. McClintock, *The American Connection: State Terror and Popular Resistance in El Salvador*; L. Zamosc, "The Landing That Never Was: Canadian Marines and the Salvadoran Insurrection of 1932", *Canadian Journal of Latin American and Caribbean Studies*, no 21 (1986).

3. D. Browning, *El Salvador: Landscape and Society* (Oxford: Clarendon Press, 1971) pp. 15–17; A. D. Marroquín, "Cambios en la agricultura y sus repercusiones sociales", *Revista Salvadoreña de Ciencias Sociales*, no 1 (1965) pp. 114–17.

4. Browning, *El Salvador*, pp. 52–65; M. J. McLeod, *Spanish Central America: A Socioeconomic History, 1520–1720* (Berkeley: University of California Press, 1973).

5. Browning, *El Salvador*, pp. 64–5.

6. Browning, *El Salvador*, pp. 66–76; McLeod, *Spanish Central America*, pp. 176–203.

7. Browning, *El Salvador*, pp. 70–2.

8. Ibid, pp. 121–30.

9. McLeod, *Spanish Central America*, pp. 121–2.

10. Anderson, *Matanza*, pp. 18–20; McLeod, *Spanish Central America*, pp. 135–8; Marroquín, "Cambios", pp. 140–1.

11. Marroquín, "Cambios", pp. 118–20.

12. Browning, *El Salvador*, pp. 128, 200.

13. Ibid, pp. 190–2; 195–6.

14. Ibid, p. 155; A. White, *El Salvador* (New York: Praeger Publishers, 1973) p. 80.

15. D. J. Rodgers, *Report on Economic Conditions in the Republic of El Salvador* (London: Department of Trade, 1929) p. 19.

16. Browning, *El Salvador*, pp. 158–9.

17. Ibid, p. 166.

18. Ibid, pp. 171–2.

19. The concept of primitive accumulation refers to the process by which capitalism is historically established through the dispossession of the direct producers, their transformation into wage labourers, and the concentration of the means of production in the hands of a capitalist class (K. Marx, *Capital*, Volume I, Moscow: Progress Publishers, 1965, part VIII). The following description is based on accounts by Browning, *El Salvador*, pp. 203–21; Guidos Véjar, *El Ascenso*, pp. 51–2; J. D. Kaestli, "Dépendence et structure de classes en Amerique Centrale", in *Dependencia y Estructura de Classes en América Latina* (Paris: Centre Europe Tiers Monde, 1972) p. 83; D. A. Luna, "Un heróico y trágico suceso de Nuestra historia", in *El Proceso Político Centroamericano* (San

Salvador: Editorial Universitaria, 1964) pp. 182–5; Marroquín, "Cambios", p. 127; and McClintock, *The American Connection*, pp. 94–6.

20. Browning, *El Salvador*, pp. 217–20.
21. P. F. Martin, *Salvador of the Twentieth Century* (London: E. Arnold, 1911) p. 291; Rodgers, *Economic Conditions . . . El Salvador*, p. 11.
22. Browning, *El Salvador*, pp. 228–9; Martin, *Salvador*, p. 301.
23. T. L. Smith, "Notes on Population and Rural Social Organization in El Salvador", *Rural Sociology*, no 10 (1945) p. 370.
24. R. Dalton, *El Salvador* (La Habana: Editorial Popular, 1965) pp. 93–7; L. Zamosc, *El Salvador on the Eve of the Great World Depression* (University of Manchester, 1977) mimeo.
25. R. T. Aubey, "Entrepreneurial Formation in El Salvador", *Explorations in Entrepreneurial History*, Second Series, vol. 6, no 3 (1969) p. 278; Smith, "Notes on Population", pp. 370–1.
26. Guidos Véjar, *El Ascenso*, p. 61; D. G. Munro, *The Five Republics of Central America* (New York: Oxford University Press, 1918) pp. 300–1.
27. During the period 1926–8, the value of Salvadoran imports was equivalent to 94 per cent of its exports (Rodgers, 1929, pp. 15–16). The distribution of the imported commodities was as follows: 73 per cent manufactured articles, 14 per cent raw materials, and 13 per cent other goods (League of Nations, *Memorandum on International Trade and Balances of Payments*, vol. 1, Geneva, 1929, pp. 41–6).
28. Munro, *The Five Republics*, pp. 114–15; D. J. Rodgers, *Report on Economic Conditions in the Republic of El Salvador* (London, Department of Trade, 1931) pp. 18–19.
29. White, *El Salvador*, p. 94.
30. Zamosc, "The Landing that Never Was".
31. Quoted from a 1932 report by consul D. J. Rodgers to the Foreign Office (British Public Records Office, FO 371 15812 A612/9/8).
32. Aubey, "Entrepreneurial Formation", p. 280; White, *El Salvador*, pp. 86–90.
33. In 1918, an American diplomat observed that the Salvadoran army and police were the most efficient and best equipped in Central America (Munro, *The Five Republics*, pp. 108–9). During the 1920s, defence and security absorbed 20 per cent of the state budget (Guidos Véjar, *El Ascenso*, pp. 96–7).
34. In 1926, a British diplomat explained the absence of political parties as follows: "The educated class in El Salvador is both numerically and relatively small . . . To such people, the system of non-party government appeals, because they can give their support to the leader of whom they approve either on the purely altruistic grounds of patriotism or on the less worthy grounds of personal advantage" (British Public Records Office, FO 371 11975 A2567/2567/8).
35. Anderson, *Matanza*, p. 7; Munro, *The Five Republics*, p. 107.
36. McClintock, *The American Connection*, pp. 97–8.
37. A. Bermúdez, *El Salvador Al Vuelo* (San Salvador, 1917) pp. 171–3; Dalton, *Miguel Mármol*, pp. 93–100, Guidos Véjar, *El Ascenso*, pp. 88–91.

38. Dalton, *Miguel Mármol*, pp. 143–4.
39. Guidos Véjar, *El Ascenso*, p. 88.
40. White, *El Salvador*, p. 94.
41. Anderson, *Matanza*, p. 7.
42. Dalton, *Miguel Mármol*, p. 99.
43. Dalton, *Miguel Mármol*, pp. 143–54; Guidos Véjar, *El Ascenso*, pp. 92–3.
44. Anderson, *Matanza*, p. 8; White, *El Salvador*, pp. 97–8.
45. This review of Romero Bosque's policies is based on the following sources: British Public Records Office, FO 371, 11971 A3714/37/8, FO 371 12744 A2644/10/8, FO 371 13472 A5756/2056/8, FO 371 14210 A2140/2106/8; Dalton, *Miguel Mármol* pp. 197–238; *Archives of the Foreign Office, American Department* (London, 1926–32); A. Cuenca, *El Salvador: Una Democracia Cafetalera* (Mexico: ARR Centro Editorial, 1962) p. 101; M. de la Selva, "El Salvador: Tres Décadas de Lucha", *Cuadernos Americanos*, no 21 (1962) p. 199.
46. Anderson, *Matanza*, p. 42.
47. Ibid, pp. 69–71; Guidos Véjar, *El Ascenso*, pp. 134–6.
48. Dalton, *Miguel Mármol*, pp. 150–61.
49. Anderson *Matanza*, pp. 42–8; Guidos Véjar, *El Ascenso*, pp. 115–17.
50. Anderson, *Matanza*, pp. 12–13.
51. Dalton, *Miguel Mármol*, pp. 157–8.
52. Anderson, *Matanza*, p. 27; Luna, "Un Heróico", p. 55.
53. The following account is based on Anderson, *Matanza*; Dalton, *Miguel Mármol*; and McClintock, *The American Connection*.
54. Cuenca, *El Salvador*, pp. 107–8; Luna, "Un Heróico".

Part II

The Transformation of Politics after 1945

Part II of this book concentrates on explanations for the development of insurgency in the 1970s and 1980s, examining in depth the nature of politics, the development of the National Security State, and, in the case of Nicaragua, the transformation of class structure. The first chapter compares Honduras and Costa Rican political developments in the period following the Second World War with emphasis on the roles of political parties.

Political and economic events are closely interrelated. This is particularly important in understanding the countries of Central America in the current period of change and conflict. Since none of the chapters deal comprehensively with the post-Second World War economic situation, a brief sketch is included here. It is followed by a discussion of the political and military issues raised by this part of the volume.

Patterns of Growth

The economies of Central America have experienced rather rapid economic growth, even as far back as 1920.[1] Export agriculture has been the motor force for such growth. Beginning in the early 1960s, it was supplemented with industrial growth derived from the Central American Common Market (CACM). That growth did not necessarily trickle down to the working- and peasant-classes – in fact it generally did not.

Table 1 indicates patterns of growth for the 1960s and 1970s. Overall economic growth was very respectable. It was somewhat lower (4.6 per cent per year) in the decade of the 1950s. In the two succeeding decades, agricultural growth exceeded that for the rest of Latin America by a full percentage point (Weeks, 1985, pp. 62 and 63). It is clear, particularly in the 1960s, that economic growth was export-led (8.1 per cent average annual increase in exports). As we will see, that decade was one in which both agricultural and manufactured products showed strong export growth.

Table 1   *Average annual growth rates by decade, Central America, 1960s and 1970s*

	1960–70	1970–9
Economic growth rates	6.5	5.9
Growth rates – manufacturing	7.9	6.1
Growth rates – agriculture	4.3	4.0
Growth rates – population	3.3	3.1
Exports	8.1	5.3
Imports	7.1	7.2

Source: John Weeks, *The Economies of Central America* (New York and London: Holmes & Meier, 1985) p. 41, Table 2; p. 62, Table 13; p. 64, Table 14; and p. 67, Table 15.

From the Second World War until 1972, Central American countries had remarkably stable currencies. In fact, except for Costa Rica, the dollar circulated as a parallel medium of exchange with the local currency until the late 1970s – suggesting an extraordinary degree of openness of these economies. The low rate of inflation was due in part to that openness. When governments have few restrictions on imports, whatever excess demand which is generated within the economy is absorbed through increased imports, thus keeping the inflation level close to that of the dollar. A complementary explanation was the presence of repressive dictatorships in El Salvador, Guatemala, and Nicaragua. In all three countries, the incomes of the peasantry and urban poor people and workers did not keep up with per capita growth, thus dampening consumption which might have put pressure on the balance of payments.[2]

The oil price increases of 1973–4 changed the picture radically, and marked the beginning of accumulation of substantial debt by the Central American countries. It also set the stage for serious problems with inflation which reached double-digit levels in the rest of the 1970s, and became rampant in certain countries in the 1980s. Table 1 shows that in the 1970s, export growth slowed – due principally to a slowing of growth in intra-regional trade – while imports continued to increase at the rate of the 1960s.

Although, as Table 1 illustrates, growth in agricultural production exceeded population growth in the 1960s and 1970s (the population growth rate was over 3 per cent per year in both decades), there appears to have been an absolute decline in per capita food consumption, even taking into account expanding food imports. Weeks estimates for the region as a whole a decline of about 11 per cent in caloric consumption of the three basic staple foods (corn, rice, and beans) between the 1960s and 1970s. He concludes:

Until other data are forthcoming, it appears that the real consumption of the poor was no greater in the 1970s than in the 1960s in three of the five countries of Central America and probably lower; in the other two countries consumption of the poor probably rose slightly.[3]

Costa Rica and El Salvador appear to have experienced increases, while the three other countries suffered decreases. Other data indicate that in El Salvador as well the bottom 60 per cent of the rural population experienced absolute decline in income during the 1970s.[4] Though the country experienced an increase in per capita consumption, that increase apparently did not occur among the "popular" classes.

In the case of Guatemala between 1970 and 1984, the top quintile of the population experienced an increase in the total share of national income from 47 per cent to 57 per cent, with declines in all other quintiles; the share of the lowest fifth decreased from 6.8 per cent to 4.8 per cent.[5] Guatemala and El Salvador experienced sharp increases in unemployment and underemployment beginning in the late 1970s. Though the civil wars, particularly in El Salvador, have contributed to such expansion of unemployment, it is clear that the trend was upward in both El Salvador and Guatemala before the conflicts affected those countries' economies. El Salvador's unemployment rate has been higher than the other countries throughout the period, reflecting the overcrowded conditions in that country. In Nicaragua, there was an upward trend in the mid-1970s, though levels of unemployment were low compared with levels during and after the insurrection. Costa Rica did not experience an increase in unemployment until the world-wide recession of the early 1980s and by 1984 had brought the level back to the rate in the mid-1970s. Data on unemployment are not available for the 1980s for Honduras. While higher than that in Guatemala, Nicaragua, and Costa Rica in the 1970s, Honduras's unemployment rate remained stable throughout that decade, varying between 7 and 10 per cent.[6]

Wage rates show a similar pattern. From the early 1970s to 1980, Costa Rica experienced a sharp increase in real wage rates, Honduras remained stable, and the other three countries experienced declines.[7]

In summary, the economic situation declined sharply in the late 1970s for the popular classes in El Salvador and Guatemala, to a lesser degree in Nicaragua, and improved or remained the same in Costa Rica and Honduras. (Honduras apparently experienced an increase in malnutrition; in any case, it remained the poorest country in the region.) Not coincidentally, the last two countries have experienced less turmoil in the 1980s than have the first three.

Central American Common Market

Industrialization, which occurred earlier in the rest of Latin America, reached Central America in the 1960s, stimulated by the Central American Common Market (CACM). It resulted in major growth in intra-regional trade, which increased about fourfold between 1963, the year Costa Rica joined the other four countries in the common market, and 1970, the year Honduras left it.[8] There was a clear bifurcation with respect to the destination of the two kinds of exports: except for some food crops, agricultural exports went to countries outside the region (food exports represented over 30 per cent of intra-regional trade in the mid-1970s) while manufactured items were exported to the other members of the CACM. Manufactures represented less than 5 per cent of extra-regional trade, excluding frozen meat and fish and refined sugar.[9]

Central American industrialization had a number of serious problems, including the following:

(1) The consumer non-durable component of Central American production was much higher than for other Latin American countries with equal or lower per capita incomes and smaller domestic markets than the five Central American countries together. Thus the development of capital goods industries and production of intermediate goods, both indicators of a solid industrial base, was minimal. As Jonas points out,[10] the US government worked long and hard to ensure that industrial planning would not take place and that foreign firms would be given the same opportunities within the CACM as Central American firms. The initial conception of the CACM was provided by ECLA (the Economic Commission for Latin America of the United Nations); the ECLA proposal included the concept of "integration industries", firms which would enjoy certain protections for ten years, including the guarantee that no direct competitor would be allowed in the five countries for that period. Since such industries would be monopolies, they would have been strictly regulated in terms of production, prices, and quality of product; integration industries would have had to be financed in part by local capital.[11] Presumably, the integration industries as a whole would have emphasized inter-

mediate and capital goods production, thus shifting the industrial mix away from consumer non-durables.

(2) Around half of the inputs for production of these goods were imported. Though the import coefficient of Central American industrial production declined during the 1960s, there was an absolute increase in imports used as inputs in industrial products due to the large expansion of industrial production;[12] this encouraged the expansion of traditional agricultural exports to generate the foreign exchange to maintain industrial expansion.

(3) Capacity utilization was extremely low, varying in the late 1960s between 24 per cent for drugs and cosmetics to 65 per cent for textiles; 75 per cent utilization of industrial capacity is considered low in developed countries.[13] The low rate of utilization of capacity was related to the *laissez-faire* approach adopted by the CACM, with strong US encouragement. Implementation of the "integration industries" concept or some regional planning of industrial growth could have increased capacity utilization.

(4) The CACM was severely crippled as a result of events in 1969 and 1970. The central issue was unbalanced industrial growth among the Central American countries. Since under the ECLA plan, no country could have had two integration industries until each had its first, its implementation would perhaps have promoted balanced development among the countries, and possibly would have kept all five countries in the common market for several more years.[14] El Salvador and Guatemala had the most positive balance of intra-Central American trade. Guatemala's trade balance with the other countries of the region was positive every year between 1961 and 1980. Honduran and Nicaraguan trade balances were the most negative.[15] Honduras, because its industrial and export sectors were the weakest of all five countries, came to perceive the CACM to be more a hindrance than help. Following the 1969 war between Honduras and El Salvador (which arose from Honduras's expulsion of Salvadorans living in that country) and the unwillingness of El Salvador subsequently to countenance major restructuring of the CACM, Honduras left the customs union in 1970.

(5) Employment opportunities did not keep up with rapid economic growth of the Central American Common Market. In Nicaragua, El Salvador, and Guatemala, industry's share of exports showed a marked decline from the first half to the last half of the 1970s, indicating that the Common Market expansion has run its course. Furthermore, industrialization was relatively capital-

intensive and industrial employment represented a small proportion of total employment.[16]

The high import coefficients and the low utilization of capacity
indicate that the Central American consumer was paying prices
above the world market. This was particularly true after the dramatic
oil-price hike of 1973, since many of the industrial input imports were
petrochemically based. The cost of such imports rose 11 per cent
per year during the 1970s. Weeks argues that the cost
for multinational companies to produce the products outside
the region would have been lower than producing them within
the CACM. Thus, his hypothesis is that the customs union was
fostered by Central American entrepreneurs (Weeks, 1985,
pp. 132 and 148).[17] Jonas emphasizes the role of ECLA and Central
American government bureaucrats in initiating the CACM. She also
indicates that multinational industrial corporations favoured the
establishment of the common market: "For these corporations too,
Central America had to develop a larger market in order to be a
worthwhile investment."[18] However, her evidence suggests that the
US government, having an ideological commitment to free trade,
rather successfully attempted to steer the CACM toward a *laissez-
faire* orientation once it was clear that the common market would
exist in some form. The direct role of multinational corporations in
shaping the CACM appeared to be minimal.

In any case, the high import coefficient of Central American
industrialization placed strains on the balance of payments:

> so that growth repeatedly brings the economy to the brink of a foreign
> exchange crisis unless exports are growing rapidly . . . intraregional
> exports in each country have been considerably more import-using
> than manufacturing as a whole. This is the worst of both worlds. The
> high import content of intraregional exports meant that the products
> could not be reoriented to the domestic markets of the countries even
> if domestic demand was sufficient . . . when the CACM began to
> collapse in the late seventies, the manufacturing sectors of each country
> suffered large negative foreign exchange balances . . . the early 1980s
> brought on a wave of factory closings in all five Central American
> countries, even in Honduras which had been the least integrated into
> the common market.[19]

Nicaragua and Guatemala had shown the greatest growth in
industrial production as a proportion of GNP during the period of
the CACM. Their industrial sectors were the hardest hit by the
economic downturn of the early 1980s.[20] Nicaragua in particular,

given the shortage of foreign exchange brought on by the US financial embargo of that country under the Reagan administration, has had to close a large portion of its manufacturing establishments.

With the collapse of the CACM, the Central American countries have gone back to being exporters of primary products. A modest amount of import substitution industrialization continues to exist, but a resurgence of industrial production – particularly for export – is highly unlikely so long as investment capital remains scarce. We now turn to the debt problem, which must be dealt with before a net inflow of capital can occur.

The Debt Problem

The strong demand for commodities in the world market in the Second World War and the Korean war period encouraged the Central American countries to diversify their agricultural exports. To coffee and bananas they added sugar, cotton, and beef. These five products remain at present the dominant non-industrial exports, and the chief products exported outside the region. While they declined from 77 per cent of total exports in the period 1960–4 to 62 per cent in the period, 1975–9, they represented 85 per cent and 82 per cent, respectively, of non-manufacturing exports in the two decades of the 1960s and 1970s.[21] Two observations are important here:

(1) while the five products represent less market risk than when there were only two main export crops, the 1980s show that reliance on those five crops can be quite risky;
(2) the manufactured exports which partially replaced the five principal commodities were less labour-using than were the agricultural exports;[22] hence, the labour coefficient of exports declined under the CACM.

During the 1960s and until the petroleum price boom, the four Central American countries excluding Costa Rica generally had positive trade balances, but all countries consistently had negative current accounts balances because of negative balances in services and profit remittances. (The current accounts balance is generally termed the "balance of payments", which includes imports and exports of commodities and services, as well as purely monetary flows of a short-term character, such as profit remittances and transfer payments.) The services category is negative because the

Central American countries must use vessels, insurance, and other export-related services from other countries – even for intra-regional trade. Only Costa Rica showed a positive services balance.[23]

Of greater importance in explaining the negative balance of payments is net profit remittances. From 1960 to 1978, direct foreign investment was $1.68 billion, some $800 million less than net profit remittances outside the region. The countries with greatest foreign investment experienced the least loss of foreign exchange through profit remittances, suggesting it is not foreign investment which leads to profit remittances. Rather, it is chiefly the profits of domestic capitalists which are being sent abroad, indicating a lack of confidence in the future stability of their own country. The exception is Honduras, where the transnational banana companies were making substantial profits in the late 1960s and early 1970s, but were not reinvesting in their operations in that country. Costa Rica, with the greatest foreign investment during the period, has had the least capital flight, suggesting that at least in the Central American case political stability and some degree of economic equality lead to attraction of foreign investors and reduction of capital flight. Paradoxically, it is Costa Rica which has the greatest per capita foreign debt of the Central American countries today. That is partly related to the fact that trade deficits were possible year after year precisely because of the greater inflow of private foreign capital – which meant that Costa Rica gradually built up a substantial foreign debt which became a major problem when commodity prices dropped precipitously. Thus Costa Rica's large debt is not due to its "welfare state" system, but to a negative balance of trade made possible by the steady inflow of foreign capital,[24] which occurred because of the stable political climate in that country.

After the oil-price increase in 1973, the balance-of-payments deficit for the region as a whole grew substantially. When commodity prices began to drop in 1978 (except for Honduras), debt service became a great burden. By the mid-1980s the foreign debt had reached alarming proportions, especially in Costa Rica and Nicaragua (see Table 2). In 1985, the per capita debt had reached $1656 in Costa Rica and $1366 in Nicaragua. Because of massive US assistance to El Salvador and Honduras (see Table 3), the per capita rate was "only" $415 in the former and $580 in the latter. Guatemala's per capita debt was a manageable $292.[25]

Whereas larger and more economically diversified countries in Latin America which experienced high debt expanded the value of their exports and curtailed their imports to obtain a positive balance of trade in the 1980s, the Central American nations were not

Table 2   *Total Disbursed Public and Private Debt by Country, Central America,*
1979–1985
(in billions of US dollars)

	1979	1980	1981	1982	1983	1984	1985
Costa Rica	1.5	2.1	2.4	3.0	3.4	3.5	4.2
El Salvador	0.9	1.2	1.5	1.7	2.0	2.0	2.1
Guatemala	0.6	0.6	1.2	1.5	2.1	2.5	2.5
Honduras	1.0	1.4	1.6	1.7	1.5	2.2	2.4
Nicaragua	1.1	1.6	2.2	2.7	3.3	3.9	4.4

Sources: All figures were calculated by the Economic Commission for Latin America and the Caribbean; cited in *Central American Report*, vol. 13, no 34, 5 September 1986 (Costa Rica); vol. 12, no 28, 26 July 1985 (El Salvador); vol. 13, no 39, 10 October 1986 (Guatemala); vol. 13, no 32, 22 August 1986 (Honduras); and vol. 12, no 36, 20 September 1985 (Nicaragua). The 1985 figures were cited in John A. Booth, "Socioeconomic Equity in Central America: Recent and Possible Future Trends", paper presented at the South-eastern Council of Latin American Studies meetings (Clemson University, South Carolina, 3–5 April 1985) p. 36.

successful in doing so. Only Costa Rica and El Salvador were able to achieve a positive trade balance in any year from 1979 to 1985; each had modestly positive trade balances in two of the six years.[26] There are at least two reasons for the persistence of negative trade balances:

(1) The Central American countries showed an extreme dependence on agricultural exports after the demise of the CACM. The particular agricultural exports of Central America experienced a precipitous decline in price. The terms of trade deteriorated about 40 per cent for the entire region between 1977 and 1983.[27] Though export volume grew in the 1980s, value of exports declined.

(2) The US government's fear of insurgency and revolution in other parts of Central America followed the successful insurrection of the Sandinistas in Nicaragua. This led to a substantial growth in economic and military assistance from the USA to El Salvador, Honduras, Costa Rica, and only recently in Guatemala, allowing the Central American countries to continue to show significant deficits in the balance of trade while maintaining foreign reserves.[28] Nicaragua also was able to obtain substantial amounts of foreign exchange through loans and grants from diverse sources. This foreign assistance also allowed the countries of the isthmus to continue to run large governmental budget deficits, since a significant portion of the aid was for budget support

Table 3 *US Economic and Military Assistance to Central America, 1980–6**
(millions of US dollars)

	1980	1981	1982	1983	1984	1985‡
Costa Rica						
Military assistance	—	†	2.1	2.6	9	9
Economic support funds	—	—	90	157	130	160
Economic assistance	14	13	31	55	48	48
El Salvador						
Military assistance	6	35	82	81	197	128
Economic support funds	9	45	115	140	211	195
Economic assistance	49	69	67	91	121	131
Guatemala						
Military assistance	—	—	—	—	—	0.3
Economic support funds	—	—	10	—	—	13
Economic assistance	11	17	14	18	33	61
Honduras						
Military assistance	4.0	9	31	37	78	63
Economic support funds	—	—	37	56	112	75
Economic assistance	51	34	41	45	97	64
Total (includes aid to Panama and Belize)	146	233	539	713	1111	1018

* Fiscal years.
† Less than 0.1
‡ The figures for 1985 were approved initially by Congress. However, increments should be considered because since 1981 there has been frequent authorization of more funds before the end of each fiscal period.

Source: *Inforpress Centroumericana*, no 627 (7 February 1985) p. 5, cited in Eugenio Rivera Urrutia, "Foreign Debt and Financial Assistance: the Case of Central America", Occasional Paper Series no 17 (Latin American and Caribbean Center, Florida International University, May 1986) p. 18, Table 3.

(Economic Support Funds), even though significant capital flight occurred, particularly in El Salvador and Honduras, because of the political and economic uncertainty caused by armed conflicts in the region. (See Table 3 for the growth in US foreign assistance from 1980 to 1986.) The magnitude of US assistance indicated that the USA was more concerned about political loyalty than about "responsible" economic policy on the part of its Central American allies, should the latter result in greater social unrest.

The International Monetary Fund and the World Bank – often in contradiction with USAID practice – pushed for their version of responsible economic policy. Both agencies began requiring "structural adjustment" in return for loans from these multilateral agencies, where in the 1970s the World Bank (as well as the InterAmerican Development Bank, and to a degree, USAID) had taken a basic-needs approach. In the 1980s, there has been a return to the orthodox neoclassical solutions of two decades ago which involve reduction of state regulation of the economy. Weeks, in criticizing the Kissinger Commission report on Central America, argues that such an approach is singularly inappropriate:

> the commission foresees a recovery of the four Central American economies based upon less government initiative, fewer regulations on private capital, and liberalization of trade policy . . . Historically, the Central American governments have placed fewer restrictions on the private sector than any governments in the hemisphere, so it is hard to see how further catering to private business interests will qualitatively improve either the "investment climate" or growth performance. Indeed for the last twenty years foreign investors have judged Costa Rica to have the most favorable investment climate in the region, and it is the Costa Rican governments which have placed more restrictions on capital than any others in Central America.[29]

Thus political and economic policy implementation by the USA in Central America are often at odds as the USA grapples for a solution to instability in the isthmus without being willing to countenance the political shifts and economic reforms which might remove the root causes of such instability.

We now turn to contemporary political–military issues, the subject of the contributions to this second part of the book.

Torres-Rivas in the concluding chapter of this book puts the role of elections in perspective: they sometimes involve competition for control of the government, but not for control of the state. Elections do not settle whether major structural changes will take place; they only settle who will control the government within defined political and economic limits. Thus, Vega shows that in Costa Rica the National Liberation Party, whose leaders redefined the course of Costa Rican politics through the Revolution of 1948, is the dominant party. While other parties occasionally win the Presidency, they are unable to change the dominant course of the Costa Rican state. Costa Rica may be compared with Mexico, though the Mexican PRI has as yet been unwilling to share control of the government. The Nicaraguan elections of 1984 can be interpreted similarly.

Control by the Sandinistas was not in doubt, and would not have been even if the Coordinadora (the coalition of right-wing political parties and civic organizations supported by the United States) had participated. This was true not because there was fraud, but because the FSLN correctly calculated majority suport for their party for the revolution.[30]

El Salvador and Guatemala have experienced long periods of control by the military. The recent elections in both countries brought Christian Democratic (PDC) governments to power. As Karl points out in her chapter on El Salvador, the PDC is a centrist party with two main objectives: reformism and anti-Communism. This means that at different times, alliances are made with the moderate left (when Duarte won the Presidency of El Salvador in 1972) when the objective is reform, and with the right (often the more progressive wing of the military) when anti-Communism is the greater concern. As Handy suggests in this volume, the PDC of Guatemala and its leader, President Vinicio Cerezo, are in the latter mode, having tacitly supported Ríos Montt (and especially the young officers who brought him to power) during his presidency, and now as junior partner with the military as it seeks the final erasure of subversion from the countryside of Guatemala. These dual goals explain Duarte's support of counter-insurgency *and* his as yet frustrated efforts to negotiate with the FMLN guerrillas (frustrated not so much by the guerrillas, as by the military and by the US government).

Honduras might best be compared with Colombia in which the two-party system of Liberals and Conservatives (in Honduras, the latter is called the Nationalist Party) remains. Since centralization–decentralization is no longer an issue, the parties have lost their ideological identification. Both parties have interest in the maintenance of the two-party system, but ideological differences must be given a voice. Hence, intra-party ideological differences are more important than differences between the parties. The military, which became professionalized in the 1950s, serves as the guarantor that no faction which would make major structural changes is able to do so. From time to time this has meant putting political party activity on "hold". While the military is more comfortable working with the Nationalist Party, it is perfectly able, when necessary, to cooperate with the Liberal Party.

What is of greatest significance with respect to the military's participation in politics is that only Costa Rica has been able to institutionalize the rule of law. The absence of a military makes it much easier for that to happen.[31]

While, as Torres-Rivas points out, elections do not ensure democracy, the perspective presented in the chapters in this part of the book is that elections are not meaningless and can, under proper circumstances, move a country closer to the rule of law. As is indicated by Karl in her chapter on El Salvador, electoral democracy may be the second choice of many of the parties (including the USA), but for the people as a whole it may be the best available alternative. While Vilas's chapter on Nicaragua does not touch directly on the question of electoral democracy in Nicaragua, electoral democracy may well turn out to be the best alternative – perhaps not one which the FSLN would have chosen, but they have found it necessary to move in that direction in order to build unity at home and support abroad. The critical question is whether the USA will allow Nicaragua to follow that path, or whether it is bent on destroying the Sandinistas.

That brings us to the issue of the National Security State and Low Intensity Conflict. The alliance of the military with the oligarchy (which Torres-Rivas, in his chapter, defines as "a backward bourgeoisie personified by large holdings, but with incomplete control over capital")[32] contributes to a continuation of inequalities, which requires repressive measures to keep down the strongly felt desire for redress of grievance by less privileged groups in the society. So long as such conditions pertain, the possibility of electoral democracy (or any kind of democracy) is nil. Thus El Salvador and Guatemala have all the trappings of electoral democracies but appearance and reality are quite distant from one another. The National Security State involves an alliance between the oligarchy and the military to prevent efforts by the popular classes (sometimes in alliance with middle sectors) to gain sufficient political power to redress some of those grievances. The National Security State is absent only in Costa Rica and in revolutionary Nicaragua,[33] and is only partly established in Honduras. Torres-Rivas points out the linkage among local private armies and paramilitary groups rooted historically in the traditional landed estate, the modern military and oligarchy, and the US security appartaus. US training of security forces in Guatemala, El Salvador, and Nicaragua began in the 1960s in response to local conditions as well as to the Cuban revolution.[34]

The conflicts precipitated by the economic situation described at the beginning of this introduction have plunged the USA into major political, economic and military involvement in Central America during the 1980s. US assistance to the national security state during the 1960s and 1970s was designed to obviate the necessity for such intervention. Since the national security state by definition does not get rid of the root causes of popular grievances, and in fact channels efforts at redressing those grievances in violent directions, it is not surprising that conditions for US intervention have developed.

The Reagan Doctrine of stopping Communism (unfortunately confused with *any* nationalist or popular-based insurgency) on the periphery, coupled with the unwillingness of the US population to support the introduction of US combat troops into Central America (the so-called Vietnam syndrome) have strengthened the position of those in the Pentagon and in the Reagan administration who advocate Low Intensity Conflict (LIC). While this doctrine is not directly discussed in this book,[35] Handy's discussion of the Ríos Montt counter-insurgency effort shows that Ríos Montt and his successors have effectively used LIC (called *frijoles y fusiles* – bullets and beans).[36] The counter-insurgency was temporarily effective (*temporarily* because the root causes of the grievances were not removed) because it delegitimized the guerrilla forces in the eyes of the peasants: first, by brutally showing that the guerrillas did not have the capacity to protect their supporters, and then by the use of carrot-and-stick programmes which encouraged acceptance of government presence and which seek eventually to transfer indigenous loyalty from the community to the nation through the delegitimation of indigenous culture. It is perhaps not necessary to point out that Low Intensity Conflict is low intensity only for the metropolitan power which practises it, not for the "host" country in which it is carried out. "Total war at the grassroots level" is an apt description of the Guatemalan counter-insurgency. It is ironic that LIC has been much more effective in Guatemala, where US military assistance since 1978 has been rather minimal, than in El Salvador, where the USA is deeply involved politically, economically, diplomatically, and militarily (though not with combat troops). This points up a fundamental problem for LIC as practised by the USA in Latin America. US military support for counter-revolution, however low-profile it may seek to be, tends to delegitimize the forces it seeks to support. The Iran–contra affair points up another problem for the LIC doctrine – the difficulty of instigating LIC from an open society. Not only are North Americans unwilling to commit combat troops to Central America, but many are unwilling to countenance the anti-democratic actions which such policies imply for US society.

Notes

1. V. Bulmer-Thomas, "Economic Development Over the Long Run – Central America Since 1920", *Journal of Latin American Studies*, vol. 15, no 2 (November 1983) pp. 269–94.
2. John Weeks, *The Economies of Central America*, pp. 59, 68–9.
3. Weeks, *The Economies*, p. 108.
4. Liisa North, *Bitter Grounds: Roots of Revolt in El Salvador*, p. 48.
5. *Inforpress Centroamericana*, 1985, cited in John A. Booth, "Socioeconomic Equity in Central America: Recent and Possible Future Trends", presented at South-eastern Council for Latin American Studies, Clemson University, 3–5 April 1985.
6. Booth, "Socioeconomic Equity", p. 19.
7. Ibid, Table 4, p. 13.
8. Edelberto Torres-Rivas, "La Integración Económica Centroamericana: Resumen Crítica", p. 14.
9. Weeks, *The Economies*, p. 66.
10. Susanne Jonas, "Masterminding the Mini-Market: US Aid to the Central American Common Market", *NACLA's Latin America and Empire Report*, vol. 7, no 5 (May–June 1973).
11. Ibid, p. 10.
12. See Flora and Torres-Rivas, p. 37 of this volume.
13. Weeks, *The Economies*, pp. 137–8.
14. Jonas, "Masterminding the mini-Market".
15. Edelberto Torres-Rivas, "La Crisis Económica Centroamericana: Ćual Crisis?" *Cuadernos de Pensamiento Propio: Serie Avances* (Managua, Nicaragua: Instituto de Investigaciones Económicas y Sociales, 1982) p. 14, Table 10.
16. Weeks, *The Economies*, p. 144.
17. Ibid, pp. 132 and 148.
18. Jonas, "Masterminding the mini-Market", p. 3.
19. Weeks, *The Economies*, pp. 141, 143, and 150.
20. Ibid, pp. 135 and 143.
21. Ibid, pp. 76 and 98.
22. Ibid, p. 79.
23. Ibid, pp. 79, 88–91.
24. Ibid, pp. 79–80, 90–5, and 186.
25. Booth, "Socioeconomic Equity", p. 36, Table 8.
26. *Central America Report*, various issues (see sources at bottom of Table 2).
27. Richard E. Feinberg and Bruce M. Bagley, *Development Postponed: the Political Economy of Central America in the 1980s*, p. 7.
28. Eugenio Rivera Urrutia, "Foreign Debt and Financial Assistance: the Case of Central America" (Occasional Paper #17, Latin American and Caribbean Center, Florida International University, May 1986) pp. 1–2.
29. Weeks, *The Economies*, p. 200.
30. See the "Report of the Latin American Studies Association Delegation

to Observe the Nicaraguan General Election of November 4, 1984", *LASA Forum*, 15, 4 (Winter 1985) pp. 9–43, which is the most reasoned and thorough report on the Nicaraguan elections.

31. See Vega, "Parties, Political Development and Social Conflict in Honduras and Cost Rica", this volume, pp. 103, 104.

32. See Torres-Rivas, "Authorization Transition to Democracy", this volume, p. 193.

33. Nicaragua has another set of security problems. Though it has violated certain accepted legal norms in an effort to fight the counter-revolutionary movement, its objectives and methods differ substantially from those of the National Security State. See *Human Rights in Nicaragua, 1986*, An Americas Watch Report (New York: The Americas Watch Committee, February 1987).

34. See Torres-Rivas, "Authoritarian Transition to Democracy", this volume, pp. 194–9.

35. The seminal study is that of Sara Miles, "The Real War: Low Intensity Conflict in Central America".

36. See Handy, "Insurgency and Counter-insurgency in Guatemala", this volume, pp. 124–9.

Parties, Political Development and Social Conflict in Honduras and Costa Rica: A Comparative Analysis

José Luis Vega-Carballo

Introduction

This study seeks to explain, historically and comparatively, the precise nature of social conflict in Honduras and Costa Rica. A useful approach to this goal is to highlight the distinct formation and trajectory of party systems and political parties peculiar to each society. Such systems, on the one hand, were obstacles to the workings of anti-party and anti-system forces, and, on the other hand, have rather successfully manipulated and absorbed the pressure for more widely-based social and political participation. The organizational *weakness* of Honduras's social classes (especially the dominant class) aided in the building of political institutions in which Honduran economic interests were subordinated to foreign capital. In Costa Rica, it was the *strength* of class structure and the need to legitimize the national economic and political supremacy of the coffee growers that led to the containment of destabilizing forces: first, the Catholic Church, and later the army, which was abolished in 1949. In Honduras, neither the Church nor the army was an obstacle to consolidation of a political party system. Since the army began to professionalize in 1949 and since the establishment of the "North American Connection" in 1954, the army has gradually developed into a strong competitor that may eventually displace the traditional political parties and other political forces of recent vintage, such as the worker–peasant movement.

Today a serious and prolonged regional crisis threatens to undermine the relative autonomy, legitimacy, and effectiveness of the civilian political systems of both countries. Still, the social polarization that leads to civil war or to low intensity conflict has not occurred – at least for the moment – as it has in the other Central American countries. This study will conclude by focusing on certain scenarios that have potential either to consolidate or to weaken the relatively democratic and competitive political systems that prevail in each society. But first, the most noteworthy contrasts in the political evolution of Honduras and Costa Rica will be introduced briefly, in order to familiarize the reader with the contexts that will be subject to comparison later on.

The Traditional Two-Party System in Honduras

Since the tardy initiation of Liberal Reforms in Honduras in 1876, the dominant social and economic class has been the smallest and most vulnerable on the isthmus. Foreign interests were encouraged by Honduran governments through exaggerated concessions, especially in mineral exploitation and in bananas. The latter surpassed the former during the first decade of this century, and the "banana enclave" transformed the country in less than two decades into the most typical of banana republics. Honduran class structure was centred on farming, animal husbandry, and commercial activities which occupied niches left to them by the two most powerful banana companies: the Cuyamel and the United Fruit Company.

After a short period of autonomy, the two political parties, the Liberal and the National, founded in 1891 and 1902, respectively, fell under the influence of the banana companies. When their conflicts could not be resolved as a result of the elections in 1923, an invasion of US marines a year later brought elections and political stability under predominantly Liberal rule, which came to an end with the economic and social crisis at the beginning of the 1930s.

Near the end of 1929 the Cuyamel Fruit Company sold its stock to the United Fruit Company (UFCO). With UFCO's support, General Tiburcio Carías and his National Party were able to control political life from 1933 to 1949 by means of a one-man dictatorship, sanctioned constitutionally and based on the system of bosses and rural client groups that dominated the National Party. The primary function of this dictatorship was to contain the wave of strikes, protests, and other pressures exerted by great numbers of labour and craft unions, which from the 1920s grew steadily in number. Taking advantage of the climate favouring civil liberties that prevailed between 1924 and 1933, these groups had acquired a certain organizational experience and capacity for struggle. The growth of unions occurred simultaneously with the development of the existing political parties, with whom they maintained and continue to maintain an ambiguous relationship of competition and subordination.

Weakened internally and from the outside as well as after the Second World War, the dictatorship saw itself besieged by ideological opponents and by anti-dictatorial public opinion that spread throughout Central America, putting an end to the personalist autocracies of the period. As a direct consequence of the murders of his opponents and the severe repression of the organized masses, Carías finally found himself obliged to accept the legal rebirth of the Liberal Party. He opened the way for Juan Manuel Gálvez, the Minister of War, Navy and Air Force, to take power through rigged elections in which the Liberals abstained from participating. Gálvez assumed power on 1 January 1949.

From that date on, important political and socioeconomic rebuilding began in Honduras. The two-party system continued to dominate, despite efforts by other political organizations to challenge it. A climate of respect was established for the rule of law and the Constitution that permitted labour unions and trade guilds to reorganize their forces. A successful strike was carried out in 1954 in the banana-producing zones, marking an important moment in the history of Honduran mass movements. The Honduran state expanded its role as a promoter of economic development, thereby giving impetus to the formation of a small, but modern business class. While breaking with the policy of Carías, Gálvez permitted incipient professionalization of the army with evident North American support, which increased after 1954 due to the events that led to the fall of President Arbenz in Guatemala and to greater militance of the Honduran labour movement that extended to the peasant lands from which banana workers came, or to which they later went in search of land and work.

The Liberal Party, under the leadership of Ramón Villeda Morales, initiated a vigorous mobilization in preparation for the elections of 10 October 1954. Villeda was rebuffed by electoral fraud and by a reaction that portrayed him as a friend of Communists and labour radicals. That produced an impasse that effectively kept the Vice-President in power, until he was finally overthrown by a military junta in October of 1956. This junta demonstrated a clear intention to decide the conflicts in Honduran society, this time as a professionalized *institution* and not as a military force at the service of an autocrat. In elections to choose the Constituent Assembly in September 1957, the Liberal Party triumphed by a wide margin. The same Constituent Assembly then elected Villeda Morales as President, a position he assumed in December 1957.

Thus began an important reformist phase along the lines of the so-called "Aprista parties" or Latin American Social Democrats, much as occurred in neighbouring Costa Rica with the National Liberation Party, founded in 1951. However, in contrast to its Costa Rican counterpart, the Liberal Party could only inscribe its statist and developmentalist views in the new Constitution and assume power with a certain calmness after first granting autonomy (*fuero*) to the army: its Chief-of-Staff would be named from a group of three candidates presented to the Congress by the Superior Council of National Defense (and not by the President). One function of the Council was to promote or remove other officials from the military hierarchy. Furthermore, the army could only receive orders from the President through the intermediary of its own Chief-of-Staff. His refusal to execute the President's orders could be overruled only through an appeal to Congress. Thus, a pact was established among the military and civil politicians to share power through dual leadership, though it was known that the armed forces were the real, effective and final depository of legalized force within the State.

Under the presidency of Villeda, reformist Liberalism led to the approval of an advanced labour code, the beginnings of a process of agrarian reform, and later the adoption of the basic principles of the "Alliance for Progress", in a climate of expanding civil liberties and labour rights. As this occurred, during the beginning of the 1960s, there was a move to diversity the production system gradually, through an emphasis on industrial development. It would soon be possible to reduce the dominance of the fruit companies, although without preventing their incursion into an infinity of new and profitable activities, including banking and manufacturing. A new urban working class began to organize, swelling the ranks of a vast people's movement, perhaps the strongest and most militant in the entire region. This movement acquired a nationalistic hue as in the 1960s foreign capital came to control about 80 per cent of the fifty largest companies and close to 70 per cent of bank deposits linked to the nascent Central American Common Market. However, since 1954 the presence of agents and resources coming from ORIT (the Regional Organization of Interamerican Workers, a pro-US regional labour federation) and the US-based AFL–CIO became stronger and stronger. These organizations tried to subdue radical labour movements by manipulating conflicts from the bureaucratized leadership levels of the organizations. They also worked to avoid the autonomous politicization of peasants and workers unhappy with the traditional two-party system.

The caretaker role of the army developed in a climate of rabid anti-Communism, promoted by government officials with the purpose of countering the impact of the Cuban Revolution. In spite of that, the proliferation of union federations and peasant associations between 1960 and 1964 demonstrated the vigour of the new forces and multiplied pressures in favour of an urgent redistribution of political and economic power. In spite of this flourishing of new social forces that culminated during the ascent of the Liberal Party and following the triumph of the Cuban Revolution, such forces were not able to break the limits of the historical two-party system. Sustaining itself principally on the clientelist model of distribution of political resources, the Liberal Party was easily able to control the votes of an electorate conditioned by a long tradition of dividing its allegiance in binary terms. Political allegiance was influenced by typical horizontal social class divisions, and much less by public opinion polls, which are quite meaningless in a society with rates of illiteracy and poverty in excess of 75 per cent, and with an adult population rooted in distant and scattered rural communities dominated by the *latifundio–minifundio* culture. Thus, regardless of how archaic the system was, it maintained its capacity to absorb and integrate new forces and pressures, moulding them into the *status quo* or accepting moderate changes that, while not ensuring perfect political stability, did not lead to revolution nor to other uncontrollable radical change.

As the connection between the labour–peasant movement and other urban professional and student forces became evident in the 1960s, there was increasing fear within the army and among the two-party élites of a generalized radicalization that might break the bounds of the narrow margin of manoeuvrability enjoyed by the traditional parties over the emerging social movements. The result was the *coup* against Villeda and the Liberal Party in October, 1963, led by General Oswaldo López Arellano. The coup was supported by the leadership of the National Party, and was celebrated with delight by the most conservative sectors of the country. The resulting repression was aimed at the peasant movement and the Liberal Party, in spite of the fact that once López was validated constitutionally in June, 1965, the government took a developmentalist turn. It justified the shift by its adherence to the directives of the Alliance for Progress, the Punta del Este Charter and by its association with various international banks and other firms that increased their penetration of financial and political spheres within Honduras.

Central American industrialization and regional integration was going full steam. In its initial phases, economic integration had favoured the diversification and economic growth of the country. However, the short growth-oriented interregnum reached its abrupt end as the famous "Soccer War" broke out in 1969. Since the Honduran army was defeated by the Salvadorans, it found it necessary to leave power and allow the political pendulum to return, as it often did, to the civilian two-party system: any seismic shift which destroyed the existing political system would threaten the military institution as well. In 1970 in response to strong anti-military sentiment and in the midst of instability, the two traditional parties agreed to form a coalition government on the Colombian model, with proportional sharing of legislative seats and public offices under the strict surveillance of the armed forces.

López Arellano mobilized the army, this time led by a group of reform-minded Peruvianist officers who decided to continue a developmentalist policy centred on agrarian reform, expanded intervention by the State in economic matters, and on redistributional policies favourable to the middle-class groups and workers. This bold move caused the pendulum to swing in the opposite direction: towards the military which this time worked in accord with progress-ive civilian groups. This did not please the leaders of the two parties, foreign interests, nor the most conservative Honduran nationals. An opposing alliance gained strength in 1974 principally in order to block implementation of Law no 8 of the Agrarian Reform Bill. Paramilitary and other pressure groups which made their first public appearance, established close ties with hard-line military officers. Manoeuvring so that the armed forces of Guatemala, El Salvador, and Nicaragua, under the leadership of Anastasio Somoza, could place a kind of fence around Honduras, this alliance managed to depose López Arellano on 15 March 1975 and replace him with General Juan A. Melgar Castro, who offered to hold elections in 1980 in order to guarantee the return to the traditional two party system after a period of "stabilization" that had many characteristics of a National Security State.

Influenced by the Cuban revolution and the theories about guerrilla tactics from the new Latin American left, a few organizations of like ideology emerged and tried to break up the political, economic, and social system. Other radical groups entered into action, especially those tied to the Catholic Church and to the preachings of the Second Vatican Council. These Catholic groups were respon-sible for the founding of unions, cooperatives, peasant leagues and eventually – in 1968 – a Christian Democrat Movement that was transformed into a Party in 1975. All this led to a threat that required that the populist reformism of the young military officers be abandoned in order that techniques of counterinsurgency be applied. This effort needed the total support of all pro-system political parties, which readily served as naive accomplices. Coordination and synchronization of military and paramilitary action in areas where both were necessary, occurred in the agrarian zones on many occasions. In this way the "marriage" between army and political parties took place.

While new measures of repression were tried in the second half of the 1970s (particularly against the peasant movement) other groups protested more and more aggressively against the increasing energy costs and trends toward recession resulting from policies of the Central American Common Market. General Melgar was not able to maintain himself in power because of accusations against him of excessive corruption, of being involved in the trafficking of drugs, and of his inability to form a broad base of social and political support. He was removed on 7 August 1978 by General Policarpo Paz García, to prevent greater internal disorder in the midst of an increase in regional conflicts centred in El Salvador and Nicaragua.

One can conclude that Honduras has been in transition from a system of shared dominance between the army and political parties (most frequently the National Party) to a military hegemony involving a weakening of the parties. This despite the fact that they appear formally to have returned to their previous level of independence and complete legality within the political scene. It is true that there have been elections in 1981 and again in 1986 where access to executive power has been contested. The military has given the impression of having retired to its specific duties of security and defence, even of guaranteeing the unexpected advance of bipartisanship and of a competitive and pluralist democracy. But in the background we witness a developing qualitative change: the historical political parties are in constant rivalry while their disputes are mediated directly by the army. Its power has multiplied by virtue of the strategic geopolitical role Honduras began to play after the ascent to power by the Sandinistas in 1979. The turn in favour of the military came from the massive military assistance that Honduras has come to receive from the USA as well as from setbacks to different reformist and populist forces that have lost their capacity to apply pressure and move freely within the political system because of a weakening economy and the prevailing physical insecurity.

The Dominant Party System in Costa Rica

As in Honduras, the origin of Costa Rican political parties goes back to the end of the nineteenth century. Their devleopment was contemporaneous with the consolidation of a Liberal and oligarchical state dominated by the interests of groups of exporters and importers. In Honduras the formation of a national State and its political parties is confounded with a weakening of the local ruling class *vis-à-vis* the banana interests. In the case of Costa Rica, not only did the opposite occur, but the state was able to reduce greatly the political weight of the army, although after 1860, it played an interventionist role that did not allow for the autonomous institutionalization of the political system. Likewise, the Catholic church, opposed to liberal reforms and to the influence of Masonic lodges, came to be subordinated to the dominant classes.

The parties that appeared originally in the presidential elections of November 1889 were to a large extent an extension through new means of the sharp struggle that was forged between the clerical sector and those liberal organizations and lay persons. From 1890 on, with the help of political parties, the liberals managed to bring about the secularization of the State and to undertake a vast reform of popular education that contributed to the emergence of a citizenry composed of a growing number of literate male voters.

But the decisive factor contributing to the establishment of a liberal democratic system was that organized opposition groups, legitimate under a State of Law, were able to compete successfully for power. This was demonstrated precisely in the crucial year of 1889, when for the first time an opposition party managed to upset the incumbent party and take the reins of government, although not without having to mobilize a broad cross-section of the populous in advance to ensure that the election results were respected. What is significant is that a legalized mechanism of containment of social conflicts began to function, almost without interruption, until 1948. The sole exception was the brief dictatorship of the Tinoco brothers (1917–19). A political culture was in place that favoured national and popular sovereignty. Negotiation and consensus were the mechanisms by which the multi-class citizenry was able to continue expanding by means of important modifications in electoral legislation, such as direct election in 1913, the secret ballot in 1925, and women's suffrage in 1949.

From 1890 until the end of the Second World War the Republican Party (and its own variants) was the great, dominant party machine, placed since 1893 at the service of the interests of a coalition of coffee growers, commercial importers, and private bankers. This coalition felt so secure that it allowed itself the luxury of breaking into successive electoral factions to contest control of the government. Of course this always was done within the limits of the liberal model of dependent agro-export development and of a foreign policy compatible with North American interests. This contrasted with the relationship of submission experienced by Honduras. Just as intra-oligarchical politics were negotiated, so was external dependence. And the arrangement worked quite well until new social forces appeared on the social and political scene of the First Republic during the first third of the twentieth century.

In the beginning, these new forces organized themselves into mutual benefit societies, in organizations for artisans, and in cultural associations. From time to time they dared to break away under the umbrella of some party willing to challenge the Republicans, as in the case of the Reformist Party in the 1920s, or the Communist Party founded in 1931. At first the Republican Party and its intra-oligarchical opposition tried to coopt the emerging movements, as in effect they did with reformism. This was not possible with the Communists. They intensified their criticism and made electoral inroads in the terrain fertilized by the economic crisis of 1929–32, and also managed to organize banana company workers who participated in the party's election campaigns and ideological struggles of those years. By 1940 the Communist Worker and Peasant Block controlled 10 per cent of the votes that customarily went to the Republican Party and its popular candidate, Dr Rafael A. Calderón.

In the face of popular pressure from different sides, the oligarchical governments made small concessions such as passing a minimum wage law, the reduction of the work week, and the creation of a Ministry of Labor; but during the Republican administration of President Cortes (1936–40), they made use and abuse of electoral fraud and police repression to wield power in the political arena. And they would have continued along that path if Dr Calderón had not changed direction unexpectedly with his policy to establish an alliance with Communism and the Catholic church, allowing him to reduce social tension somewhat by securing the approval of a labour coded and of constitutional reform, the Social Guarantees of 1943, thereby protecting the welfare and rights of workers. Conservative capitalist groups immediately shifted to the opposition. They allied themselves closely with members of an emerging Social Democratic Party which was founded in 1945. The conservatives began a counter-reform crusade contrary in content to the movement formed by the Catholic Church and its Rerum Novarum labour union, the American Embassy, the majority of commercial media, the peasant class, and the urban middle class, with whom the conservatives were allied! This disparate opposition to Calderón

Guardia was united only in its fear of the electoral advances of the Popular Vanguard Party (the old Block).

The result was the short civil war of 1948 in which the followers of businessman and intellectual social democrat José Figueres won unexpectedly with the backing of a small, improvised army. Figueres was helped by the Caribbean Legion (a contingent of men who were exiled by Central American and Caribbean right-wing dictatorships) and by arms sent by Guatemalan President Arévalo in what took shape as a serious regional conflict. East–West polarization entered through the introduction of the Truman Doctrine and within the climate of the Cold War. The agri-business oligarchy, which had lost complete control over what had been "its" Republican Party and which had no army to protect itself, had no choice but to negotiate a pact accommodating itself to the difficult circumstances. This occurred under continued strong North American pressure that justified its actions in 1946–8 along the lines of the Cold War and the necessity to detain the advances of even home-grown Communism. For that to happen, the USA had to permit the ascent to power of new classes and to allow for a change in the "liberal" orientation of the State.

After violent conflicts that resulted in close to 2000 deaths, representatives of the emerging social groups finally gained legal access to the political system, one which they would maintain from that time on. These elements reappeared in 1951 merged into the National Liberation Party. Their purpose was to deepen the reforms that Figueres and his government had initiated three years earlier with the nationalization of private banks, the constitutional abolition of the army as a permanent institution, and the creation of a great number of autonomous governmental institutions with the power to solve the technical, economic, and social problems that the Liberal State had refused to consider as objects worthy of direct intervention by the state. The traditional circles that had negotiated a way out of the crisis with Figueres never imagined that he would be capable of returning to power. He won the elections of 1953 with more than 60 per cent of the popular vote, while the old front of oligarchical parties practically disappeared. Their virtual disintegration was evidently the product of the virtual illegalization of the Communists and of the repression exerted against the leadership of the Republican Party. These followers of Calderón exiled themselves in Mexico and Nicaragua and sought to return to power, not by means of elections, but through armed force, especially if Figueres should return to head the government.

However, the two losing sides of the civil war returned slowly to legal status and electoral participation. By the 1960s their involvement in the political process was normalized. There is no doubt that 1953 marked the beginning of a new order in the political party system in which control was dominated by the National Liberation Party (PLN) with Figueres as its boss.

Nevertheless, the changes in the party system did not modify its basic form. It is true that the PLN became the dominant party which inaugurated and orchestrated a completely new age in the history of the modernization of the society. But in the past, the political system had also been dominated for fifty years by a single party, the Republican Party. Within such a system, the strongest party does not eliminate or completely absorb its opposition. In fact, it even stimulates it and allows it, from time to time, to exercise power. From this point of view the mechanism of domination is competitive, although it is skewed in favour of the most powerful group, which in turn organizes and reorganizes its hegemony by maintaining itself in the centre of the power game. It attracts new supporters to its side, avoiding radicalization, always with the objective of maintaining a substantial electoral majority. The Party merges with and blends into the State. It is sometimes difficult to establish a clear difference between the leaders and constituents of each. Even when the dominant party passes to the opposition, it does not lose its influence. It may maintain its legislative dominance, and it certainly does not lose its control over institutions and programmes that its opponents are unable to dismantle. This is precisely the story of the Costa Rican National Liberation Party.

The PLN, placing itself at the forefront of the modernization process, established its own irreversible historic plan (*proyecto histórico*). Because the opposition has always been the *PLN's* opposition, it has not been able to devise feasible alternative plans, spending its energies in maintaining a front composed of many minor parties. Though characterized by a weak and personalist structure, the opposition on several occasions still gained power: 1958–62, 1966–70, 1978–82.

The PLN shows an impressive flexibility when the time is right to attract emerging fractions of old or new social classes so that they do not align themselves with the opposition or with subversive groups. Nor have there been splits or socio-economic conflicts which were not manageable within the party or through the state machinery, though the party did experience internal divisions in 1958 and in 1970. With respect to new business sectors that emerged from import-substitution industrialization, ties to the Central American Common Market, and the diversification of national and transnational systems of production, the PLN moved adroitly in the late 1960s to attract large numbers of businessmen, thus avoiding repetition of the disaster of 1966 when the business community switched *en masse* to the opposition camp, dealing the PLN a decisive electoral defeat. And the same could be said for the action taken with respect to workers, peasants and professionals. Similarly, the flourishing government bureaucracy has been greatly rewarded by sinecures and improved salaries. It is among civil servants that the PLN has recruited most heavily, although this situation has changed recently due to the attraction the PLN has to the private sector which has discovered opportunities for advantageous involvement in the organizational structure and financial affairs of the PLN.

The preceding discussion reveals clearly the reason for the stability of the political party system in Costa Rica. Not having to compete with the military which otherwise could mediate political conflicts by use of force and confrontation, the parties (particularly the PLN) have managed to control the nature of social change in the country. The dominant party has strengthened itself through increasing public expenditure and expansion of public institutions through a symbiosis with the State apparatus and with collegiate decision-making bodies, from technical associations, to service and welfare organizations, to the universities. Without the support of these groups it is unlikely the PLN would have been able to compete with the oligarchical old guard and with private enterprise in meeting modernization needs and influencing the growth of institutions which respond to the demands of middle and popular sectors that make up the electoral majority. These sectors, which were partially excluded by the Liberal Republic, have not had to struggle in the post-war period for a place within the political panorama. Rather than, as in Honduras, having their independent organizations always at risk of repression or isolation, they have been coopted smoothly by the parties, especially the PLN. This has weakened such social forces' potential for subversion and forced them to be disciplined in their actions so that they remain within the constitutional and legal parameters as established by the political system and parties. The great "umbrella" of the party covers one extreme of the ideological and political spectrum to the other gathering every emerging sector and even occasionally reaching those marginalized by the system, thus remaining always near the system centre, exerting a kind of centripetal attraction that has maintained competitiveness and political and ideological pluralism.

From what we have examined so far, we can extract certain preliminary conclusions about the Costa Rican case for comparison with the Honduran example. We refer to factors that have operated historically to consolidate the democratization process at the level of political and electoral institutions of the State with the beneficial effect of strengthening civil society. They are the following: early institutional and legal consolidation of the centralized national State, a process compatible with the needs of economic growth in agricultural exports and those of the local dominant classes; restraints on and counterbalances to the distorting interference of foreign interests that are inclined to take possession of internal production; reformism and the relative opening up to demands for political and electoral participation that stem from ample numbers of citizens from the subordinated middle classes and the masses; the absence of polarization and fractious conflict between the élite and the fundamental social classes; considerable success in resolving ecclesiastical and social issues through negotiation, despite the break with constitutional order from 1917 to 1919, and again in 1948 (periods which led to broadened citizen participation in government); the constant intervention of the State and of political parties in civil society, and the simultaneous elimination of spaces that would be filled by subversive or extremist groups, a professional army, or a military caste seeking to resolve conflicts by means other than through the party system; and, finally, the acceptance of reformism by the dominant economic groups, making it possible to negotiate the integration of other social sectors and leaders into the power block. In the same way, the élites continue to maintain an association with foreign capital that does not deprive them of important benefits or prevent from them defining the economic politics of the State. This last strategy has experienced major setbacks because of the economic recession in the 1980s and the idea in vogue that foreign capital is indispensable to reactivate the accumulation process, a process now inevitably transnationalized.

All is not rosy in the Costa Rican case. It is very probable that in following an economic and fiscal policy with elevated social costs, the present administration and the PLN will lose popular support in the short term, thus weakening its hegemonic power. This could cause qualitative changes in the existing internal balance of forces. Since 1983, the Unity Coalition (which had gained power with strong support in 1978–82) became truly united. For the first time there existed a real possibility of an opposition group becoming a powerful competitor of the PLN. The Coalition was determined to develop a viable alternative development plan, very favourable to banking interests and private business, based on orthodox postulates of neo-liberalism, and defended by international organizations that have in their hands a great share of the destiny and welfare (or woes) of the country. Armed with populist techniques and demagogic propaganda, it would in 1990 attract ample numbers of discontented voters, which would put in serious question the continuation of Liberationist predominance, at least in its present form. The country would truly experience a bipartisan system of government in substance as well as form. The system's durability, and the parties' competitive alternation in power would be a question-mark, particularly should the model *not* be accompanied by other constitutional and institutional transformations that vitalize the democratization process. Political democratization must occur along with changes in property ownership and an increase in worker-participation in management of private firms and other productive enterprises.

More recently there has been a great deal of insistence that the country have a security force or army. These suggestions have been made by new and aggressive centre-right circles who fear the escalation of internal tensions and eventual clashes with the Sandinistas along the northern border. But domestic and foreign militaristic voices have not had much popular support to date, although the scene should be observed carefully. It is a fact that Civil and Rural Guard contingents are being trained continuously in techniques of counter-insurgency, both within and outside the country, constituting the basis of what could become a professional army. This is seen by some local politicians as a necessary evil. If this trend were to continue, and if militarization continued unchecked, the political parties would lose control of the political system. In that case a National Security State would be established, spurred by the regional geopolitical crisis and by destabilization caused by the same deflationary, neo-liberal and anti-popular policies that the PLN has carried out, in conformance with prescriptions made by the International Monetary Fund, the World Bank, and USAID.

Some Comparative Reflections Concerning the Political Development of Honduras and Costa Rica

In both countries during this century, party systems have prevailed that have followed in their *form* a relatively invariable pattern. In Honduras a *persistent bi-party system* was "frozen" from time to time in order to resolve crises caused by unrestrainable social mobilizations, or to face the danger of anti-system and anti-party forces that might undermine the political and economic system, thus leading to the eventual destruction of the military defence apparatus. In Costa Rica the *dominant party system* is just beginning to be modified in a direction that may very possibly lead to its transformation into a more mature and solid two-party system, one, however, which is being ambushed by forces that favour different versions of authoritarianism from the left or right. Of course, the Costa Rican party system has been much more stable than its Honduran counterpart, showing greater levels of institutionalization and continuity, together with more solid formal mechanisms that have facilitated negotiation and dialogue. In Costa Rica, however, there have been conflicts leading to much more profound readjustments within the society than would be possible in the apparently very fluid Honduran case. This is what happened as a result of the civil war of 1948, when the Republican Party, a product of the Costa Rican oligarchical–liberal era, gave way permanently to the National Liberation Party, causing at that time a new breakdown of the electorate into two sides that have maintained themselves without splitting along strict divisions by class. In Honduras, the historical bifurcation of the electorate had been developing many decades earlier, before the Liberal Party was remodelled by Villeda Morales at the beginning of the 1950s.

As a consequence, the two countries entered fully into periods of modernization after the Second World War with party structures prepared to absorb the emerging social groups seeking changes that for the traditional oligarchical groups were not easy to accept. The realignment of forces was more violent and profound in Costa Rica than in Honduras. In a certain way, in Costa Rica there was a "middle-class, democratic revolution" that permitted a New Class of young intellectuals, professionals, technicians and businessmen to take control of the state apparatus, to abolish the army and to pressure the agro-export oligarchy for substantial reforms and concessions. The oligarchy conceded positions and privileges, thus forging a national pact upon which the 1949 constitution and a renewed version of the dominant party system was established. The traditional groups managed to act as the opposition, and on three occasions they were able to put themselves back in power, aligning themselves with conservative agri-businessmen and industrialists of a new mould. This alliance led in 1983 to the formation of the Social Christian Unity Party (PUSC). But they were unable to dismantle the reforms introduced by the PLN.

In Honduras, on the other hand, reform movements have been much weaker. This is due to the nature of the forces that have promoted reformism and above all because the traditional groups did not suffer reverses as significant as those experienced in Costa Rica. From the beginning of the 1950s they maintained their position by tightening their alliances with the army that, after the fall of the Carías dictatorship, became more and more professionalized as it evolved into an agent against reform. Today the military threatens to be such a great counterweight to the democratization of Honduras that it could displace the political parties and other pressure groups and organizations. This situation is due to a combination of internal conditions (the inability of the parties to absorb new social groups and to renew themselves ideologically) and external ones (the geopolitical role of the Honduran army in the Central American regional crisis). The military can be characterized as a powerful anti-party apparatus, or one that accepts political parties only to the extent that they guarantee the continuity and survival of pro-system groups. It hovers over the political system, threatening to alter or to close it down unconditionally, adapting it flexibly to the demands of National Security, to a model of authoritarianism and repression.

We find ourselves, therefore, before two political and party systems that have affinities in some respects but differences in many more. Precisely through the staying power and more or less regular functioning of their party structures, both political systems have managed to overcome with relative success the poundings of social conflict unleashed by capitalist modernization during the post-war period. The system has largely stripped these struggles of their class character to ensure dominance of the multi-class patronage system. Parties have not engaged in civil confrontations with the international importance and implications for East–West polarization of those in Guatemala, El Salvador, and Nicaragua. This is not to say that the mere existence of parties necessarily prevents failures in the building of competitive, open, and democratic political systems. But without their institutionalization and continual readaptation to changing circumstances, it is not possible to maintain those processes for a generation or more.

The opening and closing of the formal and informal channels of participation in the Honduran case, in contrast to Costa Rica, has made its political system at once more fragile and aloof from the forces that operate within civilian society. In Costa Rica, the strength and the periodical renewal of leaders and policies deriving from many clientelistic or pragmatic coalitions within the parties and within the State have permitted the attainment of a degree of institutionalization greater than in Honduras. The state itself has become a medium for negotiation between social classes and interest groups. Likewise, legitimation is more generalized, with few unrepresented interests remaining. In the absence of pressures from anti-system and anti-party groups that cause hopeless polarizations, conflicts are dealt with through legal and constitutional means within the representative political system. Although the dynamism and pluralism of the Costa Rican system appears less well-developed or at least less strident than the Honduran one, what is certain is that it is a result of slower, but more ordered and predictable processes of negotiation. Corporatism, the verticality of tensions and the backing off (or isolation) of the Honduran parties from social pressures has resulted in clashes among many sectors in the society. These can rapidly exceed the normative limits of the political system and thus bring forth military intervention, causing the temporary shutdown of the party system. A diversity of conflicts arises in this way, where some actors are kept quiet or are forced to yield or to reduce their demands so that the basic class structure is kept intact, a structure that is very unequal and unbalanced in rural–urban terms when compared to the Costa Rican system.

Although the Honduran party system has been more easily overrun by corporate groups of various social class extractions, at the present time it has come to be more and more subject to the control of the military. There is no doubt that on a number of occasions the system has allowed for the channelling and defusing of conflicts that would otherwise have exploded as open class struggle, or in civil wars of national proportions such as those experienced by the three countries which form its borders.

In Costa Rica the strict electoral regime of law was achieved after 1948, under which new political and party structures favouring civil liberties and human rights were founded and survived. These structures have been an effective bulwark against destabilizing tendencis. They have strengthened nationhood, democracy, and stable pluralism. Even today the party system acts as a constant defence against attempts to subvert public order. A proliferation of new groups has been organized in relatively peaceful coexistence with old groupings and interests. Legalized and protected under the Constitution of 1949, they have adapted to the changing conditions of modernization and to the development of the Welfare State. In this way, a "polyarchy" has been formed where very different élites of business, political, ideological, cultural or intellectual extraction compete and adjust their interests, always in unstable positions of influence. Because of the crisis, these interests face each other now more directly than a decade ago in a more conflictive situation. The prize for victory is the "political booty" of control of the vast public sector. Since national income has decreased in this decade because of the economic recession and the acceptance of neo-liberal policies encouraged from abroad, political clashes could assume such importance that the folding of the political system is a plausible scenario if the parties and other collateral mechanisms for reaching understanding among the élites fail to function. Naturally, strong movements from below strive to gain greater recognition of their interests, but this has always been the case in Costa Rica. What puts the prevailing system to the test now is the accumulation and combination of internal and external factors derived from a geopolitical crisis that the political system of the Second Republic has not had to face previously. These factors include a difficult transition to a bi-party system on whose character it is too early to comment at the moment.

Finally, the two countries find themselves immersed in a regional geopolitical crisis, combined with a deep economic recession and fiscal belt-tightening of major proportions. This situation deflates and drains their resources to deal with the demands of different social groups, unhappy about the persistence of the problem and the lack of viable alternatives that benefit not only capital and the traditional and new financial institutions but, as in the past developmentalist era, extensive strata of the middle class and the masses. The Nicaraguan counter-revolution – today more than the low-intensity conflict within El Salvador – has issued a serious challenge to the sovereignty and integrity of their respective national territories. The "contras" put their illegal territorial claims and their logistical systems before whatever measures may be taken by either country to neutralize its foreign policy and experiment with development-minded policies that do not favour unilaterally dominant capitalist groups and the armed or security forces.

It does not matter which precise path the governments of each country take. What is about to be tested is the flexibility of the political party systems of the two societies to absorb and channel these tensions, without breaking down or being relegated to an inferior status by authoritarian structures that would end up eliminating completely the climate of relative freedom and political legality that forms (not without snags, of course) the underlying support for the state of law itself. Such a state is essential for competitive party systems to survive.

Further Reading

Honduras

Gustavo Adolfo Aguilar. "Honduras: situación actual y perspectivas", in *Centroamerica en Crisis*. Mexico: Centro de Estudios Internacionales, El Colegio de Mexico, 1980.

Vincent Checchi *et al. Honduras: A Problem in Economic Development*. New York: The Twentieth Century Fund, 1959.

Aníbal Delgado Fiallos. *Honduras: Elecciones 85*. Tegucigalpa: Editorial Guaymuras, 1986.

Arturo Fernández. *Partidos Políticos Y Elecciones 85*. Tegucigalpa: Editorial Guaymuras, 1981.

Victor Meza. *Historia Del Movimiento Obrero Hondureño*. Tegucigalpa: Editorial Guaymuras, 1980.

Guillermo Molina Chocano. "Honduras: la situatión política y económica reciente", in Donald Castillo Rivas, compilador, *Centroamerica: Mas Allá De La Crisis*. Mexico: Ediciones SIAP, 1983.

James Morris. *Interest Groups and Politics in Honduras*, Ph.D. dissertation, University of New Mexico, 1974 (published by University Microfilms International).

Ernesto Paz Aguilar. *Sistema Electoral Y Representación Política*. Tegucigalpa: mimeografiado, 30 May 1986.

Mario Posas y Rafael del Cid. *La Construcción Del Sector Público Y Del Estado Nacional En Honduras, 1876–1979*. San José: EDUCA, 1981.

Mario Posas. *El Movimiento Campesino Hondureño*. Tegucigalpa: Editorial Guaymuras, 1981.

Jorge Arturo Reyna. *Honduras: Cambios o Violencia*. San José, Costa Rica: Artes Gráficas de Centroamerica, 1981.

Mark Rosenberg. "Democracia en Centroamerica?" *Cuadernos de Capel*, no. 5. San José, Costa Rica, 1985.

Mark Rosenberg. "Honduras Scorecard: Military and Democrats in Central America", *Caribbean Review*, vol. 12, no 1, 1983.

William Stokes. *Honduras: An Area Study of Government*. Madison: Wisconsin University Press, 1950.

Costa Rica

Oscar Aguilar Bulgarelli. *Democracia y Partidos Políticos En Costa Rica, 1950–1962*. San José: Litografía LIL, 1977.

Carlos Araya Pochet. *Historia De Los Partidos Políticos: Liberación Nacional*. San José: Editorial Costa Rica, 1968.

John Patrick Bell. *Guerra Civil En Costa Rica*. San José: EDUCA, 1976.

Mario Carvajal Herrera. *Actitudes Políticas Del Costarricense*. San José: Editorial Costa Rica, 1978.

Centro de Estudios para la Acción Social (CEPAS). *Costa Rica 1985: Balance de la Situación*, Documento de Análisis no 4. San José: Levántico Impresores, 1985.

Jaime Delgado. *El Partido Liberación Nacional: Analisis de Su Discurso Político–Ideológico*. Heredia: Editorial UNA, 1983.

Marc Edelman. "Costa Rica: Resisting Austerity", *NACLA Report on the Americas*, vol. 17, no 1, 1984.

Wilburg Jiménez Castro. *Análisis Electoral de Una Democracia*. San José: Editorial Costa Rica, 1977.

Jorge E. Romero Pérez. *Partidos Políticos, Poder Y Derecho*. San José: Editores Syntagma, 1979.

Jorge Mario Salazar. *Política Y Reforma En Costa Rica, 1914–1958*. San José: Editorial Porvenir, 1981.

Mario Alejo Sánchez Machado. *Las Bases Sociales Del Voto En Costa Rica: 1974–1978*. San José: URUK Editores, 1985.

Jacobo Schifter. *Los Partidos Políticos En Costa Rica*. Heredia: Universidad Nacional, IDELA, 1978.

Robert H. Trudeau. *Costa Rica Voting: Its Socioeconomic Correlates*. Ann Arbor: University Microfilms, 1971.

Jose Luís Vega Carballo. *Poder Político Y Democracia En Costa Rica*. San José: Editorial Porvenir, 1982.

Jose Luís Vega Carballo. "Central America: A Choice of Bullets or Ballots", *Harvard International Review*, vol. VI, no 3, 1983.

Chester Zelaya *et al*. *Democracia En Costa Rica? Cinco Opiniones Polémicas*. San José: Editorial UNED, 1977.

Insurgency and Counter-insurgency in Guatemala

Jim Handy

From 1944 to 1954 the Guatemalan "revolution" followed a course of political, economic, and social reform. The popular organizations that blossomed under the sunny skies of the "ten years of spring" withered when confronted by the chilling blasts of government repression in the following decades. Any attempt at rejuvenating popular organizations was met with violence.

However, by the mid-1970s, the voices demanding fundamental change in Guatemalan society and economy were too incessant to be easily quieted. During the 1970s and early 1980s these voices became increasingly powerful. A number of organizations developed to help to strengthen them: Catholic Action, cooperatives, new popular organizations, and finally revolutionary armies with substantial Indian and peasant support.

The government and the military responded with increasing levels of repression. Violence was first directed at the leaders of local autonomous organizations in the countryside. This limited and almost sporadic terror in most instances only served to heighten peasant and Indian opposition to the government. Finally, following a military coup which overthrew one group of ruling officers and replaced them with another, the government counter-insurgency became more systematic, more brutal, and more effective.

Through much of 1982 and early 1983, the military attempted to reform highland village society. By forcing the peasantry into military-controlled towns, enforcing a military monopoly over all services in the highland region, and establishing a rural militia closely monitored by the army, the military sought to ensure its dominance in the region and to prevent peasants from supporting the guerrilla forces. It was, in most respects, a successful campaign.

Only after the short-term success of this operation had been proven, after the military had effective control of most of highland Guatemala and had seriously weakened the guerrilla forces fighting it, did it begin to pay serious attention to the process of democracy and elections on a national level. It allowed relatively non-violent elections for a constituent assembly to be held in 1984 and an elected civilian president to come to power early in 1986. The transfer of "power" from a military to civilian head of government was accompanied by clear warnings that the highlands were the military's special preserve. They remain so.

This chapter traces the rise of popular organizations in highland Guatemala and their increasing support for the revolutionary organizations operating there. It details the attempts by the military, first, to incapacitate and then to destroy these organizations since the mid-1970s. There follows a short assessment of current civilian/military political dynamics in Guatemala and the continuing importance which protest in highland Guatemala holds in that dynamic.

Catholic Action

The roots of the popular organizations that developed in rural Guatemala in the 1970s stretch far back in Guatemalan history. During the colonial period, a shortage of priests ensured that Indian communities, while adopting Christian teachings, infused their religion with pre-Christian native practices. This resulted in a peculiar blend of native/Catholic syncretism and a native religious hierarchy that dominated village politics and mediated between the village and local *ladinos* (non-Indians).

During the "ten years of spring", the church hierarchy searched for a means of consolidating its position in these villages in the face of government-supported peasant leagues and popular political parties. The process chosen by Archbishop Mariano Rossell Arellano was a form of religious purification known as Catholic Action.

Started in 1946, Catholic Action was meant to augment the position of priests in the villages with a concerted attack on local native religious "impurities". However, it was designed primarily as a means of combating government reforms which the church saw as communist. As Rossell expressed it, "Our small Catholic Action was one of the greatest comforts in those hours of enormous distress in the presence of Marxist advance that invaded everything."[1] Rossell proposed to forestall Indian protest by encouraging the feeling of "Christian resignation" among the poor. The church, and more specifically Catholic Action, were important in heightening unrest in village communities and strengthening opposition to the Arbenz government in the years leading to its overthrow in 1954.[2]

After the coup, the church hierarchy no longer felt compelled to combat the strength of government-inspired reform. However, in many villages the promotion of Catholic Action had initiated a reform movement that could not be easily stopped. One aspect of Catholic Action had been an attack on native religious organizations. In a number of villages this action prompted a splintering into a variety of opposing groups, fostering increased instability in village communities already shaken by the success of Protestant missionaries and the activities of reform parties and peasant leagues.[3] While the initial effect of Catholic Action varied from village to village, it most often resulted in a marked weakening of the power and control of the traditional Indian religious hierarchy, which was generally seen as a conservative influence.

The activity of Catholic Action committees in the villages had other consequences. The number of priests active in Guatemala had grown significantly during the reform decade, from 114 in 1944 to 195 in 1954. After the coup, with the church's position strengthened, the number of priests shot up to 242 in 1955 and 415 by the later 1960s.[4] This accelerated appointment of new priests led to a significant decentralization in the operation of the church in Guatemala. The Archbishop of Guatemala, his position of eminence held primarily by respect, enjoyed no formal control over Guatemalan bishops appointed by Rome. In the years immediately following the 1954 coup this inherent trend to decentralization was accentuated in Guatemala by the fact that many of the new priests appointed to districts in Guatemala were foreigners. As a result, by the late 1960s only slightly over 15 per cent of the Guatemalan clergy were native-born. The most important foreign source of priests were Spanish Jesuits and American Maryknoll fathers.[5]

Many foreign priests approached their position differently from Guatemalan ministers. With fewer ties to local and national élites, many promoted local autonomous organizations along with Catholic Action. Changes of this type in the perception which priests held of their role in the villages were also inspired by the need to compete with Protestant missionaries who were increasingly active in highland communities, and the new direction given to the international Catholic church in the early 1960s after the Second Vatican Council, which declared a preference for the poor and argued that along with the church's religious mission "comes a function, a light and an energy which can serve to structure and consolidate the human community according to divine law".[6]

Ministers in Guatemala saw this statement as encouragement for reformist activity in their parishes and became increasingly involved in social action. The most prominent activities were the organization of cooperatives and the extension of a dialogue on social and economic concerns through church-sponsored *Cursillos de Capacitación Social*. These courses began in Latin America in 1962, spread to Central America in 1965 and were quickly extended to rural areas. For some priests at least, a discussion of the social and economic problems that confronted peasants led to more active opposition to the government.

An increasingly socially-conscious Catholic Action promoted literacy through courses, scholarships and an extensive network of radio schools, encouraged local political parties that reflected peasant concerns, and, perhaps most importantly, organized an impressive series of native cooperatives.

The Cooperative Movement: A Search for Local Autonomy

At its heart the cooperative movement was anything but revolutionary. It was designed to provide an avenue for limited economic betterment without challenging the national economic structure or the distribution of income in any fundamental fashion. Nonetheless, cooperatives grew rapidly throughout the late 1960s and early 1970s. From savings and credit cooperatives they expanded to producer and marketing organizations. During the early years of the Kjell Laugerud (1974–8) administration, when the government gave limited encouragement to the concept, the movement blossomed. By September 1975, 20 per cent of highland Indians were involved in some form of cooperative.[7] This percentage increased immediately after the earthquake of 1976 as local reconstruction committees flourished.

By the mid-1970s, the combination of Catholic Action activities, an increased level of literacy among Indian youth, the economic independence offered by peasant-controlled cooperatives, and the activity of new political parties, most notably the centrist Christian Democrats, had sparked significant changes in Indian communities and Indian attitudes. In many locales the traditional religious hierarchy still functioned and the system of dual government (that is, a local Indian governmental structure that paralleled but was always subordinate to a local *ladino* one) still predominated. Nonetheless, in all but a very few communities there existed groups of natives who opposed the traditional hierarchy or who had forced it to join them in a struggle for political and economic independence through cooperatives and native-controlled political parties. For these peasants, often but not always young men or women, the usual obsequious attitude to local *ladino* authority and, ultimately, to the national government was abandoned.[8,9]

Despite the Catholic church's intention that the cooperative movement and Catholic Action should improve local social and economic conditions without challenging the *status quo*, the forging of some degree of local independence inexorably drew these initiatives into conflict with the national government. Both Catholic Action and cooperatives were increasingly opposed by the national government. During the early years of the Lucas regime, the government cancelled the registration of over 250 coops, claiming they were Marxist inspired. While the National Cooperative Institute continued to exist throughout the Lucas administration, it was slowly strangled by lack of funds and by government opposition.

Repression of Local Organizations

More direct action to discourage local autonomy was taken by death squads and the military, which throughout the 1970s and early 1980s consistently focused much of their attention on cooperative leaders and the priests most active in fostering local organizations. Beginning with the death in a mysterious plane crash of Father Willie Woods, who had helped to organize a large cooperative in Huehuetenango, these attacks became so frequent that by 1980 the Jesuits were forced to withdraw all their priests from the department of El Quiché.[10]

In that department alone, 168 cooperative or village leaders were killed between 1976 and 1978. As government repression clearly began to focus on any organization established to try to alter the *status quo*, peasant communities began to see more clearly the links between local repression and the national government. Thus, when the remnants of the guerrilla movements of the 1960s re-emerged in the mid-1970s with bases in the Indian highlands, peasant support was forthcoming in a way it had not been in the previous decade.

The Revolution Reborn

In January 1972 the Guerrilla Army of the Poor (EGP) made its first appearance in the western highlands. It began slowly to develop contacts in peasant villages and win the support of the inhabitants.

A small nucleus of combatants, survivors of the guerrilla battles in the 1960s, crossed the Ixcán river into the jungles of the northern Quiché. They began the slow process of tapping the accumulated grievances of the Indian peasants of the area and winning their trust as the first step towards revolution. According to one of them, Mario Payeras, they had learned sorry lessons from the impatience and over-confidence of the 1960s. They now saw themselves as "planters of the slow-growing tree of revolution".[11]

Working out of two fronts in the east and west of the department of El Quiché, they slowly made their way out of the jungle and into the inhabited highlands. They forswore publicity and, in the first few years, any military contact. Instead, they provided small favours for peasants, engaged in endless political discussion with Indian groups, and worked assiduously at building the strong Indian base that the revolution had lacked in the previous decade.

They found in the highlands a well-spring of discontent. Most common was anger at the greedy conduct of local landowners who had gradually monopolized land in the district and who took advantage of this monopoly to pay miserly wages. According to Payeras, one of these landlords, Luís Arenas Barrera, was particularly notorious. He had received his land immediately after the overthrow of Arbenz and kept his workers in a form of debt-bondage through advances he provided at exorbitant rates.

Consequently, the first military action of the EGP was an attack on the landlord designed to win the sympathy of local peasants. After the killing, which had been carried out on pay-day in full view of many peasants, Payeras said, "From that moment on, the word spread throughout the region that . . . [the guerrillas] had surely come to do justice, since they had punished a man who had grown rich from the blood and sweat of the poor."

The military's response to this killing also prompted increasing support for the guerrillas. Following the killing, the army began a counter-insurgency campaign in the Ixil area of El Quiché. But rather than hunting guerrillas, they began to attack local organizations in the district. In 1975 the military killed thirty-seven cooperative members in the Ixcan. By 1976 the government had announced it was waging a war against the guerrilla forces in the highlands, occupying the towns of Chajul, Nebaj, and San Juan Cotzal. By early 1977 over 100 village leaders had been killed.[12]

There are four incidents generally considered as key in ensuring Indian support for the revolution. The first was the Panzós massacre on 29 May 1978. Over 100 Ketchi men, women and children were massacred in the quiet town of Panzós, Alta Verapaz on 29 May

1978. By the 1970s, dispossession of Indian cultivators had escalated
as part of the general process of peasant expropriation in the whole
Franja. Agitation and organization on the part of the Ketchi against
arbitrary removal had been fomenting for over a year. In most cases
this type of opposition was met by the "disappearance" or brutal
torture and murder of opposition leaders. In this instance, however,
between 500 and 700 Ketchi of the region gathered in Panzos to
protest their expulsions before the mayor and an official of INTA
and to demand secure title to their land. Once the peasants had
collected inside the central square, the military, which had ringed
the square, opened fire, killing over 100 of the protestors. The bodies
of the slain were dumped into mass graves, which according to some
local observers had been dug beforehand. While the government
denied the deaths at first, and only later admitted to thirty-eight
killings, it asserted that the Indians had started the violence.
However, independent church and press reports argued that the
massacre was completely unprovoked.

With the Panzós massacre it became apparent, at least to Ketchi
and Ixil Indians in the *Franja Transversal*, that there existed no official
recourse to protect their villages against the military. Over 100 000
people gathered to commemorate the massacre one year later. Much
of the active support the EGP found in Alta Verapaz and parts of
El Quiché dated from this slaughter.

This painful lesson was further accentuated with the killing of
thirty-nine peasants and their supporters in the Spanish embassy in
Guatemala City in 1980. In late 1979 and early 1980, a number of
peasants journeyed to Guatemala City to protest against military
repression in their villages in the department of El Quiché. The first
group of 100 peasants from San Miguel Uspantan came to the city
to demand the release of seven village-leaders kidnapped by the
military.

In an interview with representatives of Amnesty International, a
group of these Indians described their grievances.[13] Four wealthy
families controlled the area but the peasants there had refused to
work for them because the wages offered were too low (50 to 60
cents a day). Consequently, the landlords called in the army who
"pounced on the peasants".

After unsuccessfully appealing for attention from the unresponsive
Lucas government throughout a long stay in the capital, many of the
peasants from San Miguel Uspantan returned to their community.
However, a second group of peasants from neighbouring areas in
the Quiché joined the protest in Guatemala City, demanding
that the army be removed from their villages and that a special

commission be established to investigate the activities of the military in the region. While this group was in Guatemala City, the original seven leaders from San Miguel Uspantán were found dead in Chajul.

After a member of the reformist FUR party was killed shortly after a meeting with the peasants, twenty-four peasants with student- and worker-supporters decided on a peaceful occupation of the Spanish embassy to publicize the violations of human rights in the region. The Spanish embassy was chosen because the ambassador had given the appearance of sympathetic support.[14] The peasants entered the embassy on 31 January 1980.

Despite demands by the Spanish ambassador that the peasants inside the building should not be attacked, the police stormed the building and thirty-nine people were killed including a former vice-president and a foreign minister of Guatemala, who were both in the building to talk with the peasants. Only the ambassador and one peasant survived. The latter was later kidnapped from the hospital where he was recuperating from his injuries. After the attack the Spanish government broke off all diplomatic relations with Guatemala and withdrew its ambassador.

Some of the peasants occupying the embassy had come from the town of Nebaj. After the death of the peasants in the embassy, this Ixil community was occupied by the military. According to one priest who witnessed the occupation, the army invaded on market day and encircled the town. On the second day of the occupation women from neighbouring communities, concerned over the fate of their men, went to Nebaj. The soldiers fired on the women, killing at least eleven. Months later Padre José María Grandes, who had been in Nebaj and had publicized the killings, was in turn killed by the army. Whole Ixil communities which until that time had tried to appeal to the national government for defence against the military decided to join the revolutionary forces.[15]

If any final goad was needed to ensure that peasant organizations would abandon peaceful attempts at change and be forced to support the guerrillas, it came in July 1981. In 1978, the Peasant Unity Committee (CUC) was established with the support of the National Committee of Labour Unity. Of particular importance was the fact that the CUC was an effective coalition of Indian and *ladino* peasants. Ethnic separation had been overcome by economic concerns and the need for common defence against the military. Directed by peasants and addressing peasant concerns, the CUC steadily attracted support. Just as steadily it became a focus of government repression. In July 1981 the leader of the CUC, Emeterio Toj Medrano, was kidnapped by the military. Toj Medrano was tortured and pressured – the soldiers threatened him with the napalming of villages – to denounce the CUC. Finally, in a daring raid, the EGP released him from the army barracks where he was held prisoner. From that point on, the implicit link between the CUC and EGP became explicit.

Indian peasants in the highlands joined the guerrilla forces in unprecedented numbers. Benefiting most from their support was the EGP, which opened seven different fronts and at times virtually controlled much of the countryside. Learning from the mistakes of the earlier revolutionary groups, the EGP refused to become embroiled in ideological disputes; instead it concentrated on immediate and pressing demands. This strategy and obvious commitment to peasant concerns proved successful. As more and more of its members and commanders were drawn from native communities, the guerrillas were even more easily able to win peasant support.

In the late 1970s, the EGP was joined by three more guerrilla groups. Two of them, the Rebel Armed Forces (FAR) and the Guatemalan Workers' Party (PGT), had direct links to the guerrilla forces of the 1960s. The most important new group, after the EGP, was the Revolutionary Organization of People in Arms (ORPA). ORPA developed through a process similar to that of the EGP but concentrated its forces in the heavily populated Indian Highlands of Chimaltenango and Sololá. After beginning activities on the Pacific coast in 1971, ORPA decided to move inland to the highlands. By 1973, over 90 per cent of the rebels in ORPA were Indians.[16] By 1982, peasant support for the guerrillas was such that ORPA could operate freely throughout much of the Chimaltenango and Sololá highlands, and controlled much of the major resort area around Lake Atitlán.

Both the EGP and ORPA rejected the somewhat ostentatious propensity of the guerrilla leaders in the 1960s continually to grant interviews to explain their position and their progress. They did this partly for security reasons and partly because they saw their primary objective as winning the hearts of the highland peasantry. In 1981 one of the directors of the EGP for the first time publicly described its goals and strategy for victory. In this statement he forcefully rejected the old strategy of *foco guerrillero*, saying, "Never did we forget the participation of the masses, not only as help in the war, but as the decisive factor, as participants and protagonists of the popular revolutionary war."[17]

By the early 1980s it was apparent that substantial numbers of Indian peasants were supporting the guerrillas, although this was not true in all areas of the highlands. In some regions, where peasants had developed viable alternative economic pursuits and where local village structures had followed a different course of development since the 1950s, active support for the guerrilla organizations remained minimal.

The whole range of changes that had occurred in highland villages in the preceding two decades – the weakening of the power of the traditional hierarchy, the more "populist" position of the church, the increasing number of educated native youth, and an experience with autonomous organizations such as cooperatives – all assisted in breaking the long-standing bonds of silence.

Brutal Counter-insurgency

The generalization of the violence in the countryside took on the dimension of race conflict. The *ladino* military commanders, the inheritors of centuries of prejudice, often saw all Indian villagers as potential enemies. Consequently, they followed a policy that drastically escalated the violence. By attacking the native population, the military drove whole Indian communities to join the guerrilla forces. By 1982, as it became obvious that some village authorities were swinging to the guerrillas, and thus that village organization was assisting the revolution, the military embarked on a deliberate policy of creating internal refugees by destroying whole villages altogether.

The survivors of these villages were then accumulated in central "safe" towns which the military could more easily control. It is only this combination of racial tension, a paranoid fear of communist subversion, the determination of the local and national landowning élite to retain its advantages, and the military's determination to retain control over highland villages, which explains the barbaric cruelty of the army in the highlands. Often this was associated with the barest evidence of support for the guerrillas.

Not all the murders in the villages could be blamed on the military. Guerrillas carried out an intensive campaign aimed at the government informants (*orejas*) in the villages. Military commissioners and large landowners were also regular targets of the revolutionary forces. The guerrillas' urban front, which occasionally bombed government offices, also periodically claimed the lives of innocent bystanders or lower-level government employees.

Nonetheless, all observers not directly linked to the government reported that the vast majority of the killings were the work of the military or right-wing death squads acting in conjunction with the government. In addition, most of the killings were not the result of government encounters with guerrillas, but were rather the fruit of military raids on peasant villages during which peasants with no connection to the revolutionary forces were killed. The thousands of deaths in the Guatemalan highlands during the 1970s and 1980s were not the result of a civil war between guerrillas and the military. They were instead the outcome of a government counter-insurgency programme that attacked the very basis of Guatemalan peasant life: the village and its social and political structures.[18]

Popular Opposition Forces Unite

By early 1982 the organizations opposing the government represented a broad cross-section of Guatemalan society. They included directors of trade unions, leaders of the CUC, organizers of *barrios* committees, settlers' committees, many academics and student organizers, and many of the left-of-centre reform politicians. Most of the leaders of these movements had been forced to flee Guatemala. Consequently, an extensive organization of leaders of popular movements was created in exile. This force unquestionably represented the majority of the Guatemalan people and served to focus international opposition on the Guatemalan government.

In order to carry out this struggle, the four rebel forces, the EGP, ORPA, FAR and PGT, formed the Guatemala National Revolutionary Union in March 1982 to facilitate a more cohesive armed struggle. In January 1982 they published a declaration of unity and detailed the principal points that would characterize a revolutionary government. They promised the Guatemalan people that a revolutionary government would put an end to repression and guarantee peace, life and human rights to the citizens; put an end to the domination of Guatemala by the rich, both national and foreign, as a first step in providing the necessities of life for the majority of the population; guarantee equality between Indians and *ladinos* and put an end to the cultural oppression and discrimination Indians had faced; guarantee a government made up of representatives of all the patriotic, democratic and popular sectors; and guarantee a policy of non-alignment and international cooperation for development in international affairs.[19]

Following this call for unity on the part of the guerrilla forces, in February 1982 the Democratic Front Against Repression, itself a coalition of over 170 organizations, joined with the Popular Front of 31 January (a group composed of the CUC, settlers' committees, and labour unions) to form the Guatemalan Committee of Patriotic Unity (GCUP). They agreed with the points expressed by the guerrilla organizations in their earlier call.

The revolutionary groups and the GCUP decided on common goals: the complete isolation of the Guatemalan government and military in the international community, and the imposition of negotiations as a first step towards a settlement that would bring democracy and economic reform to Guatemala. Their first major success along these lines was the condemnation of the Ríos Montt government by a majority in the United Nations' General Assembly in December 1982.

The Campaign in the Highlands

The military seemed unable to do anything to stem the tide of guerrilla success. Army patrols were slow to respond to guerrilla advances and major highland towns were in the hands of revolutionary forces for days at a time before the military appeared. The army frequently retaliated against the peasant inhabitants of the village. The violence of the military under the regime of Romeo Lucas García, in a programme directed by defence minister Aníbal Guevara, only served to propel more Indian peasants to support the guerrilla forces.

Military strategy changed somewhat when Benedicto Lucas García, the president's brother, was named defence minister to replace Aníbal Guevara, who was running for president in the electoral sham scheduled for 1982. Benedicto implemented a counter-insurgency policy that combined brutal attacks on peasant villages suspected of sympathy for the revolutionary forces with a civic-action programme in which the military assisted villages in local construction projects. The programme was inspired by Benedicto's training in the French military academy and from French experience in Vietnam and Algeria. Central to the programme was a scheme for forcing highland peasants to abandon their scattered communities and to relocate in concentrated villages the military could more easily control. This aspect of the army's campaign involved constant pressure and continual attacks on scattered villages to force relocation.

The Ríos Montt Regime

The fraudulent elections of March 1982 were immediately followed by a coup that brought General Efraín Ríos Montt to power. The major reason for the March 1982 coup was the fear that four years of government by the Institutional Democratic Party (PID) and Revolutionary Party (PR), in combination with the corrupt, inefficient military command, would increase guerrilla support in the highlands.

The Guatemalan military had never been able to maintain itself as a homogeneous entity. Factions within the military revolved around political parties, personal advantage and differences over the scope and brutality of military operations in rural areas. In 1982 and 1983 the army experienced even more dissension than usual. The coup in March 1982 only served to deepen the rifts between older, more conservative officers, and young officers who, rhetorically at any rate, advocated a type of rural development, but one that would be closely monitored and controlled by the military. Guatemala's political parties clustered around the edges of the various military factions.

Despite these conflicts, during 1982 and 1983 the military achieved control over the countryside and the total breakdown of village autonomy. By August 1983, when Ríos Montt was overthrown, the military had successfully ensured its national political dominance and controlled much of the national economy.

At the time of the coup four powerful guerrilla forces were in effective control of a number of regions in the country. The most powerful, the EGP, was laying plans for establishing "liberated" areas where the revolutionary forces would create nascent governments. Throughout all of the western highlands and much of the *Franja Transversal del Norte*, government control was nominal at best. Travel to Huehuetenango, one of Guatemala's major cities, was dangerous and erratic and even Quetzaltenango, Guatemala's second largest city, was difficult to reach at times. The area around Lake Atitlán, one of Guatemala's major tourist spots, was often firmly in the hands of the Revolutionary Organization of People in Arms (ORPA). Foreign capital fled the country at unprecedented rates. The tourist industry was in shambles. Wealthy Guatemalans sent their families to live in Miami and long-time American residents sold their homes and left for safer "paradises".

Following the coup, the counter-insurgency campaign initiated by Benedicto Lucas was pursued with a vengeance. After an initial period during which the government offered amnesty to guerrillas and their supporters, Ríos Montt declared on national television: "Today we are going to begin a merciless struggle . . . to annihilate the subversives that have not understood the good intentions of the government."[20] This phase of the government campaign was called "Victory 82". Villages throughout the highlands were occupied; all peasants suspected of subversive tendencies were killed, or were forced to flee to the rapidly growing refugee camps in the Mexican state of Chiapas. As always the military definition of subversive was wide-ranging. As Ríos Montt explained: "The problem of war is not just a question of who is shooting. For each one who is shooting there are ten working behind him." According to that logic, with guerrilla forces estimated at between 3000 and 6000, that left the military with up to 60 000 "subversives" in the highlands to "deal" with.[21]

Many villages in the department of Huehuetenango, villages in the Ixil triangle around Nebaj and in the Quiché were particularly hard hit. Many virtually ceased to exist as peasants fled to refugee camps in Mexico or wandered in the hills. By the end of that year up to 200 000 refugees had fled to Mexico and somewhere between 300 000 and 1 million peasants had fled their villages and were surviving in the mountains or in the ghettos of Guatemala City.[22]

According to the testimony of survivors, army attacks on villages were horrific in their total disregard for the lives of innocent people who could have had nothing to do with guerrillas. Any village which had strong, autonomous institutions, that is, a cooperative or peasant union, was suspect.[23] The reports were enough to prompt the Bishop of San Cristóbal de las Casas, in Chiapas, Mexico (near the site of most of the refugee camps) to confirm publicly: "Yes, there is genocide. I collected the testimony of various refugees giving proof of it. Neither children, women nor old people were respected." The bishop went on to give the details of a massacre on 17 July 1982 in the village of San Francisco, Huehuetenango, in which only twelve of the village's population of 350 were thought to have survived.[24]

The campaign by the military left much of Guatemala a deserted graveyard with burned-out caskets of adobe huts as silent testimony. The basic ingredients of the campaign in the highlands were made clear in a presentation submitted to the ministers of the Ríos Montt government by the army Special General Staff in early April 1982. The plan, entitled the National Plan for Security and Development, was meant to work in conjunction with the Fundamental Statute which Ríos Montt has issued to replace the 1964 constitution. The plan and the statute gave greater powers to the executive and the military. The military's anti-subversive campaign was to be directed by the Institutional Coordinating Group of the General Staff, which was not only to oversee all military operations in rural areas but to coordinate all government institutions and agencies. Along with greater military control the plan proposed:

> to structure and regulate nationalism to promote and encourage it in all organs of State and to propagate it in rural areas; to ensure that it is included in the education and training given to the people as a doctrine opposed to International Communism; to ensure that programmes to reduce the level of illiteracy be carried out in order to make the population more receptive to new ideas and to increase the effectiveness of actions taken to create nationalism and maintain it.[25]

According to the Guatemalan Committee for Justice and Peace, this programme was aimed primarily at Indian children in the areas of conflict – in 1982, 455 000 native children were taught Spanish as part of the campaign. "Alongside this, through assassination of the elders of the native communities, who are the repositories and guardians of their culture, an attempt is being made to stop it being preserved and handed on to the younger generations."[26]

The desire to destroy the strength and vitality of the native culture in the highlands and thus more easily extend military control over the area was the key to the second stage of the government programme entitled "Firmness 83". The military campaign hinged on two elements: the creation of model villages and strategic hamlets, and the formation of civil guards to be commanded by the army. The model village scheme was first espoused by Ríos Montt early in the spring of 1982, when he declared that the villages would be funded by huge donations to Guatemala from the American fundamentalist churches, especially the Christian Broadcasting Network. While the treasure of donations he envisaged was never forthcoming, the military embarked on its own programme of model villages. The camps clearly were part of the government campaign to destroy the foundation of village life and to reform it with substantial military control.

The military's decision to create a system of strategic hamlets was inspired by a similar desire. In these instances, an existing village, usually a municipal capital, was reinforced with an army garrison, and peasants from the surrounding countryside were forced to relocate there. The military hoped in this manner to stop the guerrillas from recruiting among the population or from receiving provisions from the outlying hamlets. The peasants forced from their land and relocated in these villages were often in dire straits.

Even the military officer in charge of the National Reconstruction Committee, while arguing that these people had grouped around the bases for their own security, admitted that there were about 250 000 peasants, "among them children who are forced to eat dirt", who were in need of assistance.[27] Much of the worst violence perpetrated by the military in the highlands was associated with the government programme to force relocation in the model villages or the strategic hamlets.

The second aspect of the military's programme to extend its control over rural areas, and probably the most ambitious, was the creation of civil patrols. All male residents between certain ages in highland villages were forced into civil patrols under the authority of the local army commander. These patrols blossomed in the highlands. By the summer of 1984 they were estimated to be 700 000 strong. The army spokesperson argued that the patrols "are not just fighting the guerrillas, but are also organized to develop their villages, distributing food, building materials, setting up schools and health centres".[28]

While the patrols did perform these tasks in a number of villages, their main purpose was to increase army control over highland Guatemala. All men in villages were required to participate in the patrols. The military kept lists of the men in the patrols, and was able in this manner to keep close tabs on the activity of most men in the highlands. In many ways the civil patrols fulfilled the long-held military dream of virtually complete control of rural Guatemala by replacing existing village government with a military instrument.

As well as providing an element of control, the civil patrols were the army's first line of defence against the revolutionary groups. A common saying in the western highlands in the spring of 1983 was that the "civil patrols protect the army". In many ways this was true. They were required to carry out extensive campaigns along highland trails in search of guerrilla enclaves, as well as to report any suspicious activity in their village. The army kept these patrols on a short leash and, reportedly, meted out quite drastic punishment if there was any indication of a lack of zeal in performing duties.[29]

On occasion the civil patrols fostered heightened violence in the highlands. Most Guatemalan *municipios* traditionally carried on a more-or-less running feud with neighbouring communities, the result of hundreds of years' competition for limited land. In many areas this took the form of racial conflict as *ladino* communities, most of them established during the nineteenth century, deprived the older Indian municipios of much of their land. After the civil patrols were established, *ladino* patrols, generally better armed than those from

Indian communities, on a number of occasions took advantage of the opportunity afforded them to attack neighbouring communities.[30]

There were also reports that the military forced these patrols to attack neighbouring villages. A commission of Canadian church representatives which visited Guatemala in August and September 1983 stated that it had received testimony from two "trustworthy people" which confirmed that members of a civil patrol from a neighbouring area had been compelled by the military to kill a number of people in a small hamlet – people who had refused to join the civil patrols.[31]

The fiercest violence associated with the government's campaign had begun to wane by September 1982. In most districts the military was prepared to move to the second stage of its campaign against the guerrillas. A significant portion of the junior officers who had led the coup against the Lucas government had publicly complained about the generalization of counter-insurgency violence under that government, warning that the indiscriminate violence was pushing peasants to support the revolution. They called for a programme to win the hearts of the peasants, particularly in areas with a high percentage of Indians. By the summer of 1982 they were threatening the Ríos Montt administration if military strategy did not shift in that direction.

The shift away from the focus on imported communist aggression as the root cause of unrest indicated a new emphasis for the military. One result of this new emphasis was seen in the increased stress placed on the *frijoles* part of the *"frijoles* and *fusiles"* (beans and bullets), as the government had labelled its counter-insurgency campaign. The stress on *frijoles* was designed as a means of improving the image of the military and national government in rural areas and of attacking some of the most immediate causes of peasant unrest. It was a continuation of the campaign barely begun by Benedicto Lucas, but also borrowed heavily from the US-inspired civic-action programmes employed in the 1960s in Zacapa.

In its 1982 incarnation, the army in the initial stages offered food, assistance in reconstruction, worked to provide water, and, on occasion, offered temporary medical clinics for peasants in villages recently repopulated.[32] The next step of the programme was more ambitious. Headed by Colonel Eduardo Wohlers, the Program of Aid to Areas in Conflict (PAAC) required permanent army occupation of strategic villages. Through the military, the government offered increased credit to small farmers, and prepared a programme to encourage cooperatives and to stimulate the adoption of new labour-intensive vegetable crops. Small-farm experts from Taiwan began to advise the programme's coordinator in early 1983.

This "social side" of the counter-insurgency was a mix of civic-action ideas and the "developmentalist" policies followed briefly during the Kjell Laugerud administration. Much of the funding for the programme came from international aid agencies, especially US AID and CARE, but all of it was directed by the military-controlled National Reconstruction Committee, the only agency which the government allowed to operate in the highlands. At its heart, however, was military determination to maintain control of highland villages. Colonel Wohlers explained, "Under the previous governments the problem was that we pulled out, leaving the subversives to take advantage of our absence to win back villages."[33] With this new strategy the military was to maintain a permanent presence, a presence that alternated brutal repression with carefully measured benevolence.

In its early stages the emphasis on the *frijoles* aspect of the programme seemed to take dramatic effect. Reporters from *Newsweek* in December 1982 cited the example of one Quiché woman who described a massacre in her village in which many people were killed and her children burned. She first assumed they were soldiers "because they wore uniforms and acted as soldiers have always acted". But as the military's civic-action began to be implemented in her village she had doubts. She finaly decided, "It must have been the subversives because now the soldiers are feeding and protecting us and why would they do that if they wanted to kill us."[34] By carefully nurturing this image the military hoped to dry up guerrilla support in rural areas.

The Ríos Montt administration did all it could to foster the impression that the military had gained control of disputed areas and that villages had accepted military assistance and protection. Despite army successes it was a hard image to maintain while tens of thousands of refugees lived across the Mexican border and, even though the torrent of fleeing peasants had been reduced, more continued to arrive at Chiapas refugee camps weekly.[35]

Political Conflict and Opposition

While the government's campaign in the highlands was the aspect of the Ríos Montt administration that was felt most painfully by the bulk of the Guatemalan population, a number of other issues created conflicts within the government and the military. The most serious of these were disputes over a "return to democracy", the government's economic policies and – intermingled with these two – an increasingly bitter conflict between two powerful factions in the military. It was the last of these which most directly led to Ríos Montt's overthrow and in the process clearly showed the severely restricted possibilities for reform in Guatemala.

Much of the rhetoric surrounding the coup of March 1982 was couched in terms of "reinvigorating the democratic principle" after a decade of electoral fraud. While the more important impulse for the coup was military concern over a poorly waged civil war, there were still expectations that new elections would soon follow. These expectations were quickly dashed by the attitude of Ríos Montt and the Advisory Council of Officers. While one political party tacitly supported the Ríos Montt administration, most of Guatemala's right-wing politicians opposed what they saw as an attempt to entrench more firmly the military's dominance over the political process.

Throughout the Ríos Montt regime a careful distinction had been drawn between rural and urban Guatemala. Ríos Montt counted on the urban middle class for much of whatever support he enjoyed. Consequently, the fiction of being a responsible, moral government – a fiction made more preposterous by the military campaign in the highlands – was pursued vigorously in urban areas.

Ríos Montt's campaign against the right-wing death squads won him support among the middle class, particularly from people aligned with the Christian Democrats, and muted some of the demands for elections and constitutional government. He led a vigorous attack on the interior ministry, which during the Lucas administration had been especially corrupt and responsible for much of the government-orchestrated urban violence. Close to 300 people in the ministry were fired in the months immediately following the coup.[36]

Violent incidents in Guatemala City during the early months of the new administration fell by over 90 per cent. The city, which had been silent and dark after nightfall for almost two years, slowly came back to life. A similar process occurred in other urban areas.

Ríos Montt also won support from the urban middle class for his campaign against government corruption. In the first months after the coup over fifty people were arrested for corrupt practices under the previous administration.[37] The campaign rested heavily on religious and moral responsibility. It was a popular campaign, especially among the urban middle class, even though there was some complaint that the "big fish" behind the corruption in the Lucas regime had escaped unscathed.

The administration fared less well with the economic policies it initiated. These policies quickly alienated large landowners, leaders of the business community and eventually much of the middle class. Ríos Montt took over the government with the Guatemalan economy seriously depressed. During the early 1980s the world-wide recession had reduced the demand for and price of Guatemala's exports.

Shortly after taking power the new administration prompted opposition from the business élite by implementing new taxes and rationing foreign exchange. During the last three years of the Lucas García government, Guatemala had suffered a disastrous increase in its debt and a severe decline in its foreign reserves. The problem was aggravated by a reduction in the export tax on coffee, a measure forced on the Lucas government by the coffee oligarchy.

Consequently, the coup in March 1982 was meant partly to prompt support for renewed aid for Guatemala, both economic and military through the installation of a government more acceptable than the widely condemned Lucas regime. While US military aid was consistently denied the new government despite the attempts of the Reagan administration to have congress approve such aid, Ríos Montt was remarkably successful in grabbing sizeable loans from international agencies. Despite these loans the Ríos Montt administration was forced to ration foreign exchange.

During the eighteen months of his administration, Ríos Montt was increasingly opposed by Guatemala's right-wing political parties, but retained throughout the tacit support of the Christian Democrats. With the PID/PR coalition effectively discredited by the overthrow of Lucas, the most powerful of the right-wing parties was MLN. Given the policies proposed by the Ríos Montt administration, particularly the tax measures and rumours of agrarian reform, this party's attacks on the government were not surprising and, hoping to take advantage of the PID/PR collapse, the MLN continued to push for quick elections following the coup.

The Conservative Military Hierarchy Reasserts Itself

The differences in the way political parties viewed Ríos Montt reflected a more serious division in the military. Ríos Montt's firmest support came from a group of junior officers, most of them key participants in the coup of March 1982 and many represented in the Council of Junior Officers that advised the president. While much of Ríos Montt's support within the military came from these junior officers, he continually sought to lessen his reliance on them and to develop his own base of support. The junior officers themselves supported Ríos Montt as a compromise with the traditional conservative hierarchy, and only as long as he followed policies they approved of. In the end he lost the support of many of the junior officers and was overthrown by the traditional military hierarchy reacting both against the continued influence of the junior officers and his economic policies, especially the rumours of agrarian reform.

The coup that had brought Ríos Montt to power had seriously divided the military. From the overthrow of Jacobo Arbenz in 1954 to the early 1970s, the two most powerful factions in the army were the technocrats who had been instrumental in forming the PID and who by the late 1970s clustered around Lucas; and the more conservative and traditional officers linked to the MLN who had in common an obsessively paranoid anti-communism. During the 1970s a third group had arisen which was more prepared to countenance some limited reform and had links to the Christian Democrats. This group had supported Ríos Montt in the 1974 presidential elections.

During the 1970s the MLN, with its "organized violence" and openly fascist pronouncements had lost support among the military until by 1978 there were few officers who would openly back it. Nonetheless, there remained a core of officers who held political and economic views closely akin to those of the MLN politicians. With the PID officers completely discredited after the overthrow of the Lucas administration, the two opposing factions within the military – the junior officers and the conservative hierarchy – confronted each other.

This division was most clearly represented by the Advisory Council of Junior Officers on the one hand and the defence minister Oscar Humberto Mejía Víctores and chief of staff Héctor Mario López Fuentes on the other. Some of the contradictory aspects of the military's operations in the highlands can be traced to the conflict between those two elements. In particular, many of the junior officers opposed the more brutal aspects of the counter-insurgency campaign. It is no coincidence that the shift in emphasis in the *frijoles* and *fusiles* programme occurred shortly after Ríos Montt was presented with a petition from fifty field commanders calling for less brutality.[38]

To a considerable extent, Ríos Montt's position depended on how well he could respond to the junior officers' demands without completely antagonizing the more senior officers. It was clear that he was unable to do so. The military hierarchy that reasserted itself after the coup of August 1983 was predominantly composed of conservative senior officers with links to the MLN and the traditional rural élite, the most violent and rabidly anti-communist of Guatemala's officers.

On 8 August 1983, General Mejía Víctores and General Mario López Fuentes, supported by the bulk of the military command, forced Ríos Montt from office.[39] None of Mejía Víctores's movements upon taking power was unexpected. In many areas the level of brutality again increased. One Indian leader in the highlands told reporters a month after the coup: "Our people are once again being forced to flee their villages into the mountains to save their lives."[40] The most far-reaching civil-action activities in highland villages were curtailed, and the emphasis of government rhetoric shifted from combating social causes of revolt to striving to "eradicate the Marxist–Leninist subversion threatening our liberty and sovereignty".[41] Death squads began once again to operate more or less openly in urban areas and attacked what elements of internal opposition still remained in urban Guatemala; university faculty and students, members of the church and trade unionists were gunned down in Guatemala City with distressing frequency.[42] In contrast to Ríos Montt's attempts to keep US policy in the rest of Central America at arms length, Mejía Víctores encouraged an expanded US presence in the region.

Perhaps the most vigorous measures following the coup were directed at internal military discipline. Immediately after taking power, Mejía Víctores warned junior officers: "We are aware of the need to preserve and strengthen the unity of the army, upholding the principle of hierarchy and subordination to frustrate the attempts of some elements to fracture and confuse the armed institution."[43] In December 1983 the military command passed a new army code which placed greater stress on discipline and adherence to the hierarchical levels of command. It also demanded the retirement of all officers who held employment outside the military within two years of the passage of the code (an attempt to reduce tension within the military from officer-involvement in business deals), and the retirement of all generals who were not actively performing duties in the high command.[44]

Mejía Víctores also promised quick elections. The first step along that path was voting for a constituent assembly to draft a new constitution. These elections were held without serious mishap, and apparently with little fraud, in July 1984, giving a small plurality to the Christian Democrats in the assembly. The influence that this strength gave them was severly limited, however. Mejía sharply warned that he would react decisively if the Christian Democrats tried to do anything more than draw up a new constitution, advising against any meddling in his administration.

Nevertheless, presidential elections were held on schedule in November 1985. The perennial Christian Democrat presidential candidate, Vinicio Cerezo Arévalo, handily won these relatively fair elections and was allowed to take office in January 1986.

The Cerezo Administration

The election of Vinicio Cerezo seemed to portend a new era in Guatemala politics. Cerezo, long a fixture in the Christian Democratic party, was from the party's "left wing" and was perceived to be a committed reformer. The army had been relatively impartial during the voting that brought him to power and seemed to be taking a back-seat to the civilian administration for the first time since early in the administration of Julio César Méndez Montenegro in 1966. However, as Mejía Víctores made clear in his speech at Cerezo's inauguration, the military was passing elected office to the Christian Democrats on probation; unspoken but completely understood limits on his power were passed along with the office. It was also clear that the battleground over which the military was most determined to maintain its control was highland Guatemala.[45]

The first two years of the Cerezo administration was a period of apparent contradiction in the political dynamics between the military and the civilian government. Cerezo himself on a number of occasions admitted that the military had acquiesced in his election because it suited their own purposes and that he wielded less than the full range of power generally associated with the office he occupied.[46] The military clearly held substantial national political influence.

But little of this discussion focused on the highlands, and it was there that the military most assuredly continued to dominate. The military maintained its monopoly over services to highland communities through the agency of the military-dominated National Reconstruction Committee and the Programme of Aid to Areas in Conflict. The system of strategic hamlets and civil patrols remained intact. While the overwhelming brutality of the military campaign in 1982 was no longer apparent, this was so simply because the military no longer needed to rely upon it in the apparently pacified highlands.

The military followed an aggressive campaign designed to instil patriotic sentiments in Indian children and to erase the elements of Indian culture and Indian autonomy that had survived and developed in highland communities since the initial Spanish conquest. This "cult of nationalism" was meant to ensure that Indians in highland Guatemala would more readily link their aspirations to the state and state agencies as well as ensure that they no longer possessed the internal cohesion necessary to mount effective opposition to state agencies in the future.[47] Nationalism was another aspect of the military's determination to retain absolute control over rural Guatemala. The irony apparent in a nation embarked on a "new democratic opening" at a time when the most important governmental structure in the country, that of the municipality, was less representative and less autonomous than it had been at any time in its history, did not receive the amount of attention it deserved.[48]

Despite the military's determination, its control over highland Guatemala was less than complete. The guerrilla organizations were neither destroyed by the military counter-insurgency in 1982 and 1983 nor were they prepared to accept the limited democratic opening provided by the 1985 elections as a serious attempt to alter the structures they had emerged to combat.[49] While the counter-insurgency ensured that their support among the highland peasantry was subdued (there was some resentment among the peasantry that guerrilla promises of protection and assurances of their ability to stand up to the army had proven unfounded and helped result in the destruction of many of their communities) it was clear that at least part of that support smouldered beneath the surface. By the summer of 1986 guerrilla operations, which had never completely ended, were increasing in many areas in northern Huehuetenango and El Quiché.[50]

Many Indians in the highlands were prepared to wait a little while to see if the change in government led to any significant alterations in local structures of domination and repression. In this regard the challenge to these structures presented by the increasing clamour for agrarian reform was the most serious. A movement threatening land invasions (and combining that threat with some actual occupations) led by Padre Andrés Girón on the Pacific Coast forced the Cerezo government to divide some purchased *fincas* among Girón's followers in the summer of 1986. The Cerezo government walked a fine line between appeasing these peasants and not antagonizing landowners.[51]

Padre Girón's movement, despite its significance as a symbol of peasants taking their own action to remedy local situations, is no solution to the problems confronting Guatemala. They can only be addressed through a comprehensive programme of agrarian reform that not only redistributes land, but redistributes economic and political power along with it. The Cerezo government is neither prepared nor powerful enough to implement such a programme; any indication that it is prepared to do so would bring a swift end to the current "democratic opening" in Guatemala.

Conclusion

At first glance the impressive rebirth of popular organizations that occurred in Guatemala in the 1970s appears to have had little positive results. Sporadic attacks on the leaders of these organizations helped to propel significant numbers of peasants to support revolutionary forces hoping to effect significant structural change through violent revolution. When it appeared that this revolution might succeed, the military thrust aside, momentarily, the schisms that had divided the institution and the fiction of democratic government to deal with the revolutionary threat. Having done so with quite remarkable brutality in the early 1980s, the military determined to ensure that no other such threat would develop by reshaping highland Guatemala with significant, and permanent, military control. Confident of its supremacy there, it acquiesced in the holding of national elections for congress and president in 1985.

But the experience of popular organization and the hard lessons learned in the 1980s are not easily wiped out. The only step that could prevent a resurgence of popular protest and eventually a new challenge by revolutionary armies is not repression in the highlands but decisive steps to alter the prevailing social and economic structures and to address the problems denounced by these popular organizations during the 1970s and early 1980s. Neither the civilian government of Vinicio Cerezo nor, most assuredly, the military, was prepared in the 1980s to countenance such steps. Until they are taken, revolt will continue to be endemic in Guatemala, snuffed out in one corner, only to flare up in another.

Notes

1. Cited in K. Warren, *Symbolism of Subordination* (Austin: University of Texas Press, 1978), p. 89.

2. For example, the Catholic Action newspaper, *Acción Social Cristiana*, constantly published articles attacking virtually all aspects of the government's programme of reform. See 19 July and 19 August 1945. Also see pastoral letter of Archbishop Rossell, 25 May 1950, in *El Imparcial* (Guatemala City) 26 May 1950; and pastoral letter of 14 April 1954, enclosed in W. Krieg, first secretary of the US embassy in Guatemala to State Department (14 April 1954) in State Department Archives, Guatemalan Records.

3. See for example E. M. Mendelson, "Religion and World View in Santiago Atitlán", University of Chicago, microfilm collection of manuscripts on Middle American Cultural Anthropology, 1957, p. 52; and his *Los Escándalos del Maximón* (Guatemala City: Seminario de Integración Social Guatemalteca, 1965).

4. F. Turner, *Catholicism and Political Development in Latin America* (North Carolina: University of North Carolina Press, 1971) pp. 135–6; and B. J. Calder, *Crecimiento y cambio de la iglesia católica Guatemalteca: 1944–1966* (Guatemala City: Seminario de Integración Social Guatemalteca, 1970).

5. R. Adams, *Crucifixion by Power*, p. 294; see also Calder, *Crecimiento*, pp. 148–9.

6. Cited in Adams, *Crucifixion*, p. 294.

7. Cited in *New York Times*, 14 September 1975.

8. Warren, *Symbolism*, pp. 107, 165. The most complete study of the effects of Catholic Action on Indians in the highlands is R. Falla, *Quiché Rebelde: Estudio de un movimiento de conversión religiosa, rebelde a las creencias tradicionales, en San Antonio Ilotenango, Quiché (1948–1970)* (Guatemala City: Editorial Universitaria Universidad de San Carlos, 1978).

9. D. Brintnall, *Revolt Against the Dead*, p. 141. Also see P. Diener, "The Tears of St Anthony", *Latin American Perspectives* (Summer, 1978) for a somewhat unconvincing argument concerning the manner in which Indians are forced by *ladino* merchants to continue with local celebrations.

10. Cited in *Noticias de Guatemala* (Costa Rica) 28 July 1980.

11. M. Payeras, *Los días de la selva* (Mexico, 1980); this has been translated and appears in *Monthly Review* (July–August, 1984).

12. Shelton Davis and Julie Hodson, *Witness to Political Violence in Guatemala: The Suppression of a Rural Development Movement*, p. 47; *Latin America*, 25 July 1975; 23 July 1976.

13. Interview in *Amnesty International Bulletin*, 8 February 1980.

14. *Frente*, vol. 1, p. 1.

15. Sean McKenna, cited in article by Tommie Sue Montgomery, for *Network News*, reprinted in the *Toronto Star*, 16 October 1982.

16. "Historia de ORPA", reprinted in *Guatemala: Un pueblo en lucha*, edited by José González and Antonio Campos (Spain, 1983) pp. 178–87. Also see FAR bulletin, edición internacional, p. 29, año. 3, febrero 1983, edited by José González and Antonio Campos (Spain, 1983).

17. Declaration of Rolando Morán, made in 1981 and reprinted in *Guatemala: Un pueblo en lucha*, pp. 154–67.

18. For example, only two of the 115 respondents to the Oxfam Study thought that the increase in rural violence could be traced to the presence of guerrillas (p. 2).
19. See "Declaration of Revolutionary Unity", *Latin American Perspectives* (Summer 1982); interview with FAR director, *Uno mas Uno*, 12 October 1982; and "Proclama unitaria de las organizaciones revolucionarias EGP, FAR, ORPA, y PGT al Pueblo de Guatemala" in González and Campos (eds) *Guatemala: Un pueblo en lucha*, pp. 201–14.
20. Cited by Allen Nairn, "Guatemala Bleeds", *New Republic*, 11 April 1983.
21. Cited in *New York Times*, 17 October 1982.
22. The Mexican government officially recognized the presence of 35 000 refugees in 32 camps. But, others suggested there were closer to 100 000 in 60 camps. See Ignacio Ramírez, "Tropas Mexicanas forman un cordón de seguridad tras el ataque Guatemalteco", *Proceso*, 7 February 1983, cited in Grupo de Apoyo a Refugiados Guatemaltecos, *La contra-insurgencia y los refugiados Guatemaltecos* (Mexico: Grupo de Apoyo a Refugiados Guatemaltecos, 1983) pp. 9–10, p. 71. The new Archbishop of Guatemala, Próspero Penados, estimated there were 500 000 internal refugees in Guatemala; Enforprensa, *Guatemala Faces 1984*, p. 34. The Human Rights Commission of Guatemala estimated in September 1982 that there were 1 million refugees. *Noticias de Guatemala*, 12 October 1982, p. 10.
23. See, for example, *Los Angeles Times*, 14 October 1982; Davis and Hodson, *Witness to Political Violence; El Gráfico* (Guatemala City), 8 October 1982.
24. Cited in *Proceso*, 4 October 1982, in Grupo, *La contra-insurgencia*, p. 27.
25. Comité Pro Justicia y Paz de Guatemala, *Human Rights in Guatemala* (February 1984) pp. 10–11.
26. Ibid.
27. *El Día*, 4 August 1982.
28. Cited in *Los Angeles Times*, 19 September 1982.
29. *Guatemala Update*, April–May, 1984; *Toronto Star*, 15 July 1984.
30. For example, in Chiché, El Quiché, throughout the month of January 1983 there was increasing friction between the civil patrols in town – primarily *ladino* – and the Indian patrols in the cantons surrounding it. This friction erupted in a number of pitched battles in which twenty-five Indian peasants were killed; *Prensa Libre*, 4, 5, February 1983. Similar tension was also apparent between patrols near the Mam village of Todos Santos; conversation with patrolmen in April 1983.
31. *Why Don't They Hear Us?*, Report of the Canadian Inter-Church Fact-Finding Mission to Guatemala and Mexico, 22 August 1983 to 8 September 1983, p. 10.
32. Reports of the military distributing food and offering other services occurred frequently in Guatemalan newspapers throughout 1982 and 1983; see for example, *Prensa Libre*, 11 and 15 January 1983.
33. Cited in *Latin American Regional Report, Mexico and Central America* (LARR) 6 May 1983.

34. *Newsweek*, 13 December 1982.
35. Conversation with Mexican relief worker in refugee camp near Comitán, Mexico, 29 April 1983.
36. *LARR*, 30 April 1982; *El Día*, 17 August 1982; *Uno mas Uno*, 15 and 18 August 1982.
37. *LARR*, 30 April 1982.
38. *LARR*, 29 October 1982.
39. Francis Pisani, "L'éviction du General Ríos Montt fuite en avant au Guatemala", *Le Monde Diplomatique*, 30 September 1983; *LARR*, 15 July 1983. See also *Prensa Libre*, 21, 24 and 26 March 1983; and *Guatenoticias*, 15 January 1983.
40. Cited in *Washington Post*, 22 September 1983. See also Inter-Church Committee on Human Rights in Latin America, Toronto, news release, 8 November 1983; Guatemalan Human Rights Commission, news release, 15 May 1984.
41. Cited in *LARR*, 19 August 1983.
42. Enforprensa, 27 April–3 May, 25–31 May 1984.
43. Cited in *LARR*, 19 August 1983.
44. *LARR*, 13 January 1984.
45. Mejía's speech cited in *Excelsior* (Mexico City) 21 January 1986.
46. Cerezo cited in George Black, "El Señor Presidente", *NACLA*, no. 19, November–December, 1985) p. 25.
47. Comité Pro Justicia y Paz de Guatemala, *Human Rights in Guatemala* (February 1984) pp. 10–11.
48. For a fuller discussion see Jim Handy, "Resurgent Democracy and the Guatemalan Military", *Journal of Latin American Studies*, vol. 18, No. 2 (November 1986), pp. 383–408.
49. "La apertura democrática, un engaño mas", *FAR Bulletin*, no. 3, año III.
50. One need only visit the Ixil triangle area of Nebaj, Chajul and San Juan Cotzal to see the evidence of continuing and increasing battles with the EGP.
51. "Piden calma a Padre Girón, *La Hora*, 5 January 1987; "No a golpe de Estado", *La Hora*, 14 January, 1987; J. C. Cambranes, *Agrarismo en Guatemala* (Guatemala: Editorial Servitrensa, 1986).

The Christian Democratic Party and the Prospects for Democratization in El Salvador[1]

Terry Lynn Karl

Introduction

One of the major issues in the debate over the prospects for democracy in El Salvador is the nature and role of the Christian Democratic Party. To the Reagan administration and others in the USA, this party represents the moderate centre, a viable ally that can lead its country through the twin shoals of military authoritarian rule and revolution. To its critics, the party is little more than a surrogate of the USA, willing to carry out the bidding of an administration intent upon blocking a negotiated settlement of the civil war and preventing the victory of the opposition FDR–FMLN (Democratic Revolutionary Front – Farabundo Martí National Liberation Front).

As always, reality is more complicated, reflecting the complexity of the "centrist" role the Christian Democratic Party (PDC) has chosen for itself. Although the party has grown increasingly dependent upon the USA, both politically and economically, in the period from 1980 to 1987, it has also demonstrated a certain degree of autonomy at critical junctures. For example, President José Napoleón Duarte's sudden decision to meet with the FDR–FMLN on 15 October 1984, took the Reagan administration and most political observers by surprise. This decision to commence negotiations, albeit short-lived, had its roots in both Christian Democratic ideology and practice, not in the wishes of the USA. It reflected the view that the party's own long-term survival ultimately depends upon the successful construction of an anti-authoritarian alliance that can forge a compromise on the procedures for democraticization and the parameters for a future regime. As we shall see, this view places the PDC in a state of permanent tension between its electoral base, on the one hand, and its allies in the Salvadoran military and the USA, on the other. Such tension can represent both opportunity and disaster. Because transitions to democracy are contingent upon the ability of antagonistic domestic political actors to produce acceptable interim negotiations or pacts about the new rules of the political game, and because pacts are usually put together by parties that occupy the "centre" of the political spectrum, the PDC has the chance to play a unique role in Salvadoran history. Yet precisely because it is the fulcrum of political tensions, it also runs the risk of irreversible political decline.

The Christian Democratic Strategy to Democratize El Salvador

There can be little debate over the PDC's credentials for playing a centrist role in El Salvador. Since its inception, the party has played a pact-making game – first with the left until 1972, then with the right after 1980, and briefly again in 1984–5 it sought accommodation with the left. Formed in 1960 when international Christian Democracy was showing substantial gains throughout the continent – especially in Venezuela and Chile – the PDC rapidly demonstrated its ability to construct a durable organization, build a mass base in largely urban areas, and govern the city of San Salvador. Its successes resulted in part from the popularity of party leader Napoleón Duarte. By March 1972, the PDC was able to produce a national electoral victory in coalition with two other parties, now represented in the FDR–FMLN. This victory was subsequently snatched away through electoral fraud by the armed forces.[2]

Although the PDC's critics emphasize recent US influence over the party to explain its political behaviour, the PDC's current strategy for democratization owes far more to Christian Democratic ideology and its own participation in that international movement than it does to direct US pressure. The PDC's guiding principles for democracy are based upon certain key Christian Democratic tenets: anti-communism; belief in the need to build consensus; a reformist conception of private property rights, which results in advocacy of land reform; the right of individual political expression primarily through the right to vote; and the rule of law. This vision has a strong conservative bias stemming from Catholic precepts of ordained order and zealous opposition to the spread of atheistic thought represented by communism; yet the emphasis upon socio-economic change gives the movement a reformist cast. In many Christian Democratic parties, the ideological discord between these twin preoccupations of order and reform has often resulted in confused political definition, strong internal factionalism, and party divisions. The Salvadoran party is no different in this respect.

The PDC's strategy of democratization has been influenced by the party's two decades of political practice. During its formative years, the PDC was forced to grapple with the question of whether or not to ally itself with the military. At that time, it rejected any type of collaboration, preferring to continue to build its own separate political base. In 1960 Duarte sealed his status as a major party figure by maintaining party unity during the strong debate over a possible alliance with the military. The party adopted a policy of non-cooperation with the military, which it maintained until after the 1972 election when the military denied the PDC its victory. Forced into exile in Venezuela, Duarte and other party leaders came to the conclusion that any future reform in El Salvador could only be achieved in alliance with the army, particularly the young officers. As early as 1973, they were discussing the possibility of an interim government that could unite civilians, including the PDC, and military progressives. By the coup of October 1979 most of the PDC leadership had set aside its reluctance to join with the military. In a highly controversial decision in 1980, the Christian Democratic Party, led by Duarte, joined the military government at the very moment when army-led repression was forcing other civilian parties into open, armed opposition.[3]

To a unique extent, the experiences of other Christian Democratic parties, particularly those of Chile and Venezuela, have affected the Salvadoran party's strategy and perceptions of reality. The Venezuelan example of regime transformation in the aftermath of 1958 has had a particularly strong impact. During his seven years of exile in Caracas, Duarte absorbed significant lessons through his close political relationship with the founders of the Venezuelan Christian Democratic (COPEI) party, who had participated in a regime transition led by Acción Democrática's Rómolo Betancourt. Because Venezuela's own democracy was an élite-negotiated enterprise, party officials there emphasized the importance of political pact-making with the army, the private sector and other political parties as well as the need to relinquish certain reformist aspects of the original party programme. Duarte, noted for his highly personalistic and messianic style, was particularly taken by the Venezuelan model and considered himself El Salvador's equivalent of Rómulo Betancourt.[4]

For the Salvadoran party, the Venezuelan experience provided an important instance of an undefeated military withdrawing voluntarily from power. In exchange for an amnesty for past human rights violations and political crimes as well as substantial economic benefits, the Venezuelan Armed Forces had accepted a new self-definition as an "apolitical, obedient, and non-deliberative body". True, in 1957–8 that military was already deeply divided over its own role in government and chose to withdraw from power in order to maintain its institutional integrity. Yet Betancourt's legendary artfulness was of critical importance; he courted the military, nurturing its leaders' allegiance to his own emerging regime. When a guerrilla war broke out after the establishment of democracy, Betancourt was able to translate his widespread popularity into broad national support for the military's effort to quash the uprising. Among Venezuelan politicians, this produced a strong belief in the possibility of "democratizing" a country's armed forces – a belief they willingly shared with their Salvadoran counterparts.

There were additional lessons for El Salvador in the Venezuelan agreement that established the "rules of the game" in the political realm. The Pact of Punto Fijo, signed prior to the holding of any elections, was a classic example of an interim agreement to create a formula for compromise. It guaranteed that all parties would respect the result of the elections, whatever they might be, and established a political truce between parties previously in dispute, particularly the Christian Democrats and the social democrats. At the same time it successfully excluded the Communist Party. Although the pact did not commit the parties to explicit quotas of power-sharing, as did a similar pact in Colombia, it did recognize that the benefits of state power must be equitably distributed to guarantee the prolonged political truce necessary for the formation of a coalition government. Thus, regardless of who won the elections, each party was promised a share of the political and economic pie through access to state jobs and contracts, a partitioning of the ministries, and a complicated spoils system that would assure the political survival of all signatories. In 1982, the Salvadoran PDC would attempt a similar agreement through the Pact of Apaneca.[5]

The Venezuelan parties had also negotiated an economic pact with the private sector that established the broad outlines of a development model – an important means for limiting uncertainty during the formative stages of a democracy. All political parties in Venezuela agreed to respect foreign and local private capital accumulation as well as to subsidize the private sector. The agreement thus rules out the possibility of expropriation, but it did provide for a programme of land reform based on compensation paid for by Venezuela's petroleum wealth. In return for their support of basic property rights, the parties won the élite's acquiescence to the expansion of the state, the right of workers to organize, and a policy of guaranteed benefits in health, education, social security, and wage rates. Given US interests in Venezuelan oil, the economic pact was closely tied to an informal *modus vivendi* with the USA. In exchange for assurances that US holdings would not be expropriated and that Venezuela would maintain a pro-US foreign policy, the US government refrained from intervening to support its previous ally, Pérez Jiménez, and eventually promised its full backing to the new regime. PDC leaders hoped that a similar arrangement could be made in El Salvador, providing reassurance to both the Salvadoran agrarian élites and the US administration.

To a lesser extent, the experiences of Chile, whose democratic political system was overthrown by the 1973 coup, also influenced the Salvadoran Christian Democratic Party. Unlike their Venezuelan counterparts, the Chileans in their advice to Duarte were sceptical about the possibility of democratizing a military like El Salvador's through simple persuasion; instead, they stressed the importance of the US role in producing a military withdrawal from government. In addition, they were aware of the deep divisions likely to be caused by a substantive agrarian reform – particularly one lacking the petroleum revenues that had financed the Venezuelan programme.

Chilean Christian Democrats spoke from their own experiences of democratic failure in Chile. They traced this failure to their inadvertent debilitation of a pragmatic centrist party during the mid-1960s before the election of Salvador Allende, and warned the Salvadoran PDC against a similar mistake. In particular, these Chileans felt that their party had failed to continue the practice followed by its predecessor, the Radical Party, of occupying the political centre by forming alliances with both the left and the right. On the one hand, the party had become sectarian, adopting a *partido único* majoritarian strategy that polarized politics, making it more difficult to formulate compromises. This factor, combined with party tactics emphasizing mobilization at the expense of clientelist relationships, upset the normal rules of Chilean democracy by encouraging popular organization and real political competition in previously unincorporated rural areas. On the other hand, the party could see in retrospect – given the power the Communist Party had gained and the 1970 victory by the Popular Unity Coalition – that it had been unnecessarily intransigent toward those factions of the left that wanted to play by electoral rules, contributing to a destabilization through polarization, mobilization, and the break-down of a centre. "We have to avoid that here," argued José Miguel Fritis, a Chilean PDC member working in El Salvador, "by building a pragmatic center-right coalition in this country."[6] Once cemented, this alliance could later turn its attention to negotiations with the left.

This combination of Christian Democratic ideological predisposition and party experience in several countries produced clear if inconsistent guidelines for the democratization of El Salvador. First and foremost, the Salvadoran PDC believed that it should try to "turn enemies into partners" by forming an alliance with the military in order to convince it to leave power. This explains the PDC's 1980 decision to govern with the traditionally repressive military, to give unqualified support to the Salvadoran armed forces while attempting to conduct serious political work inside the government, and to renounce all active efforts to seek a political solution not voluntarily sanctioned by the military. In light of this strategy, it became unlikely that the party would risk alienating the Salvadoran High Command in the future by entering into agreements that could strain the nascent PDC–military relationship.

Second, the party has been committed to occupying the centre of the political spectrum, wherever that might be, through pragmatic policies, and alliances with both the left and the right which explicitly avoided mobilizational tactics. But because the PDC's association with the military prohibited political negotiations with the left, this strategy called for the formation of flexible and frequently-changing alliances that were aimed at assuaging the fears of the private sector and the political right and that resulted in the gradual abandonment of the PDC's centrist position. At some time, however, it could be expected that, in order to regain the centre, the party would make some move toward the left – to the extent permitted by the Salvadoran Armed Forces.

Third, the PDC has always believed in the importance of pursuing a careful programme of agrarian and technocratic reforms to improve the efficiency of the market and the state while solidifying a social base for a conservative political democracy. Yet this goal collided with the desire to soothe anti-reformist agrarian interests and the effort to build a centre-right coalition. In practice this meant that the party's position on the importance of and timetable for various reforms shifted constantly according to the strength of organized interests of the moment, a behaviour that would be unlikely to change even with a strong electoral majority. Ironically, the party's own constant vacillation has made the achievement of such a majority less and less likely. This became an important impetus for the La Palma talks as we shall see, and foreshadowed the backpedalling that would occur as reaction to negotiations intensified.

Finally, like all other forces in El Salvador, the PDC believed it should seek international support for its own programme – an awkward task as the party twisted and turned through these other imperatives. On the one hand, potential democratic allies in Latin America and Europe had trouble with the PDC's decision to join a repressive military regime; on the other hand, the Reagan administration found it difficult to support a programme of state-led reform, given its own militant bias in favour of free enterprise. As the PDC's fortunes dipped throughout 1982, its only firm ally until the 1984 elections remained its sister-members of International Christian Democracy who best understood its policy twists and turns. Most other international actors, including the USA, measured out their support for the Salvadoran PDC according to their own foreign policy positions regarding the desirability of a political settlement.

Stalemate and the 1984 Elections

Political and military stalemate, which defines the situation in El Salvador today, can facilitate democratization under some conditions. Democracies are usually made "on the instalment plan", as events unfold. They result from concrete steps and sequential decisions, unintended consequences and pure luck, which, when taken *in toto*, increase the probability of a competitive or semi-competitive polity. In general, transitions to democracy have been a by-product of other goals and intentions on the part of reactionaries and revolutionaries. For anti-democratic actors, democracy is by definition a second-best option chosen only when no single other regime preference can prevail. A democratic compromise can emerge from and terminate a prolonged and inconclusive struggle that would otherwise bring significant losses to all political forces involved. Indeed, democracy's greatest attraction may well be this institutionalization of stalemate through the construction of a polity based upon uncertain outcomes yet offering the possibility of future change. Thus the clear perception of stalemate can be conducive to democracy's emergence — a situation that began to take shape only in 1983.

The period from 1980 to 1983 marked a clear failure of Christian Democratic strategy described above. The decisive pressure from the Carter administration, rather than any subtle "democratization" of the military, had convinced the armed forces to accept the PDC as a junior partner in the ruling junta in 1980 and to lend some support to land reform. The military's subsequent agreement to the holding of elections in 1982 was a means to deflect international pressure for negotiations and a concession to the USA, not to the military's hated Christian Democratic allies.[7] When these US-sponsored elections took place in 1982, the Christian Democrats, tarnished internationally and domestically by their complicity with a repressive regime, were unable to win the electoral majority they needed to govern. They could not defeat the ultra-right, represented by the National Republican Alliance (Arena). Indeed, only open US intervention in the selection of the country's president kept ultra-rightist Roberto D'Aubuisson out of the nation's highest office; he was replaced by a compromise candidate, Álvaro Magaña, who had not even participated in the elections. The right, furious at US interference, retaliated by appointing D'Aubuisson President of the Constituent Assembly and promptly adopted legislation that effectively annulled much of the Christian Democratic land reform. By 1983, each pillar of Christian Democratic strategy – the alliance with the military, the occupation of the political centre, the insistence upon reform, the desire for international linkages — was in serious trouble.

What changed this context in 1983 was the dawning realization of a political and military stalemate, a stalemate defined by several mutual vetoes. The Reagan administration, pursuing a hard-line strategy in Latin America, remained committed to the defeat of any revolution on its watch – a fact that rules out a military victory by the FDR–FMLN. At the same time, the US Congress, which controls the strings on the purse that is the sole maintenance of the Salvadoran government and economy, refused to condone an alliance with the violent ultra-right, represented by Arena, or military escalation in El Salvador, with its potential for involving US troops. This ruled out both the total defeat of the opposition and the full restoration of the old regime. Finally, the FDR–FMLN demonstrated that it was too strong, both politically and militarily, to be defeated by the Salvadoran military alone. Since it could deny an economic recovery or peace until its political demands were met, the FDR–FMLN retained the power to prohibit a successful centre-right alliance in El Salvador. In sum, El Salvador faced a series of international and domestic vetoes that effectively prevented either military authoritarianism or revolution.

By 1983 this system of vetoes began to translate into crisis for both El Salvador and US foreign policy. Inside El Salvador, the temporary breathing-space opened up by the 1982 elections and the subsequent formation of a government of "National Unity" had closed by January 1983. The FDR–FMLN had launched a highly successful military operation in October 1982; this culminated in an intense campaign at the new year.

The FDR–FMLN offensive, coupled with increased US pressure to hold down human-rights violations, exacerbated existing divisions within the armed forces. Appalled by losses through death and desertion up to 20 per cent of enlisted personnel, and hindered by supply shortages caused by congressional unwillingness to fund the war adequately, the Army Command was torn between a hard-line and a semi-reformist course. An expanding faction, led by Defence Minister García, began to support land reform in order to assure continued access to US aid. The January 1984 rebellion of Lt. Col. Sigifredo Ochoa, supported by the rightist party, Arena, signalled the discontent of the country's ultraconservatives with García's leadership, the continued talk of land reform, and human-rights-related restrictions on US aid. This revolt was terminated only by a delicate military compromise involving the transfer of Ochoa and the eventual removal of García. Although different factions of the army eventually agreed upon General Vides Casanova as the new commander, the fragility of the army's unity could no longer be discounted.

The governing political parties were also deeply divided over the prosecution of the war, the state of the economy, and the extent to which reforms should be permitted. In early 1983, the alliance between Arena and the National Conciliation Party (PCN) – two rightist parties that had dominated the Constituent Assembly since the 1982 elections – collapsed in a shambles, leaving the country virtually ungovernable and weakening the base of Arena and the ultra-right. After considerable turmoil, the Christian Democrats stepped in and, drawing upon their pact-making experience, joined with the PCN to forge a fragile, one-vote working majority in the Assembly. But it is clear that the PCN's association with the Christian Democrats was a stopgap measure, intended to prolong a deadline for the land reform. Crisis erupted at mid-year over the Constituent Assembly's adoption of the new constitution. Arena and the PCN reunited to block future land reform in the constitution, using death-squad threats as part of their "legislative" tactics. In return, the PDC tried to defend its programme of agrarian reform by resorting to the unusual tactic of mobilizing peasants to march into San Salvador. In the tense period that followed, the Christian Democrats were forced to accept a constitution that blocked the PDC party programme by raising barriers to changes in land-tenure patterns.

The Reagan administration faced a similarly bleak situation in 1983. Heightened pressure for political negotiations instead of a military solution came from a variety of sources: the unexpected strength of the FMLN offensive, the deterioration of the Salvadoran military and government, the visit of the Pope to Central America, the formation of the Contadora Group, and the positions of European allies. In addition, US public opinion was strongly opposed to increased military involvement in Central America. Harris Polls from 1982 and 1983 showed that 79 to 85 per cent of the respondents were against the introduction of US troops into El Salvador; this figure dipped to 54 per cent after the invasion of Grenada, but stayed at that level only briefly. To show its displeasure with administration policy, Congress began to block additional US funds to the Salvadoran army, cutting a $60m aid request in half to protest the Salvadoran government's lack of progress in the investigations into the deaths of four church-workers and other US citizens.

In general, support for the Reagan plan of massive military and economic aid aimed at producing military defeat of the opposition had waned badly—a trend the president was unable to reverse through his unusual address to a joint session of Congress in April. Even the May shake-up of the Central America team with the removal of Assistant Secretary of State of Latin America, Thomas O. Enders, the visit of President Magaña to Washington, the formation of the Kissinger Commission, and the roving ambassadorship of Richard Stone did little to stem rising criticism. By November 1983, Reagan was forced to veto a bill that renewed the human rights certification requirements on aid to El Salvador since his own avowals of Salvadoran progress in curbing repression had become a political embarrassment.

As early as March 1983, the Reagan administration was seeking new elections in El Salvador both to escape from its own policy dilemma and to alleviate the country's internal crisis – a tactic that had proved at least temporarily effective in 1982. This time the Reagan administration made certain not to leave their outcome to chance. Fearful that Roberto D'Aubuisson might win an electoral majority, which would permanently jeopardize congressional approval of US aid, and realizing that the Christian Democrats offered the best public relations advantages, the Reagan team poured over $10m into the elections, paying for electoral technology and administration and the air fares of international observers. It gave support funds to the Unión Popular Democrática (UPD), a confederation of unions allied with the AFL–CIO that backed the PDC and cooperated with Venezuela's COPEI government and the

Konrad Adenauer Foundation of West Germany to channel money to the Christian Democrats through a Venezuelan-sponsored public relations firm.[8]

The 1984 electoral results were satisfactory for both the USA and the PDC. In the final run-off between Roberto D'Aubuisson and Napoleón Duarte, the Christian Democratic candidate won 53.6 per cent of the valid votes. The party, which had only nominally governed from 1980 to 1982 and had remained on the political sidelines in 1983, was given another chance.

The Road to Negotiations

The 1984 elections reshaped the political game in El Salvador to the advantage of the PDC, giving its programme the international and domestic credibility it had lacked during the 1980–2 government. Duarte's first task as president was to bring in massive amounts of new funding to finance the war. His success was resounding, indicating a broad range of international support. The Reagan administration, delighted that it finally had an elected ally to present to Congress, sent Duarte to the House and Senate committees that had previously slowed or blocked aid and arranged for him to address the Senate. The new president was an effective campaigner in Washington as well as in El Salvador. Duarte won immediate supplemental military and economic aid. The amount set for the fiscal year 1985 brought the total aid figure secured by the Duarte government to almost half a billion – an amount second only to Israel's. After his Washington stint, Duarte travelled to Europe, where he received aid from West Germany's Christian Democratic government, and from Portugal, Belgium, and Britain.[9] Even France and Mexico, the FDR–FMLN's strongest backers except for its Soviet, Cuban, and Nicaraguan allies, softened their positions toward the new government.

Using this international backing as leverage, Duarte moved quickly to clarify the new conditions that would prevail under his government: the foreign aid the country desperately required depended on curbing the extreme right inside both the armed forces and the political parties. Although in the past, there had been pressures on the military to clean its own house, Duarte's success in Washington brought home the message that to receive substantial increases in US aid El Salvador had to maintain a government acceptable to the US Congress. The Salvadoran Armed Forces, having previously been directly pressured by Vice President Bush, responded positively to this message by restructuring the military command. Four leading rightist officers linked to death-squad activity were transferred to posts outside El Salvador. In addition, the military agreed to dismantle the intelligence unit of the Treasury Police (the reputed centre of death-squad activity) and to separate the command of the regular army from the security forces – a manoeuvre that would bring the security forces under closer governmental control.

Arena also felt immediate pressure to lower its extremist profile. When threats of a plan to overthrow Duarte surfaced, the new president quickly turned to his US allies. In the past, the Reagan administration had been reluctant to intervene against Arena. But the administration took a new stance, dispatching General Vernon Walters – an expert at dealing with recalcitrant militaries – to El Salvador to tell D'Aubuisson that a coup would not be tolerated. In June, the State Department accused D'Aubuisson of complicity in a plot to assassinate Thomas Pickering, US Ambassador to El Salvador, and subsequently denied D'Aubuisson a visa to enter the USA. Reagan feared that the ultra-right might upset the US diplomatic victory represented by the 1984 elections and demonstrated that his government now had a stake in Duarte's success: Arena would have to play by the recently established party rules or risk the open wrath of the region's dominant power. Since US displeasure centred on D'Aubuisson's notoriety, new divisions began to appear in Arena over D'Aubuisson's future role in the party. Some conservatives turned their support to other rightist parties, such as the PCN.

Thus Duarte's election marked an important shift in the balance of power among the USA, the Salvadoran Armed Forces, and the Christian Democrats. In a sense, the least powerful member of this alliance – the PDC – temporarily gained the upper hand. While this realignment did advance democratization by propelling party politics into a more central role and restricting state violence, the actual changes it introduced were still quite tentative. The private sector continued to block land reform in the Constituent Assembly and to oppose the attempts of workers and peasants to organize. Death-squad activities slowed but did not stop. The Duarte government knew it was walking a fine line. As rumours of a leadership purge based on political sympathies spread throughout the armed forces, one high commander publicly warned, "If it stops here, it is okay, but if it continues, it could become worrisome."[10]

Yet the new president could not stop at this point if he wanted to succeed in the future elections. Despite his initial actions, Duarte faced intense pressure from his party and electoral base. Worker and peasant organizations grew increasingly angry at his constant efforts to placate landowners at their expense. Impatient for change and trusting that repression would slacken under the new government, these groups became more active after the 1984 election. Strikes and labour disputes increased at an alarming rate and demanded solutions.[11] At the same time, trouble arose in the PDC's relations with the UPD, an umbrella organization of labour federations and peasant unions that had faithfully backed Duarte in the past. In the 1984 elections, the Christian Democrats had given promises of accelerated land reform in exchange for the UPD's support. But the PDC found itself unable to keep this commitment. Although Christian Democratic leaders argued that the peasant unions would have to build support for the party in order to win a majority in the 1985 Assembly elections that could reintroduce the land reform programme, the Secretary-General of the nation's largest peasant union publicly threatened to withdraw support from the PDC if it did not deliver on its promises.

Other factors weakened the PDC's hold on its electoral base. The 1984 elections had communicated an important message: the party's constituency, and the Salvadoran population in general, favoured some form of political negotiations with the opposition to bring peace and economic recovery, and the party did not seem to be making progress in this area. Pre-election polls showed that 70 per cent of all Salvadorans considered the war and the economy to be the country's principal problems; 51.4 per cent favoured dialogue as the best means of resolving the war – a surprisingly high percentage to be openly expressing agreement with what was the formal position of the FDR–FMLN. Only 10.3 per cent advocated military annihilation of the armed opposition, while just 10 per cent called for a military intervention by the USA.[12]

One does not have to look far for the underlying causes of these trends in public opinion. The rapid deterioration of the economy since 1979 had dramatically affected the living standard of most Salvadorans. The price index rose about 25 per cent per year. Yet since 1980, wages had been frozen by government decree: between 1979 and 1983, real minimum wages declined by 65 per cent and consumption levels by 50 per cent. Almost 80 per cent of the population was either unemployed or underemployed.[13] The war and the uncontained human rights abuses had taken an additional toll on the country. By 1984, it was generally acknowledged that there had been over 50 000 deaths and over 1.3 million persons displaced in this country of only 5 million inhabitants. Faced with extreme poverty and war, the popular base of the Christian Democratic Party was clamouring for some visible and significant change.

Thus the 1984 electoral victory created a painful dilemma for the governing party. On the one hand, it was restricted by its key allies – the USA and the Salvadoran military – who had been opposed to any form of negotiations with the FDR–FMLN. On the other hand, its electoral base had given Duarte a mandate to negotiate. To the extent that voters had been free to choose – given the exclusion of the FDR–FMLN and the abstention or failure to vote by a third of the eligible electorate – they had voiced a preference for a programme of reforms, an end to the war, the termination of human rights abuses, an opening toward the FDR–FMLN, and the defence of the right of association.[14] Throughout the campaign, Duarte had claimed that D'Aubuisson had produced nothing but economic chaos and death during his 21-month tenure as president of the Constituent Assembly. The alternative Duarte had offered – the linchpin of his campaign – was a *"pacto social"*, a government that would reconcile and integrate all Salvadorans into an effective plan for peace. Now Duarte had to deliver on this promise or else be vulnerable to the same charges he had levelled at D'Aubuisson.

Compounding all these difficulties was the continued pressure of the FDR–FMLN. It engaged in a heavy sabotage campaign through June and July, repeatedly seized control of the nation's roads, and launched a spectacular attack on the Cerron Grande dam, demonstrating a military capability that surprised US advisers Despite a lull in combat as the FMLN adjusted to an escalated air war – and despite frequent pronouncements in the US press about the new successes of the Salvadoran armed forces – the enormous influx of aid following Duarte's election did not appear to diminish the opposition's capacity to continue fighting and disrupting the economy. The FDR–FMLN made its position clear: there would be no peace or economic prosperity until the fundamental issues of the distribution of power and wealth were resolved.

The Christian Democratic leadership was aware that the period of grace opened up by the presidential elections would soon expire: the Constitutent Assembly elections scheduled for March 1985 would determine the fate of reform and of the PDC. If the party could not gain majority control of the legislature, it could not hope to implement a land reform. Its tenuous position was obvious. As PDC leader Eduardo Molina explained:

> There is no military solution to our conflict now, unless it is a military
> victory by the guerrillas. . . If we continue to attempt to resolve
> the conflict militarily, we will lose. Only a dialogue and eventual
> incorporation of democratic elements of the left into our ranks offer
> any exit for us now.[15]

President Duarte, faced with another election and pushed from
all sides, saw only one way out. The guerrillas had an apparently
limitless capacity to maintain the war, while the PDC position could
only deteriorate if the party failed to show some results before the
1985 Assembly elections. A coup by the right or a victory by the
left perpetually threatened to bring down the Christian Democrats
or to provoke a US military intervention – which from the viewpoint
of the PDC's nationalist members would be a disaster. Yet continued
backing from the USA, if it could be contained, was critical. Duarte
understood that the two leading forces historically opposed to
negotiations – the Salvadoran military and the Reagan
administration – needed him in order to extract aid from the sceptical
US Congress. Especially with US elections around the corner, and
with the Contadora process revitalized by Nicaragua's acceptance
of a regional peace agreement, the Reagan administration could not
oppose Duarte. After surprisingly little consultation with the USA,
Duarte gambled on his own indispensability to US and Salvadoran
hard-liners: in a dramatic speech to the United Nations, he invited
the FDR–FMLN to negotiate.

Negotiations and the 1985 Assembly Elections

In early 1985, the prospects for democracy, peace, and reform in
El Salvador were greater than at any moment since the outbreak of
civil war. The political stalemate in the USA over policy toward
Central America and the military stalemate that has prevailed in
El Salvador since 1983 began to create a different set of probable
political outcomes and to change the perceptions of most important
political actors. What was new in El Salvador's political equation
was the temporary increase in the PDC's autonomy, as marked by
the La Palma and Ayagualo talks. The FDR–FMLN, having openly
called for negotiations since 1981, responded promptly to Duarte's
invitation. Although the FDR–FMLN may have believed in the
possibility of an all-out military victory just after the Sandinista
defeat of Somoza in nearby Nicaragua, those heady days had passed

and for some time the FDR–FMLN had been ready to discuss a settlement.

Unexpectedly, some factions of El Salvador's traditional oligarchic alliance also gave tentative backing to the Duarte initiative. Affected by international pressure and the strains of continued combat with the FDR–FMLN, the Armed Forces initially agreed to attend talks with the opposition, though it insisted that all discussions be limited to the parameters established by the 1983 constitution. Certain groups in the agrarian private sector also gave Duarte's initiative lukewarm approval – a departure from their attitude in the past, when they feared the Christian Democrats as much as or more than the FDR–FMLN. Suffering economic losses and aware that they were losing their historic grip on the military, some agrarian élites increasingly resorted to conservative political parties rather than death-squads to represent their interests and to control the rural poor.

Yet the barriers to democratization remained great. The majority of the military and the ultra-right did not commit themselves to negotiations. Conservative army officers were reported to have privately criticized Duarte for his decision to open talks with the FDR–FMLN and demanded that the president refuse to discuss military activities, the combining of the Salvadoran army with the guerrilla army, and any form of power-sharing – the basic issues facing the country.

During the actual negotiations, the distance between Christian Democratic and FDR–FMLN visions of democracy represented another substantial obstacle to compromise. As we have seen, the Christian Democrats emphasized élite pact-making generally with parties of the right, electoral mechanisms, clientelistic relationships, the importance of individual political rights over the right of workers and peasants to organize, and slow reform. The competing vision of the FDR, whose members span a political spectrum from dissident Christian Democrats to Marxists, was mass-based and stressed political organization and mobilization as tools to achieve rapid socioeconomic reform. Within the FDR–FMLN itself, there were disagreements over the most desirable type of political regime, with some guerrilla factions contending that a Leninist party was a viable model for the future – a view not shared by the majority of the leadership of the FDR.

These distant visions created substantively different interpre–tations both of the current situation in El Salvador and of the steps necessary to achieve a basic compromise. On the one hand, Duarte's government maintained that profound changes had actually taken place between 1979 and 1985: that human rights violations were slowly being brought under control, that the anti-democratic character of the armed forces had changed, that the power of the landowners had been broken, and that all political parties – including those of the opposition could now participate freely in fair elections. Asserting that the conditions that brought about civil war no longer existed, Duarte offered a general amnesty to the FDR–FMLN if it would lay down its arms, assistance in resettling those who wished to leave the country, and the right to participate freely in future elections based on rules established by the 1983 Constitution. In Duarte's view, the basic rules of the 1983 Constitution could not be abridged.

The FDR–FMLN offered a radically different interpretation. While agreeing with Duarte that certain changes had occurred in El Salvador, it maintained that the military and the death-squads continued their systematic violations of human rights, that land reform had been blocked, and that as long as the country's repressive forces remained intact, the safety of opposition leaders and supporters could not be guaranteed during an election. Rejecting a settlement based on the 1983 constitution, which was designed without their participation under the leadership of Roberto D'Aubuisson, FDR–FMLN leaders offered a three-stage plan, to be implemented over an extended period. In the first phase, the government would present a concrete formula to guarantee security, end human rights violations, stop weapons imports, and send US advisers out of the country. In exchange, the FDR–FMLN would agree to an arms freeze and to the termination of economic sabotage. During the second phase, there would be a formal cease-fire, with territorial concessions to both rebel and government forces. The final phase would include a broad national dialogue, the formation of a new government, a new constitution, and the reorganization of the armed forces. Only at this point would national elections be held.[16]

The actions of the US government exacerbated the distance between El Salvador's power contenders. The Reagan administration refused to lend solid backing to negotiations, encouraged an escalation of the war in the days following the La Palma talks, and sought to weaken the position of political forces that called for dialogue. Worried by the "leftist tilt" of mass organizations allied with the Christian Democratic government, US officials fomented a split in the UPD and subsequently created a new, less reformist, union which openly competed with Duarte's labour base. When the government continued to resist US pressure to implement an economic programme which favoured traditional economic élites,

US embassy officials began to talk openly of the desirability of a victory by the right in the 1985 elections "to give balance to El Salvador's democracy".[17] In addition, the Central Intelligence Agency refrained from providing funds to the Christian Democrats for electoral support as it had in the past. By early 1985, relations between the USA and its PDC allies dropped to their lowest point, exacerbated by differences over economic policy.

The Reagan administration's response to dialogue and its subsequent criticism of the Duarte government encouraged a renewed political challenge from the right. The army, disabusing the government of its notions of civilian control over the military, refused to abide by Christmas truce agreements negotiated by President Duarte and the rebel leaders. The High Command subsequently set extremely narrow parameters on the president's freedom to negotiate, conditioning its support of the government upon these limitations. It ruled out any formal cease-fire, declared that purely military matters were out of the hands of the executive, and specified that any future settlement be based strictly on the 1983 Constitution – a document drawn up largely by the ultra-right. Without US pressure on the Salvadoran Armed Forces, the Duarte government alone could do nothing to win greater flexibility or exercise control over the military.

In March, in the midst of the build-up of these complex tensions within the US/Armed Forces/Duarte government alliance, the Christian Democratic Party swept the legislative elections in an unexpectedly large victory. It gained a small majority in the sixty-seat legislature, thus overturning the rightist veto of the past, and won control of over 200 of El Salvador's 262 municipalities. Although the issue of negotiations was carefully kept out of the campaign, Duarte had unquestionably gained popularity through his peace initiative. In addition, the Christian Democrats benefited from a combination of other factors: their control over the resources of the bureaucracy, the electoral neutrality of the army, certain changes in electoral laws, the tendency of Salvadorans to vote "*oficialista*" and deep divisions within ARENA.[18]

On the surface, the 1985 Assembly elections represented the culmination of the Christian Democratic Party's bid for power. For the first time, the party controlled both the executive and the legislative branches. More impressive, immediately following the vote it won a dramatic public expression of support from the Salvadoran Armed Forces. When a coalition of ARENA and the PCN tried to challenge the electoral results in order to retain their control of the legislature, the entire Army High Command made an unprecedented public appearance to rebuff the manoeuvre of the ultra-right and demand an end to partisan struggles "in the face of a common enemy". Given its popular mandate and its apparent control over the central institutions of the state, it appeared that the PDC could finally and effectively implement its programme of democratization and agrarian reform which had been blocked since 1980.

The formal governmental picture, however, was deceptive. Despite three elections between 1982 and 1985, power resided in a struggle between forces that did not formally participate in the electoral process and which owed no permanent allegiance to the Christian Democratic government – the US/Salvadoran Armed Forces, on the one hand, and the FDR–FMLN, on the other. Each side retained a powerful veto over government policy since neither of the central issues facing the country – the economy and the war – could be alleviated without their cooperation. With elections out of the way, the political–electoral cycle began to reverse itself. The Christian Democratic Party, having once been pushed into initiating peace talks to placate its electoral constituency, now shifted to the right as it sought to govern with its allies – the USA, the Armed Forces, and the private sector.

Once the elections were over, the Army High Command promptly clarified the parameters of acceptable policy space for political and military matters. It would support the construction of a formal democratic order, even one dominated by Christian Democracy, as long as Duarte kept to the letter of the conservative 1983 Constitution and limited dialogue with the FDR–FMLN to the procedural aspects of incorporation into future elections. In its view, a negotiated end to the war, the formation of a new government, or the integration of El Salvador's two armies were not issues for discussion.

The parameters of economic policy were also largely pre-established for President Duarte. The Salvadoran economy had become completely dependent on US aid which was conditioned upon economic policies acceptable to the Reagan administration. Immediately following the election, Duarte began to cede ground to the USA and traditional Salvadoran élites by devaluing the colón, providing huge incentives to the coffee-growers, and channelling major portion of development funds into the traditional private sector – measures contrary to the campaign promises of 1984–5. Although Duarte sought to implement a tax reform which would affect economic élites, they continuously attempted to block his efforts. Indeed, emboldened by their access to an extraordinary level of US funds, these élites also renewed their pressure against a negotiated settlement or a political opening and for an eventual military victory over the FDR–FMLN.[19]

If Duarte's room for manoeuvre in the government was surprisingly limited, the electoral picture presented by the Christian Democratic victory was also deceptive. Although the party had won by a surprisingly large margin, the 1985 election was characterized by a sharp decline in voter turnout. Of the 2.7 million eligible voters, less than 1 million actually voted – a drop of one-third compared with the 1984 election. Approximately 17 per cent of the ballots that had been cast were spoiled or invalid. The increase in non-voters appeared to reflect either sympathy with the FDR–FMLN or a growing disillusionment with the government.[20] Since President Duarte could no longer tell his constituents that a rightist veto in the legislature was responsible for policy failures, this trend was bound to increase in the future if the Christian Democratics could not deliver on their campaign promises of peace, land, political rights and jobs. Paradoxically, by winning formal control of the executive and the legislature during a civil war, the Duarte administration now had the most to lose.

Christian Democracy, US Policy and the Future of Democracy in El Salvador

There is no viable political democracy in El Salvador today, despite the semi-competitive elections that took place in 1982, 1984, and 1985. Democracy depends on the achievement of a compromise protected by law – a fundamental agreement over a set of secure rules that determine who wins and who loses, that guarantee the game can be played again in the future, and that set the broad parameters of a model for economic development. Clearly, such an agreement has not been reached. Nonetheless, this period is especially instructive for demonstrating the dilemmas of the so-called centrist option in this deeply divided country. To the extent that the Christian Democratic Party moves towards a political settlement to the civil war, it solidifies its electoral base but runs head-on into the opposition of the armed forces, the oligarchy, and, most important, the USA. To the extent that it eschews negotiations and lends its weight to the war effort, it alienates the party base.

In the end, though, the ability to tilt forces and events toward a political solution in El Salvador lies beyond the control of the PDC. Despite Duarte's insistence upon a national solution for national problems, it is the USA that frames the structure of incentives that either encourage or discourage democratization. For this reason, the Reagan administration's encouragement to the military to escalate the war just after the La Palma talks seriously undermined the tentative and fragile move towards negotiations. Supporting the assumption of Salvadoran military officers that "there are times when you have to make war to achieve peace", the administration provided the Salvadoran Air Force with new helicopter gunships specially designed for attacking FDR–FMLN strongholds and, for the first time, allowed US military operations whose explicit purpose was to sabotage the talks.[21] Reagan officials have played down the significance of a dialogue, requested new increases in military aid, and reiterated their claim that the armed forces could defeat the FDR–FMLN by 1986, despite indications to the contrary.

To actors inside El Salvador, these steps, when combined with a series of inadequate and rhetorical US responses to violent actions by the ultra-right, demonstrate the intention of the Reagan administration to seek a military victory – a posture that only threatens efforts toward compromise.[22] The Reagan administration's logic is, of course, to force the FDR–FMLN to accept Duarte's terms for negotiation. But the effect is precisely the opposite. US-sponsored militarization merely increases the incentives for the anti-democratic right to seek a "winning" solution while decreasing the probability of democratization through compromise.

In the final analysis, ironically, the policies of the administration may breathe new political strength into the FDR–FMLN while simultaneously undercutting the Christian Democratic Party by leaving its only "acceptable" ally to pay the political price of ongoing civil war. As long as FDR–FMLN cannot be eliminated – an act that would require the involvement of US troops – the pressure to implement a negotiated settlement lies most heavily on the Christian Democratic government. In the long run, continuing the war would favour the FDR–FMLN – a fact recognized by all contending forces. The rebels do not have to win the war; they simply need to remain strong enough to prevent the consolidation of any regime that might intend to exclude them. "The heart of this is the war", one opposition delegate remarked at La Palma, "and we are not losing the war."[23] Indeed, attempts by the Duarte government to eliminate the opposition by military means end up weakening the Christian Democrats more than they do the rebels. Bombing by the Air Force, and army sweeps into contested territory are currently the cause of civilian deaths; the PDC government is held accountable for these attacks, which are unlikely to increase its popularity among the people who are affected. Moreover, La Palma has opened a political space that now cannot easily be closed, despite the intensification of the war on other fronts. If the government claims that democracy and the rule of law now prevail in El Salvador, it can no longer rely on repression and maintain its credibility. Instead, it must address the buregoning demands for reform and peace from labour, peasant organizations and Christian base communities or risk electoral and other setbacks down the road.

Eventually the growing untenability of the government's position and current US policy will most likely force stark choices on US policy-makers: to support dialogue and a negotiated settlement or to face increasing involvement and the eventual prospect of sending US combat troops to El Salvador to attempt to eliminate the FDR–FMLN. As long as domestic and international opposition to a US war in Central America translates into a congressional majority that prohibits a military solution, democracy via negotiations is still on the agenda. Thus if Congress or a new administration takes a more positive stance by cutting military aid and tying increases in economic support funds to progress in negotiations, human rights and socioeconomic reforms, it can tie the hands of the ultra-right and encourage the eventual incorporation of the opposition – steps which keep alive the possibility of a democratic outcome. In the past, Congress has successfully, albeit sporadically, demonstrated to the military and the ultra-right that it will not support forces that systematically violate human rights in order to block reform – a stance that once helped to create the political space for the La Palma talks. It can do so again.

The prerequisite to successful negotiations is the recognition by all sides of a military and political stalemate after seven years of war whose basic parameters are unlikely to change, given the mutual vetoes in place from the USA and the FDR–FMLN. With encouragement from the hegemonic power in the region, this recognition could lead key contending actors to accept a "second-best" solution, one which guarantees the political survival of all parties and the permanent victory of none. Once negotiations begin on the nature of this "second-best" solution, any faction that chooses not to play the democratic game could be isolated from domestic and international support. Those groups that refuse to compromise and continue to fight for the restoration of the past or the implementation of a non-democratic model in the future could be effectively marginalized.

Negotiations do imply, however, that the USA might have to accept a "second-best" solution as well. Indeed, if negotiations are successful, the USA could be faced with a democratic compromise in El Salvador that is significantly more broad in scope, participatory in means, and indigenous in content than previous Latin American democracies. This new democracy, forged through a compromise between warring parties, could play an important role in mitigating regional tensions. While this outcome is optimistic, given the traditional forces against change in Central America and the militarist cast of Reagan policy toward the region, the alternative is a civil and regional war without resolution that is strongly opposed by the Salvadoran population. In the USA, efforts by the Reagan or any other administration to maintain the war at a low level in order to avoid a difficult political solution will result at minimum in continuing battles with Congress and at a maximum in a US military intervention strongly opposed by the majority of Americans. In El Salvador, it will produce continuing devastation. Faced with these choices, an uncertain democracy in El Salvador might not look so bad.

Notes

1. This chapter is a revised, condensed, and updated version of "After La Palma: The Prospects for Democratization in El Salvador", *World Policy Journal* (Spring 1985). To save space, citations providing general references have been omitted. Also see "Imposing Consent? Electoralism *vs* Democratization in El Salvador", by the same author in Paul Drake and Eduardo Silva (eds) *Elections and Democratization in Latin America, 1980–1985* (San Diego: University of California, Center for Iberian and Latin American Studies, 1986).
2. For a historical description of the party, see Stephen Webre, *José Napoleón Duarte and the Christian Democratic Party in Salvadoran Politics, 1960–1972.*
3. This treatment of Christian Democratic democratization strategy is drawn from interviews conducted by the author in El Salvador, Mexico, and Venezuela. Discussions with Napoleón Duarte, Fidel Chávez Mena (PDC), Héctor Dada (former leader of the PDC), José Miguel Fritis (IVEPO), Rafael Caldera, (former president, Venezuela) and José Rodríguez Iturbe (CAREF, Venezuela) were particularly useful.
4. Interview with Napoleón Duarte, San Salvador, October 1983. This description of the influence of the Venezuelan model of democratization was also drawn from interviews with COPEI members and officials from the Foreign Ministry and CARE in Caracas, Venezuela, November 1983.
5. On 3 August 1983, the PDC, ARENA, the PCN, and the PPS signed this agreement as a means of easing tensions and reaching some form

of governability during the civil war. The pact pledged to lower the level of inter-party disputes, established a timetable for a new constitution and the next elections, and set up a political commission to work out disagreements. See Thomas R. Campos, "El Pacto de Apaneca, Un Proyecto para la Transición", ECA, September, 1982.

6. Interview with José Miguel Fritis, Chilean Christian Democrat working in IVEPO, San Salvador, October 1983.
7. Raymond Bonner, *Weakness and Deceit: US Policy and El Salvador* (New York: Times Books, 1984) pp. 290–3.
8. The US government also gave money to the PCN to help to draw votes away from ARENA, *Boston Globe*, 4 May 1984; *Time Magazine*, 21 May 1984. Interview in IVEPO, San Salvador, October 1983.
9. For a report on Duarte's international trip and subsequent aid statistics, see *Central American Bulletin*, July–August 1984, and *Latin America Weekly Report*, 27 July 1984.
10. *New York Times*, 25 May 1984.
11. This was the first strike activity in El Salvador since the virulent repression against the labour movement began in 1980. See the *Central American Bulletin*, July–August 1984.
12. See Ignacio Martín-Baró and Victor Antonio Orellana, "La Necesidad de Votar: Actitudes del Pueblo Salvadoreño ante el Proceso Electoral de 1984", *Estudios Centroamericanos: Las Elecciones Presidenciales de 1984*, April–May 1984, pp. 255–6. This entire edition contains several excellent analyses of the 1984 elections.
13. See Segundo Montes, "Condicionamientos Socio-Políticos del Proceso Electoral", *Estudios Centroamericanos*, April–May 1984 and *NACLA Report on the Americas*, vol. 18, no 2 (March–April 1984).
14. Ricardo Chacón, "Las Campañas de los Partidos", in *Estudios Centroamericanos*, April–May 1984, pp. 229–52.
15. *Christian Science Monitor*, 8 March 1984. Similar views were also expressed by President Duarte in *Playboy*, October 1984, and by leading party officials in interviews held in San Salvador, October 1983.
16. See FDR–FMLN Political–Diplomatic Commission, La Palma: A Hope for Peace, November 1984.
17. *New York Times*, 12 May 1985; interview with Political Officer, US Embassy, April 1985.
18. Interview with PDC leader Adolfo Rey Prendes, San Salvador, April, 1985; interview with Hugo Barrera, former member of ARENA, San Salvador, April 1985.
19. Interview with official of ANEP, San Salvador, April 1985.
20. *Central America Bulletin*, June 1985, p. 7. Interview with high-level Christian Democrat, April 1985.
21. *Washington Post*, 19 October 1984.
22. A week before the La Palma talks, Under-secretary of Defence Fred Iklé announced that the Salvadoran military had broken a long stalemate with guerrilla forces and could "neutralize" the insurgents by the end of 1984. *New York Times*, 7 October 1984. General Paul Gorman, the

commander of US military forces in Latin America, has maintained that the Salvadoran military could have 80 to 90 per cent of the country under control within two years if Congress approved sufficient military aid. These comments, taken in the context of mild responses to new activity by the ultra-right – the mobilization of Colonel Ochoa in La Palma the day before the first talks, death-squad threats against President Duarte and members of the private sector for favouring negotiations, and the acquittal of a known rightist officer widely believed to have murdered two US officials – keep alive the hope of a military solution in El Salvador.

23. *New York Times*, 6 December 1984.

The Impact of Revolutionary Transition on the Popular Classes: The Working Class in the Sandinista Revolution

Carlos M. Vilas

This article analyses several aspects of the Sandinista revolution's impact on the popular classes which are its main support.[1] Most studies of revolutionary processes emphasize the effects of revolutionary policies on the old ruling classes. However, little is known about changes affecting the popular classes during the transition, such as socio-demographic variation, their political and economic claims, levels and styles of organization, and strategies for accomplishing desired goals. This article seeks to enhance understanding of this aspect of the Sandinista revolution in Nicaragua.

The word *transition* generally refers to the transformation leading to socialism: thus it is anti-capitalistic in context. It would be difficult to call the Sandinista revolution (in its present stage) anti-capitalist. Instead, it is an anti-oligarchical, anti-imperialist national liberation revolution, whose major aims are to affirm national sovereignty, develop productive forces and improve the standards of living of the popular majority – all within a framework of a mixed economy, class coexistence and popular participation. The transition is from underdevelopment to greater justice, social well-being, development, and nationalist self-determination, within a national and popular, rather than a proletarian and socialist, framework.

This chapter examines the revolution's impact on the popular classes in general, and on the working class in particular. The peasant and urban informal sectors are outside the chapter's focus, although they inevitably arise indirectly.

The Popular Classes at the Time of the Sandinista Triumph

At the end of the 1970s, Nicaragua was an agrarian society in economic, though not in demographic, terms. While nearly 50 per cent of the population lived in urban centres, almost 80 per cent of production was generated by agriculture. In Central America at the end of the 1970s, only Costa Rica had a smaller percentage of its economically active population (EAP) in agriculture.[2]

Agro-export capitalism created a complex class structure in Nicaragua, and an unevenly developed proletariat. Proletarianization was greater in the country than in the cities; more extensive in agro-export sectors than in production for domestic markets. Furthermore, export-oriented agricultural employment was subject to strong seasonal fluctuations. On the eve of the revolutionary triumph, class structure in the countryside was dominated numerically by poor peasants lacking sufficient land to provide for family needs, forced to support their families through seasonal labour in export activities. Approximately 40 per cent of the economically active rural population (around 165 000 people) fell into this category. There was also a rural proletariat, largely in agro-export activities, which constituted nearly 30 per cent of the rural EAP (around 125 000), so that nearly 70 per cent of the EAP was made up of proletariat and poor peasants. The rest of the rural population consisted of middle income and rich peasants and a very tiny agrarian bourgeoisie. Representing approximately 20 per cent of the rural EAP, the middle and upper peasantry generated nearly half of agricultural production and owned more than half the farmed land.[3]

In the cities, the proletariat working in production and basic services numbered approximately 130 000 workers, or 20 per cent of the urban EAP; however, less than half of these were industrial proletariat. But small employment growth from industrialization occurred during the 1960s within the framework of the Central American Common Market. A large share of the burgeoning urban EAP was directed towards self-employment, handicrafts, small business and personal services. At the start of the 1970s, nearly 70 per cent of the industrial sector consisted of artisans and only 6 per cent were actually industrial workers, though the meagre available information indicates a relatively rapid deterioration and proletarianization of artisan production. On the eve of the revolution, nearly 50 per cent of Managua's EAP belonged to the urban informal sector (UIS). Since most industrial plants were in Managua and its immediate environs, it can be assumed that the relative influence of the UIS was even greater in other cities.

Medium-scale production was not so pronounced in the industrial sector as in the country. Almost from the inception of industrial production, capital, production, and the labour force in that sector were heavily concentrated. In 1979, 75 per cent of employment and 86 per cent of total aggregate value came from the largest establishments, which represented 17 per cent of all industrial establishments.[4]

The socio-demographic and occupational profile was reflected in the revolutionary movement by the high participation of the popular groups in the urban insurrection. The Sandinista revolution is more a revolution of the poor than of the proletariat. The FSLN was stronger in the neighbourhoods than in the factories. At the same time, there were proportionately more workers involved in producing the new society (the insurrection) than in reproducing the old society (the economy).[5]

The Sandinista revolution evolved through a rural guerrilla stage to the final urban insurrection, but there was never a peasant guerrilla movement such as that seen in China, Algeria, Angola and Mozambique, Vietnam, El Salvador, and parts of Guatemala. Those revolutions were characterized by liberated zones with organized civil life and developed production systems. In Nicaragua, the mountains were the "crucible where the best cadres were formed",[6] but the decisive blows were struck in the cities. Political power, like the population, became urbanized in Nicaragua.

Popular Classes and State Policies: Intervening Factors

Various elements have intervened in the revolutionary state's policies towards the popular classes. We may divide these roughly into four: (i) the way the FSLN and the revolutionary government conceived of certain classes and fractions within those classes in their political design; (ii) the previously described uneven urbanization process; (iii) adoption of a mixed economy in which the state became the dynamic accumulation axis; (iv) external pressures and tensions, including, primarily, the counter-revolutionary war pushed by the US government.

(i) Characterization of Various Segments of the Popular Classes   Any state policy directed toward a particular social group must be based on an explicit or implicit characterization of that group: who its members are, what position they occupy within the social structure, their claims, interests and demands. In Nicaragua, attention has been given mainly to "intermediate" groups within capitalist social polarization, i.e. groups that define their identity by criteria other than material production alone. These would include:

the poor peasantry and landless workers, the informal urban sector, and the indigenous population of the Atlantic region.

Toward the end of the insurrection and early in the revolutionary government, the tendency was to treat everyone as part of the proletariat. In a popular and anti-imperialist revolution, it was easy to conclude that these groups would eventually melt into the working class. Thus, they were a kind of incipient proletariat.

Several factors seem to have helped to create this interpretation. In the case of the poor peasantry, such a view encouraged seasonal hiring of labour in the agro-export sector or for personal services in urban areas or small towns. The salary obtained through seasonal employment was considered vital for family sustenance. The function of the smallholding was simply to tide the worker over to the next harvest, relieving the capitalist of maintenance expenses during the non-productive season. To quote Lenin, this was a type of "salary in kind".[7] Thus, the poor peasant could be characterized as a semi-proletarian.

The informal urban sector was considered part of the proletariat because the working class was defined as including all the poor, e.g. manual labourers and people employed at various tasks but who lacked stable employment or income. This concept was widespread within the Sandinista Front, in the Marxist cultural politics of pre-revolutionary Nicaragua and in the early years of the revolution. It doubtless expressed the type of capitalist development and urbanization which occurred after the Second World War, but also reflected the participation of the impoverished masses from the cities in the final insurrection.[8]

Finally, generalized ignorance of ethnic matters led to a strictly material focus regarding the country's Indians, who were seen as impoverished farmers, workers in the mines and lumber companies, exploited by foreign capital and traders. They were viewed only as producers, while ignoring cultural elements that differentiated them from the poor of other ethnic identities. The revolution initially stressed salaries and the extreme poverty of the indigenous labour force on one hand; on the other hand, it interpreted cooperative production practices, the non-inheritance of property, and distribution of the fruits of production among all villagers as vestiges of primitive communism.

This focus led to policy decisions meant to accelerate or consolidate the proletarianization of these groups and fractions. Both the poor peasantry and the Indian villagers were included in the Association of Farm Workers (Asociación de Trabajadores del Campo; ATC), together with the rural proletariat. Cooperative organization, based on these groups' supposed collective culture, was promoted. The poor peasantry later had its own organization, but the case of the Indians was more complex. Also, attempts to introduce some type of organization for the informal sector failed, though initially a sizeable part of this group joined the Sandinista Defense Committees (CDSs).

Although these remarks describe the revolutionary state's main approach to these fractions, certain technical sectors within the movement held an opposing viewpoint. In their view, the large peasant mass made substantial contributions to production, including agro-export production.[9] Some argued that there was virtually no agricultural proletariat.[10] This perspective implied that there was virtually no working class in Nicaragua.

In its simplest terms, the first viewpoint led to postponing land demands by calling them petty bourgeois, inefficient, backward-looking. The second viewpoint, however, de-emphasized the question of wages. In the best Sandinista style, polar positions finally fused into policy measures which attempted to articulate the best elements of both sides, although one or the other tended to prevail at any given time.[11]

(ii) Uneven Urbanization   The Sandinista Revolution has sometimes been called an urban revolution in a rural country. This is because many policies of the revolution, especially those meant to raise living standards of the popular classes, were oriented more towards the cities than the country. Chief beneficiaries from those policies, then, were not the workers – who constituted an urban minority – but the informal sector, lower white-collar employees, and the middle class.

On the other hand, structural policies of the revolutionary government, meant to cause profound socio-economic change, are perforce rurally oriented. Large accumulation projects, designed to transform relations of production and develop productive forces, are geared towards agriculture: agrarian reform, agro-export development projects, and others. The same is true of Sandinista social development programmes, such as literacy, adult education, and expansion of health services.

Nonetheless, many of the immediate benefits were quickly appropriated by city-dwellers even though the costs were shared by all. Certainly urban dwellers could take better advantage of social policies, although, as described below, emphasis was directed towards the countryside. When economic crisis and other limiting factors appeared, the cities offered more alternatives for adaptation to the new situation.

Perhaps the most notorious example is the case of consumer subsidies, which began with the revolutionary government and continued until early 1985 – though some still remain. Subsidies were established as a way to reconcile farm income and consumer needs; however, more attention was given to the income of the urban masses pressured by inflation, resulting in a deterioration of real farm-product prices and a decline in farm income, while consumer prices remained frozen.

Similarly, landless farmers were forbidden to take over land, while spontaneous settlements were allowed to be established on urban terrain. While one branch of the state discouraged direct actions by landless farmers, other branches of the same state quickly furnished construction materials, water, connections to electricity, and other services to urban land invaders.

This is not the first time a social revolution in an agrarian society has had such results. People in the cities can generally exercise more pressure: they are nearer to each other and generally interact more. They are also closer to the seat of government; thus governments are always attentive to the opinion of the urban popular sectors. Furthermore, the country's few professional cadres live in the cities, and it is considered important to improve their living conditions.

Another, perhaps more important, factor in Nicaragua is the urban insurrection's decisive role in overthrowing dictatorship. Although the economy is agrarian, half the population is not. Major operations in the critical state of the revolution did not take place in an agrarian setting. The common people became involved in the revolution in the belief that their lives would improve: investments in urban development of the neighbourhoods of Managua, Leon, Masaya, etc., doubtless discriminated against rural populations, and may have indirectly stimulated migration to the cities, but these measures can hardly be called excessive, extravagant, or inopportune.

(iii) The Strategy of a Mixed Economy with the State as the Dynamic Axis of Accumulation
The revolution's social base is a broad alliance which includes not only the working class, the peasantry and the urban and rural poor, but also the middle classes and patriotic bourgeoisie. This multiclass concept, which Sandinista political discourse calls national unity, is a correlate of the mixed economy strategy.

This means, first, that relations between the revolutionary

government and popular classes are included in the more complex set of relations that the revolutionary government hopes to maintain with the bourgeoisie and middle classes whose interests are, at some level, contradictory to worker and peasant interests. Thus, the pace and content of policies beneficial to the popular classes may be subordinated to the need to maintain broad alliances with these other sectors, making hegemony of the masses a secondary consideration.

A second issue is that elements of the popular classes may agree with elements of the propertied classes in certain areas. For instance, a vertical alliance of agrarian producers – peasants, middle producers and the large agrarian bourgeoisie – on credit policies, rural input supply, and other matters, could counter urban consumer claims, including those of the urban proletariat and small artisans, but excluding farm workers.

Third, multiclass features may be repeated within the state sector, the revolutionary government and the FSLN themselves. There was varying concern within the revolutionary government as to how satisfaction of certain popular demands would affect behaviour of the patriotic bourgeoisie. Repeated reference to poor labour discipline, unmatched by similar concern for employer discipline as well as the mechanical association of higher wage demands and increased inflation reflect an entrepreneurial vision within many state cadres and in the FSLN, as well as the idea that more can be expected of workers' patience than of employers' patriotism.

The state's efforts to curb worker and peasant movements against decapitalization by the agrarian and industrial bourgeoisie in 1981, reflects the fact that such demonstrations alarmed those bourgeois sectors that were not decapitalizing, but who feared ideological questioning of private property. The slow application of agrarian reform between 1981 and 1983, can also be at least partially explained as a state attempt to still fears among the agrarian bourgeoisie remaining in the country and continuing to produce. However, slow distribution of land to peasants prior to 1983 was also due to the fact that organization of the state sector in the countryside was assigned top priority.

(iv) External Pressures and Tensions Third World vulnerability to international market fluctuations and to economic pressures within nations which control that market are not overcome by revolution. Rather, they tend to increase, since the vulnerability caused by extreme product and export specialization, a highly open economy, technological and financial dependency, outdated procedures and techniques, etc., remain and are aggravated by destabilizing neocolonialist manoeuvres. For example, the same international organisms that provide financial assistance to nefarious Third World dictatorships until just hours before their overthrow, refuse to finance development projects of popular regimes. In addition, US opposition to Third World revolutionary change rapidly turns what is initially a political and economic confrontation into military aggression. International experience shows that the popular war of national defence constitutes a necessary stage of social revolutions in imperialist times.

The counter-revolutionary war against Nicaragua, impelled, financed and equipped by the US government, obviously hinders development and transformation policies. This is compounded by the effects of the trade embargo and blockage of funds by international credit organizations. The war not only causes a vast amount of resources to be channelled to national defence – approximately 50 per cent of the government's budget and 10 per cent of the EAP – but also destroys lives and property, and distorts the nation's activities.

At the same time, the war has encouraged shifts which led to greater compatibility between state policies and the revolution's popular bases. Growing emphasis on production for the domestic market, greater attention to peasant and farm-worker demands, and concern for more efficient administration of scarce resources, are changes caused by the conflict since 1984. Thus, defence needs limit the resources available for developing the revolution's policies and programmes, but also modify their content so that they fit better with the strategic focus of revolutionary transformation. Giving priority to defence means giving priority to areas where the war is fought – the countryside – and to the classes that fight the war, e.g. peasants and farm workers.

Characteristics of State Policies Towards the Popular Classes

Immediately after the revolutionary triumph of July 1979, the government initiated a broad policy to satisfy mass demands for improved living standards. The policy was supported by mass participation, and significant foreign financial assistance was obtained.

For example, in the area of public health, massive vaccination campaigns wiped out endemic diseases such as malaria and dengue, and virtually eliminated measles and polio. Enthusiastic mass

participation through the CDSs facilitated widespread environ-
mental health campaigns. New institutions, such as the Ministry
of Social Welfare, and strengthened pre-existing ones, such as the
Institute of Social Security, provided attention to a massive and
historically neglected sector.[12]

Medical consultations nationwide rose by over 15 per cent between
1980 and 1984; Managua's share dropped from 44 per cent of total
consultations during the first year to 32 per cent in 1984, a fact
which emphasizes the expansion of medical services towards the
countryside. Hospital services were similarly expanded; the number
of beds grew by 10 per cent during this period. Managua's share of
beds remained stable in absolute terms and fell in relative terms
from 36 to 32 per cent of the total.[13]

Educational gains have been well publicized. Enrolment in
primary schools rose from 411 515 in 1980 to 536 656 in 1983: this
figure dropped slightly in 1984 because of declining enrolments in
the war zone. Enrolment in Popular Adult Education averaged
nearly 87 000 per year between 1981 and 1984. During the same
period, almost 2000 school centres (primary and pre-school) were
built and numbers of teaching staff increased by 6000 (an increase
of 30 per cent in five years).[14]

One of the more relevant aspects of this policy was the wide
popular participation it generated. The development of people's
health days, adult education, and other activities, helped to
strengthen public organization. Accelerated growth of the CDSs
during these years can be largely attributed to the close links between
revolutionary government policies and mass participation. This
was clearly goal-oriented participation, but had wide political
reverberations by providing opportunities to discuss and even
question decisions made by the state.

This policy demanded financial backing, made possible by access
to soft funds from international cooperation. The juxtaposition of
economic crisis and rising foreign military aggression caused strife
over the allocation of funds among defence, the public investment
programme, and social expenditures, ending in the drastic reduction
of the latter. Public investment in the social sector, representing 29
per cent of the total from 1980–2, fell to an average 13 per cent in
1983–5, and to 11 per cent (budgeted) in 1986.

It is difficult to evaluate the degree to which different classes and
fractions felt the impact of recession and budgetary restrictions, but
Table 4 gives an indirect view, through per capita consumption
figures.

It is clear that during rapid decline of private consumption, basic

Table 4   *Evolution of real per capita consumption, 1980–5 (base year 1980 = 100)*

	1980	1981	1982	1983	1984	1985
Total consumption	100	92	85	82	84	81
Public	100	106	122	164	187	195
Private	100	88	76	62	60	55
Basic	100	100	92	80	77	74
Non-basic	100	71	53	36	34	26

Source: INEC and *Secretaría de Planificación y Presupuesto.*

consumption has dropped more slowly than non-basic consumption. To the degree to which different types of consumption represent different social groups, it may be hypothesized that the lower income groups' situation first improved, and in more recent years, has suffered less than that of higher income groups.

Since greater deficiencies in health, education, and social security existed in the rural environment, social policies benefited this group relatively more. Likewise, the impact of budgetary restrictions since 1984 has been felt more in the country than in the city, as has the absolute reduction of services caused by the war.

The war has had a strong impact on development programmes and social services. According to the Ministry of Agricultural Development and Agrarian Reform (MIDINRA), by the end of 1985 the war had displaced some 79 000 persons. These were nearly all peasant families, whose relocation has greatly affected productive activity and has curtailed the food supply. This massive resettlement has also tested the revolutionary government's ability to respond to urgent needs for new land, basic infrastructure, and a minimal provision of services.

The destruction of assets has been too large for the Nicaraguan economy to absorb. Up to the end of 1984, in social services alone, counter-revolutionary attacks had destroyed eleven rural child-care centres; 840 adult education centres had to be closed; 247 members of these centres were assassinated. Fourteen schools were totally destroyed and 359 had to be closed. In 1984 alone, 98 schoolteachers were killed and 171 kidnapped. Forty-one health stations were destroyed and forty-nine health workers assassinated, kidnapped or wounded.[15]

The Working Class Within the Revolution

Certainly the working class has been very vulnerable to tensions and contradictions inherent in transition to a different society. This situation has been complicated by the combined economic crisis and counter-revolutionary war, but it is also the objective result of class configuration, i.e. the recent and incomplete proletarianization, the heavy weight of agrarian and peasant economies, and state policies toward workers. This subject will be explored in four dimensions: organization, employment, wages, and labour productivity and attitudes toward work. Other relevant questions, such as worker-participation in company administration, and the relationship among the worker movement, the FSLN and the state, have been discussed previously by the author.

Organization The revolutionary triumph favoured the rapid growth of labour unions. Although exact figures are difficult to obtain, it is estimated that the union movement included less than 27 000 workers prior to 1979, representing 11–12 per cent of all salaried workers. In mid-1983, approximately 145 000 workers belonged to unions, i.e., 41–2 per cent of the total,[16] and by mid-1986 around 56 per cent, or 260 000 salaried workers were unionized.[17] Some 80 per cent of unionized industrial workers belong to unions affiliated to the Sandinista Workers' Confederation (CST) and nearly all unionized farm workers belong to the Association of Rural Workers (ATC).[18]

The growth in membership and numbers of unions was accompanied by the institutionalization of union contracts, the expansion of social security, and improved benefits. The atmosphere of organizational freedom and general improvement in working conditions contrasted with the repression prevailing during the dictatorship, imbuing the unions with a great sense of efficacy, which doubtless furthered the rapid growth of the worker movement. The Ministry of Labour played an active role in enforcing labour legislation, health and occupational safety norms, and in providing technical assistance to unions on collective agreements, labour rights and general working conditions.

The strengthening of worker organizations occurred in spite of two major contradictions. The rapid escalation of the class struggle became very intense in 1981 due to private decapitalization. This may have been the moment when the workers' movement, particularly the CST, adopted more explicit class-based, i.e. anti-capitalist positions. Decapitalization was denounced as a manoeuvre by the bourgeoisie, in complicity with the US government, to weaken the economy and weaken the revolution: the workers demanded confiscation of relevant property, stricter legislation, and the institution of worker-vigilance of private entrepreneurs. The revolutionary government was sensitive to the demands of the worker movement, and, in general made most of them law. However, it was also sensitive to the alarm this caused among private businessmen. The government deemed company and land takeovers to be illegal, and, in declaring a state of economic emergency, suspended the right to strike (September 1981).

Between 1979 and the end of 1981, an intense struggle took place among the diverse political currents of the worker movement. This was essentially an urban–industrial phenomenon. In the country, the workers' movement was directly linked to the political work of the FSLN. There had been no farm workers' movement prior to the creation of the ATC in 1978, thus, the FSLN had no competition. Such was not the case in the cities, where since at least the early 1950s there had been a small workers' movement, operating clandestinely or on the border of legality. This was basically a "bread and butter" unionism. The federations did not play a significant role in the political struggle against Somocismo – although there were several important union struggles. The political affiliations of the various unions generally reproduced the partisan spectrum.[19]

Difficulties of the CST position are evident. On one hand, its explicit affiliation with the FSLN identifies it with a revolution which responds, in general, to the political expectations of most workers. This same identification, because of FSLN alliances with private enterprise, reduces the CST's capacity to advance workers' claims immediately and effectively. Under these conditions, the CST favours the overall Sandinista revolution, compromising by adopting a low profile regarding "sectarian" claims of the working class. Minority union federations – mainly communist, socialist and social-Christian in orientation – insist on short-term claims and ignore, or relegate to a secondary role, the overall revolutionary project. The minority unions reduce class to its labour aspects, while the CST dilutes labour on behalf of national unity. The high priority given to agricultural production has allowed the ATC to operate more autonomously, thus rather effectively reconciling its adhesion to the revolutionary process with an aggressive stance on wages.

The state of economic emergency, declared in September 1981, led to a demobilization of the working class which today is recognized by the CST itself.[20] The CST, in effect, strengthened its links with the state, reduced its class-based stance, and further de-emphasized salary claims on behalf of a more national focus. From that time on, emphasis was placed on more labour discipline, high productivity and incorporation of workers into the country's military defence. Thus, its activities became concentrated in priority areas defined by the FSLN and the government.

At the end of 1984, there was evidence of uncontrolled, increasingly autonomous speculation. Sandinista unions called for action against speculators and unnecessary intermediaries.[21] This CST line of action took place within the government's general reorientation of economic and financial policy, meant to curb the transfer of human resources and capital into the commercial sphere.[22] Informal sector activities, which the government had tolerated as contributing somewhat to effect distribution of goods and services, became the target of policies meant to reduce them. Those in the informal sector were now considered parasitic contributors to the black market.[23] Evidence of salaried workers' participation in these activities emphasized the importance of CST participation in the campaign against the informal sector.

The agenda of the IV National Union Assembly of January 1985, convoked by CST, summarizes current positions of the workers' movement: defence of basic provisions; struggle against usury and speculation; boosting of production and productivity.[24] It is interesting to note that the assembly's message included all producers as part of the working class and of "the people". (In Nicaragua the farm *producer* refers to all types of agricultural entrepreneurs – small, medium and large.) National unity is now expressed in terms of the unity of all productive classes against the "parasitic" classes. The need to maintain national cohesion against class divisions, always a major theme of Sandinista ideology, becomes stronger under foreign military aggression, and is a recurring topic in the FSLN's dialogue with the workers.

Employment Early reactivation of the economy was reflected in uneven employment growth: it grew more in non-farm activities than in farm activities; more in the public than in the private sector, and more in non-productive than productive activities. General unemployment dropped between 1980 and 1983, and though the relatively greater capacity for job creation outside the productive sectors was later to generate economic and financial tensions, at the time it allowed a partial solution to unemployment. Unemployment increased from 1984 onwards, due to three main factors:

1. restrictions on non-productive investments in response to the growing economic crisis;

2. reduced capacity of public investment to generate employment;
3. the decline of private investment.

Table 5 shows the change in overall employment and trends in agricultural and non-agricultural employment. The unemployment rate grew more for the non-agricultural sector than for agriculture. This suggests that the rise in unemployment is more a product of crisis (in foreign exchange, production input) than of the war, or in any case that the war's effect is felt indirectly, through competition for extremely scarce resources. Furthermore, unemployment affects salaried workers more than non-salaried workers, inasmuch as the crisis is harder on the industrial sector than on trade and services. In the industrial sector, where employment fell by more than 13 per cent between 1980 and 1983, small establishments were affected more than medium-sized and large ones.

Table 5   *Unemployment rate, 1980–5* (in %)

	1980	1981	1982	1983	1984	1985[a]
General	22	19	20	19	21	22
Agricultural	28	23	28	24	25	19
Non agricultural	18	16	14	15	18	24

[a] Preliminary
Source: INEC, INSS.

Wages Following an initial readjustment, the revolutionary government adopted a policy of relatively firm salary control, which remained virtually intact until 1983. This policy, together with accelerated inflation which began in 1981, caused a quick decline in real salaries. Between 1980 and 1985, real wages fell by nearly 40 per cent against the general consumer price index (cf. Table 6), and by 40–50 per cent when considering the cost of several alternate consumer baskets as a deflator. During the first half of 1986, the

Table 6   *Evolution of real wages,* 1980–5* (Base year: 1980 = 100)

	1980	1981	1982	1983	1984	1985
Index	100	101	89	77	77	63

* Salaries and wages paid to social security holders.
Source: Compilation of INEC and INSSBI figures.

dizzy pace of inflation caused an additional drop in purchasing power of nearly 70 per cent.

This control policy was felt to be a necessary evil to avoid the inflationary inpact of wage increases. However, the decision was also intended to provide higher profits and thus stimulate private production, while allowing state entities a financial breather. In any case, this cautious policy evidently surprised most workers and encouraged confrontations between the CST and the government, on one hand, and between the CST and other labour federations on the other.

An early attempt was made to palliate the more irritating effects of wage control through the so-called "social wage" – i.e. an expansion of social services. The name was inappropriate, since no contribution was required for use of these services which, as already seen were available to all who needed them, wage earners or not.

Financial restrictions caused a rapid reduction in the social wage cushion, and by 1981–2, the expression was no longer in use. The government then resorted to wages in kind, which meant that workers received partial payment in merchandise they produced: cloth from textile factories, footwear, soft drinks, milk and dairy products. The idea was that workers could acquire these items at cost, for their own use. Later they were allowed to buy a few extras for resale; and in many cases products were also given to their families. It became obvious that a large part of company production was being channelled to the black market.

According to estimates, in some branches of industry payment in kind in 1984 constituted more than 45 per cent of a worker's real income.[25] Goods were also allocated in this way to technicians, professionals, and administrative employees. However, the practice occurred almost exclusively in APP companies (APP = People's Production Areas; state-owned firms) where wage norms were much stricter than in the private sector.[26] Wages in kind began as a short-cut for APP companies to overcome state wage-policy limitations, and as a way to retain qualified personnel who would otherwise have transferred to the private or informal sectors. In practice, the procedure rapidly became a much more important source of income than monetary pay.

Payment in kind peaked in 1984. By this time it also involved a complex system of barter, in which part of one firm's production was exchanged with products from other companies; the system allowed the personnel of each company direct access, at cost, to goods included in the exchange.

Payment in kind has many implications. First, wages cease to reflect the cost of reproduction of the labour force, and become the monetary symbol of a labour relationship which allows the worker access to private commercial capital via state subsidy.[27]

Second, labour discipline declines, and the development of conscientious attitudes becomes very difficult. Competition over merchandise breaks out among the workers. Earnings from the resale of goods are much higher than wages that can be earned by working longer and harder. At the same time, the Sandinistas were exhorting workers to work harder, surpass goals, and produce more.

In the third place, ties between wage earners and the informal sector and black market are stimulated and expanded.

These ties are strengthened because most popular-class urban families rely on both wages and non-wage earnings, and a high proportion of industrial workers also own small farms, workshops, or corner stores. Under these conditions, maintenance of workers' standards of living depends not so much on wages as on social security benefits, the chance to purchase goods at official prices in the company commissary, etc.

The magnitude of these exchanges, their black-market impact, and resulting short supplies in official channels, as well as the discord such exchanges generated among wage-earners not accorded this privilege, led to their elimination in mid-1985. This difficult decision was obviously resisted by former beneficiaries, who lost a large share of their incomes. In some factories there were mass resignations; in FANATEX textile mill, for example, the elimination of payment in kind caused the mass exit of 300 workers – nearly 20 per cent of its workforce.

Wage conditions stimulated the shift of workers to the urban informal sector, reducing the mass of wage-earners. Between 1981 and 1982 alone, 5000 to 9000 non-farm workers quit their jobs,[28] and although there is no systematic information for later years, this movement appears to have continued. Reduction in industrial activities caused by the crisis, and higher earning potential from other activities discouraged wage-earners, who were also enticed by the fewer controls on individual activity, less political and institutional pressure, and other factors. However, the high rate of unfilled jobs in manufacturing, especially in the APP, indicates that workers left the formal sector because of the steady drop in real remuneration, and not because industrial activity was curtailed by the crisis.

High personnel turnover among firms and institutions, particularly in the public sector, is also attributed to the drop in real wages. Workers have become more alert to possibilities of better salaries or working conditions; employment becomes a privileged lookout point from which to spot a better job. This attitutde is particularly strong among technical and professional groups, but does not exclude skilled workers.[29]

In the early years of the revolutionary government, farm-workers' wages were lower than those of urban workers, and provisions less readily available. Informal sector alternatives open to urban workers, such as wages in kind, are nearly non-existent in the countryside. The author has previously described this situation's impact on the labour deficit for agro-export crops.[30]

However, in recent years the government has attempted to reduce these differences. The average urban–rural salary ratio of nearly 2.4 in 1980 fell to 1.8 in 1984, because of a wage policy that favoured the latter group (a nominal increase of 97 per cent for this group, as opposed to only 56 per cent for urban workers). The mean salary/production-per-worker ratio in the agricultural sector had deteriorated by 3.5 per cent between 1980 and 1985, while in the industrial sector the mean salary/production-per-worker ratio shrank by nearly 20 per cent during the same period.[31] At the beginning of 1985, coinciding with greater flexibility in age policy, the FSLN decided that farm workers – both permanent and seasonal – would have priority for wage increases.[32]

The extension of the social security system to agriculture improved working conditions; there was also more concern for enforcement of occupational health and safety provisions. The ATC is now developing a campaign meant to increase the proportion of permanent workers and progressively reduce seasonality of rural employment. In any case, working conditions are hardly satisfactory, and this seems to affect the performance of the labour force.

Although no systematic information exists, it is plausible to assume that the "temptation" of the informal sector is greater for city workers than for farm-workers. De-proletarianization of farm workers seems to be tied to expectations of obtaining land through agrarian reform. These expectations had risen because, prior to 1984, agricultural wages had declined more than industrial wages – even though during this period production per employed person in agriculture remained relatively constant. In fact, agricultural salaries shrank more acutely than real prices of farm products.[33] Attraction to farm employment could conceivably increase because of changing agrarian reform and agricultural development policies since mid-1985, which emphasized accelerated land distribution, substantial real price improvements, a more agile banking system, and greater state attention to the food supply.

Labour Productivity and Attitudes Toward Work   Capitalism and socialism have many differences, but are alike in one thing: in both ideologies, a good worker is a hard worker. To be sure, this is not the workers' image of socialism or national liberation, and thus the matter of worker-productivity becomes a central theme in the early stages of any revolution.

During the first years of the revolutionary regime, manufacturing productivity increased, but this occurred mainly in the largest firms and in the private, rather than the public, sector. This increase was basically due to general economic reactivation, and occurred within a context of deteriorating real salaries and income transfer from wage-earners to non-wage-earners, and from productive to non-productive workers.[34] Inasmuch as the productivity increase occurred under adverse material conditions, much of the workers' response would appear to be due to political convictions, or at least favourable expectations.

The situation was different in the countryside, where general productivity fell. One reason was that perceived emancipation resulted in less commitment to work. The length of the working day was acutely reduced, and labour intensity dropped considerably.[35]

Productivity has also been affected by the crisis. Restriction of foreign exchange for importing parts and supplies, policies of workforce retention and a decline in general activities undermined previous productivity levels. The lack of raw materials and other supplies puts firms in the bind of either maintaining production rhythms while reducing labour time, or avoiding strikes by slowing production.

There is currently debate in Nicaragua as to whether these objective factors are aggravated by subjective factors emanating from the workers themselves: lack of job interest, motivation, and discipline. This may be a passive but collective expression of social discontent. Indicators abound: between 1983 and 1984, for example, absenteeism rose from 33 to 50 per cent.[36] Personnel turnover is equally appalling. In the countryside, the pre-revolutionary six-hour working-day was reduced to two or three hours.[37]

The war has also affected productivity. At present a significant share of the industrial labour force has defence duties. They have been recruited for military service, or drafted into the reserves, territorial militia, etc. In some cases this means that the worker leaves the firm for up to two years; in other cases, he must participate periodically in mobilizations and shorter training manoeuvres. Obviously, these conditions make it hard for a firm to maintain a steady production rate.

The serious deterioration of real salaries and inadequate supply weakens the relationship between productivity and wages. During the years studied, salaries dropped far more than productivity; at the end of June 1986, wage purchasing-power was only 20, compared with a base of 100 in 1980. Under these conditions productivity operates independently of any wage consideration. Insistence on tying wage increases to productivity and the extension of the working-day make sense when wages allow access to certain material benefits. When the real wages are so low that this is not the case, and the market is under-supplied, higher wages offer little or no incentive. This is particularly true when alternative employment possibilities, and expectations of higher income, exist in the informal sector.

The effectiveness of ideological calls for extra effort may be limited by the existence of a mixed economy and consequent need to direct part of the surplus – i.e. part of the workers' additional effort – to the patriotic bourgeoisie. In any case, a contrast arises between dollar incentives for patriotic producers and the incentive of *gallo pinto* (rice and beans) for worker and combatant wage-earners.

Such differentiated stimuli imply that social inequalities are reproduced within the revolution. This is troublesome in a socialist transition and also, though for different reasons, in a development transition. In a transition towards socialism, one objective is assumed to be the reduction, and even elimination, of class inequalities. In the transition towards development, concern arises because social inequalities detract from the development of a productive conscience.

The compound effects of crisis and war tend to enhance social inequalities in the framework of class alliances. Perhaps the workers' willingness to take on additional defence and war efforts is not entirely inconsistent with their reluctance to exert the same efforts for production. Demobilized workers who once battled heroically against the counter-revolution, return to their jobs and rapidly become accustomed to the prevailing low level of exertion. It is easier to offer one's life to the revolution than to give one hour of extra work on the job. Within a strategy of national multiclass unity, workers are willing to defend sovereignty – and thus the revolution – but ideological appeals are not heeded in the context of the mixed economy.

A 1986 policy of offering higher monetary rewards for surpassing production goals appears to be achieving higher productivity.[38]

Crisis, War and Class Reconfiguration   The economic crisis – particularly as it reduces productive activity and employment –

together with escalation of the war, have also changed the size and composition of the working class.

National defence has become one of the largest sources of salaried employment. Assuming that 10 per cent of the EAP is involved in defence,[39] this means that between 105 000 and 110 000 people are engaged in the war in some capacity: as combatants, in logistical support, etc. By mid-1986, approximately 23 per cent of wage-earners were involved in national defence. Apart from the fact that no productive activity occupies such a massive number of wage-earners, this situation separates the wage question from the question of reproduction of the labour force, since defence workers have priority in food allocation, which is guaranteed for soldiers.

The war has also boosted feminization of the rural labour force, which was already rising because of male migration to higher-paying jobs in the cities. With the massive incorporation of men in the territorial militia and military service, women's share of rural employment has grown rapidly. This phenomenon is more developed in the APP than in the private sector, and more marked in seasonal than in year-round activities. During the 1983–4 agricultural cycle, it was estimated that women accounted for 42 per cent of total employment, and this increased to nearly 50 per cent in 1984–5. Women's labour participation was even higher in some areas: 70 per cent in tobacco cutting, 60 per cent in cotton harvesting, 70 per cent for coffee.[40] Women's participation is also increasing in APP manufacturing industries, although to a lesser degree.

The Future of the Working Class

The previous sections have offered some general considerations for discussion of the future development of the working class within the revolution.

First, there has been an undesirable shift in class sizes. Although no statistics exist, it is reasonable to state that there are fewer workers today than seven years ago. This is the result, first, of simultaneous crisis and war, although the war has generated a new kind of salaried employment. In any case, war and crisis have caused a sharp decrease of productive wage-earners, who constitute the proletariat in a strict Marxist sense. Pressure on the workers was first felt in industry, and although these factors remain, depletion of the labour-force is likely to have bottomed out, barring the possibility of additional drastic cut-backs in the already weakened industrial sector. War and crisis have caused a significant redirection of the original rural transformation and development strategies, reducing the emphasis of agro-export activities and increasing the relative importance of production for the domestic market. This can be simplistically described as more of a peasant than a worker strategy.

The informal sector, until at least two years ago, was the main refuge of workers who abandoned productive activity or wage-earning jobs. This option was particularly feasible for urban workers, although it also existed for some rural workers who migrated to the cities. Current government policies aim to reduce the vast size of the informal sector and impede its development. In Managua, at least, such policies have had some success, creating the new problem of what will happen to workers displaced from the informal sector. In some cases, when rural ties have not been totally severed, "returning to the land" is an option, enhanced by the recent push for agrarian reform.[41] For the majority, informal employment may be the only possibility, even with lower income and greater instability.

Government and FSLN commitment to a policy of wage-containment during the early years generated a large lag in remunerations which helped to reduce the number of salaried workers, particularly blue-collar workers. This reduction was felt most strongly in the APP. The private sector managed to avoid Ministry of Labour controls and paid higher wages. Thus it could attract qualified employees from the public sector, while discrediting the government's wage policy, the government itself, and the FSLN, which backed the policy.

There is evidence that some public sector institutions also resorted to implicit over-payment of wages in order to retain personnel, or to obtain skilled workers for priority development projects. There may have been no choice, but certainly such state actions against its own wage legislation did not sell this legislation to the workers. Furthermore, wage incentives and perquisites are higher and more readily available to technical and professional staff, although a more balanced trend has appeared recently in some APP companies engaging in essential production.

Imbalances generated by the wage policy make one wonder why it was adhered to so firmly. The position maintained almost unanimously by the government, FSLN and Sandinista union leaders was that higher salaries, if not accompanied by greater productivity, would directly affect price levels and bolster inflation. This argument is theoretically disputable and, in Nicaragua, is empirically refutable as well: inflation occurred when nominal salaries were rigidly controlled, so that wages were operating as an adjustment variable within the overall economic system.

Although many factors were doubtless involved, we wish to stress those of a more ideological nature.

First, the revolution's leaders, on the basis of solid evidence, were convinced that more could be expected in terms of workers' sacrifice than of entrepreneurs' patriotism. In other words, the working class, in its support of the revolution, is more able to postpone certain gains. This is a variation on the argument that the present generation must sacrifice for the sake of future generations, and is based on the assumption – a questionable one in this case – that wage-earners have a narrower range of alternatives. A similar assumption applied to farm producers.[42] This argument is compatible with the revolution's initial interest in making the APP the driving force of what was then called the "new Sandinista economy". It was understood that broad wage-claims would not allow the future APP companies to obtain needed minimum profitability. The example of Chile during *Unidad Popular* was generally cited as an additional argument for a cautious wage policy.

A second factor was confusion regarding the role of wages in the revolution's present stage and, more generally, regarding the nature of the work process. In some FSLN sectors, it was assumed that the Sandinista triumph and conquest of political power by a block of national–popular forces, eliminated labour exploitation. Some attempts were made to differentiate between a supposedly new type of labour relations within the APP, and private sector labour relations. In general, however, it was explicitly or implicitly felt that the socio-economic content of labour relations had been politically transformed. In some cases this concept was reinforced by the counter-revolutionary war: defence priorities and national unity would transform the nature of labour relations.[43]

Third, we may also be witnessing the survival of a pre-capitalist concept of wage labour, in which the worker is a source of expense rather than of value added. This view is more widely held than one might think,[44] and is appropriate to the industrial sector's net importing nature. In times of economic crisis and acute outside restriction, the legitimacy of a wage increase is weighed against the cost to society as a whole.[45] It is easier to pay producers higher prices – in the belief that these will directly increase production – than to declare wage increases for those who are actually considered as net consumers.

In turn, the multiclass strategy of national unity and mixed economy affects claims of the working class. Under growing economic crisis and greater autonomy of the commercial sphere the FSLN emphasized national unity not only *vis-à-vis* military aggression by the US government, but as unity of the productive *versus* the parasitic classes. This may be closer to St Simon's socialism than to that of Marx. If social concepts originate from social beings, the type of dependent capitalism developed in Nicaragua, more obvious in the commercial than the productive sphere, is closer to St Simon, and indeed to Ricardo.

Under these circumstances the type of alliance formed between workers and peasants is unlike that found in conventional textbooks or in other social revolutions. First, because rural workers constituted a large proportion of the worker class, the alliance acquires a rural–rural rather than the traditional urban–rural composition. Second, pressures on urban workers caused by war and crisis, and the consequent changes in economic strategy, mean that the city workers subsidize the peasantry and farm-workers in general, rather than vice versa.[46]

We should add that this occurs within a multiclass framework in which workers and peasants must subsidize the patriotic bourgeoisie and urban middle sectors. Deterioration of living conditions of these latter groups has been notorious, as seen in the abrupt drop of non-basic consumption and as confirmed by daily observation. In addition to adverse living conditions, these groups are obliged to smuggle their sons out of the country to avoid military conscription, so it is clear that the present situation is far from ideal. However, within this uneven deterioration it is clear that workers start in a lower position and are far more vulnerable.

This unequal footing and internal jockeying to disperse effects of the crisis has a certain logic within the revolution's social complexity. The middle groups, the petty bourgeoisie, constitute a relatively large part of Nicaraguan society, especially in the urban areas. These groups helped to overthrow the dictatorship, are represented in the revolutionary government, and form part of the FSLN – although certain segments of these social layers identify with the opposition and even with the counter-revolution. It is not surprising, then, that they press for policies favouring their own interests, and that these interests can be identified in many of the revolutionary regime's policies and approaches. At the same time, the government's concern in responding to these demands is coherent with the overall revolutionary strategy.[47]

The FSLN and the government have tried to keep the crisis and war from disproportionately affecting the workers. However, the FSLN has been more receptive than the state to workers' demands.

State institutions have tended to back APP company administrators whenever there is conflict with the unions, even when unions complain of poor management of the company's interests. The state seems most concerned with consolidating the principle of authority in the face of what it considers a lack of worker-discipline. Union demands are answered slowly, and procedures are carried out one by one, until the union or CST appeals directly to the FSLN.

Although the distinction appears subtle, deterioration in living and working conditions have affected the workers as workers more than as people. Individual consumption has fallen more than collective consumption, which does not require a labour contribution. Employment and wage income have contracted more than employment in informal activities and non-wage income. Rather than a shift from employment to unemployment, the Nicaraguan economic crisis implies an increase in working-time spent in informal activities and a higher share of family income derived therein. Life is certainly more difficult than it was two or three years ago, but the informal sector is like a big lake where everyone can fish.

Surely this is not what the revolutionaries originally had in mind. We must ask, though, whether anything much greater or very different is possible in an anti-oligarchical, national liberation revolution which takes action against capitalism only in its most unjust, outdated and dependent forms; where regional economic crisis is aggravated by internal transformations; in a backward, impoverished and wounded nation possessing more courage and imagination than resources, pitted against the greatest military power in history.

More than for any other class or sector of society, the Sandinista revolution still represents a political victory to the workers, the poor, the masses. There is no longer a National Guard. Union activity is not repressed or clandestine. A worker can differ with his employer or manager without fear of being fired. One can settle on empty land and put up a dwelling without destruction and eviction by the police. The peasants have land. The children go to school.

Notes

1. In Spanish, the popular classes (*clases populares*) include the working class and artisans (both urban and rural), the peasantry including semi-proletarianized peasantry, and persons in the informal sector, sometimes including the marginal elements of the middle class, such

as owners of small stores and medium-sized farmers. There is no direct equivalent term in English. Perhaps "masses" comes the closest, but that term implies an undifferentiated group, rather than a linking of many different groups. The Spanish adjective *popular* might be translated as populist, but populism has a more specific historical political meaning than is implied by *popular*. Thus we have chosen to translate the term into its English cognate, recognizing that the adjective "popular" in English normally means something quite different (editor's note).

2. For Nicaragua, the figure was 43 per cent, compared with 50 per cent in El Salvador, 55 per cent in Guatemala, and 63 per cent in Honduras.
3. C. M. Vilas, *The Sandinista Revolution: National Liberation and Social Transformation in Central America* pp. 60ff.
4. Instituto Nicaragüense de Estadísticas y Censos (INEC) *Anuario estadístico de Nicaragua* (Managua: INEC, 1981).
5. Vilas, *The Sandinista Revolution*, chap. 3.
6. H. Ruiz, "La montaña era como un inmenso crisol donde se forjaban los mejores cuadros", *Nicarauac* (May–June 1980) p. 24.
7. V. I. Lenin, *Contenido económico del populismo* (Madrid: Siglo XXI, 1974).
8. cf. Vilas. *The Sandinista Revolution*, pp. 101ff.
9. cf. Baumeister, Eduardo, "The Structure of Nicaraguan Agriculture and the Sandinista Agrarian Reform", in R. Harris and C. M. Vilas (eds) *Nicaragua: A Revolution under Siege* (London: Zed Books) pp. 10–35.
10. C. D. Deere y P. Marchetti, "The Worker–Peasant Alliance in the First Year of the Nicaraguan Agrarian Reform", *Latin American Perspectives*, 29 (Spring 1981) pp. 40–73.
11. C. M. Vilas, "Reforma agraria, agroexportación y empleo rural en Nicaragua", *Canadian Journal of Latin American and Caribbean Studies*, vol. 9 (1984) pp. 111–32.
12. UNICEF–OPS, *Análisis de la situación económico-social de Nicaragua* (Managua: UNICEF, 1984).
13. cf. INEC, *Anuario estadístico de Nicaragua* (Managua: INEC, 1984).
14. Ibid.
15. Insituto Nicaragüense de Seguridad Social y Bienestar (INSSBI) *48 meses de agresión extranjera* (Managua: INSSBI, 1985).
16. Vilas, *The Sandinista Revolution*, p. 178.
17. Stahler-Sholk, R. *Política salarial en Nicaragua, 1979–1985* (Managua, unpublished mss, 1985).
18. C. M. Vilas, "The Workers' Movement in the Sandinista Revolution", in R. Harris and C. M. Vilas, *Nicaragua: A Revolution under Siege* (London: Zed Books 1985) pp. 120–50.
19. Ibid.
20. Interview with the organizational secretary in *Pensamiento Propio* 33, (May–June 1986).
21. See, for example, *Barricada* (21, 23, 24, 28 and 30 December 1984).
22. In 1983 the mass of capital circulating through channels beyond governmental control represented more than one-quarter of the

country's real product, or six months of exports, and in 1984 amounted
to nearly half of the national product, or one year of exports. See C. M.
Vilas, "Nicaragua: The Fifth Year – Transformations and Tensions in
the Economy", *Capital and Class*, vol. 28 (Spring 1986) pp. 105–38.

23. *El Nuevo Diario* (30 July 1986).
24. *Barricada* (1 May 1985).
25. According to a report by the Ministry of Industry, in 1984 five APP
    (public sector) enterprises in the footwear industry delivered 77 750
    pairs of shoes to their 1070 workers (nearly 73 pairs per year per
    worker). Initially, one pair per month was delivered, but later the
    average rose to six pairs per month. The ratio of the factory-assigned
    price to the price that could be obtained for each pair on the black
    market was between 1:10 and 1:12. The state-owned clothing company,
    Enaves, distributed nearly 23 000 garments to its 978 workers (nearly
    24 per year), especially blue jeans made for export. Here the ratio of
    factory-assigned price to black market sales price was estimated at 1:18.
    In textiles, the APP's FANATEX company delivered 270 000 yards of
    cloth to its 1600 workers, and TEXNICSA, also an APP company,
    delivered 205 000 yards to 1150 workers. It is interesting to note that
    cloth consumption by all small and medium-sized garment
    manufacturers – representing around two-thirds of total garment
    production – is 1 million yards per year. This means that during 1984,
    2750 workers received as much cloth from two companies as was needed
    by small and medium-sized clothing manufacturers for six months of
    production. MILCA, the Coca Cola bottling company, delivered up to
    forty 24-bottle cases per month to each worker. In this case, the price
    difference was a more modest 1:2.4. (*Barricada* and *Nuevo Diario*
    newspapers from May, June and July 1985).
26. In the private industrial sector, double bookkeeping for salaries is not
    unusual: the "white" books follow official salary levels, while the "black"
    books reflect payment of salaries above legally permissible levels. See
    G. Dijkstra *La industria en la economía mixta de Nicaragua* (Managua,
    mimeographed, 1985).
27. The point was made inadvertently but formally by an officer of state-
    owned MILCA (the Coca Cola bottlers) when, in the midst of criticisms
    of wages in kind, he announced that his company would continue
    delivering soft drinks at cost only to workers who owned taverns and
    had commercial licenses issued by the Ministry of Domestic Commerce
    (*Barricada*, 15 April 1985).
28. Vilas, *The Sandinista Revolution*, p. 245.
29. According to preliminary results of a recent study on the public sector,
    personnel turnover during the first half of 1986 affected 34 per cent of
    construction workers, 34 per cent of Ministry of Labour personnel, and 48
    per cent of the Central Bank's staff. (*El Nuevo Diario*, 19 September 1986).
30. Vilas, "Reforma agraria. . .".
31. R. Stahler-Sholk, *La normación del trabajo en Nicaragua, 1983–1986* (Man-
    agua: unpublished mss, 1986) Table 5.

32. V. Tirado López *La primera gran conquista: La toma del poder político* Managua: Ediciones de la CST, 1985).
33. Vilas, "Reforma agraria".
34. Vilas, *The Sandinista Revolution*, pp. 208–12.
35. A study by the Center for Research and Study of Agrarian Reform (*Centro de Investigaciones y Estudios de la Reforma Agraria*) found that although all administrators interviewed noted that farm productivity had declined from pre-revolutionary levels, none recommended a return to those levels. In general, their production recommendations averaged 10–15 per cent below pre-revolutionary levels, although after 1979 their recommendations were higher than were actually achieved. This may implicitly recognize that higher previous levels were largely due to repressive conditions of dictatorship.
36. Statements by Commander Víctor Tirado in *El Nuevo Diario*, 15 May 1985.
37. Declarations of Commander Tirado in *Barricada* (20 November 1984), and Commander Jaime Wheelock, Minister of Agricultural Development and Agrarian Reform, in *Barricada* (17 June 1986).
38. A preliminary study of the Ministry of Agricultural Development and Agrarian Reform reveals that the length of the farm labour working-day had increased from previous years. So far in the 1986–7 farm cycle, the working-day has increased by an average of 9 per cent over that in 1985–6. During these two periods, achievement of government norms and working-days was 98 per cent and 90 per cent, respectively. According to the report, the average working-day for 1985–6 was slightly over $4\frac{1}{2}$ hours, increasing during the present cycle to an average of over 5 hours. According to the Ministry, wage increases (average 37 per cent) and bonuses for surpassing production goals (50 per cent) help to explain these differences, apart from ideological considerations.
39. See *Barricada* (17 June 1986).
40. Criquillón, A. *et al.*, *Revolución y mujeres del campo* (Managua: Asociación de Trabajadores del Campo, 1985) p. 22.
41. In some areas land is now being given to workers in the informal sector, i.e., small artisans, small merchants (*Barricada*, 21 April and 21 September 1986).
42. Until very recently farm-price policy was far more beneficial to agro-export producers than to producers of basic grains. Within agro-exporting, policy benefited cotton and sugar-cane producers more than coffee growers. In social terms, large and medium capitalist producers and the state sector benefited more than coffee- and grain-producing peasants. In general, policy favoured those producers who could exercise more pressure on the government.
43. For example, an editorial from the newspaper *Barricada*, the official FSLN publication, stated: "While before, greater production efforts meant enriching the owner, the new social production relations that Nicaragua is building mean that every extra effort helps free society from outside pressure. This is a substantial difference. If, under the dictatorship, man was merchandise, selling his labor so as to survive,

workers today produce to contribute to a common life, out of social responsibility. They are not producing only to satisfy their food and reproductive needs, but to obtain a new dimension of self, through their work." (1 February 1985)

44. For example, in the study of the impact of agrarian reform on rural employment, the author found that several leaders of the Unión Nacional de Agricultores y Ganaderos (the organization for small and medium farmers and cattlemen) from León and Chinandega, felt negatively about rural workers, believing that they were lazy, did not know how to work, wasted resources, and mistreated equipment.

45. Tirado López, *La primera gran conquista*, p. 132.

46. The basis for this strategy can be seen in the speech by Commander Luís Carrión, national FSLN leader, at the inauguration of the First Peasant Congress (*Barricada*, 26 April 1986).

47. Failure to bear this in mind has caused a logical contradiction in interpreting social revolutions in such societies. On one hand, it is recognized that the dominant form of capitalism and its articulation with pre-capitalist forms of production generates a complex social structure in which the proletariat is a very small minority. On the other hand, these regimes are harshly criticized for furthering what are considered petty bourgeois strategies and policies. See, for example, A. Astrow, *Zimbabwe: A Revolution that Lost its Way?* (London: Zed Books, 1983).

Authoritarian Transition to Democracy in Central America

Edelberto Torres-Rivas

After comparing the varying attempts made at analysing Central American politics, it is reasonable to conclude that the political crisis is in essence an armed criticism against the traditional power structure – one that has taken different forms in Guatemala, El Salvador, and Nicaragua. The authoritarian oligarchical tradition of Central American origin fused with the modern counter-revolutionary mind-set of North American origin to produce a new form of political regime within the historical framework of the bourgeois state.

The most serious accusation that can be made against the Central American bourgeoisie – landowners, businessmen, and others involved in agricultural export – is their lack of ability effectively to promote political and social integration within society. This historical offence involved the repeated loss of opportunities for capitalist development: in a national sense – the opportunity to integrate different classes in an internal market — as well as in a bourgeois sense – to take advantage regularly of different opportunities to accumulate and invest wealth. As a result of more than a century of frustrated opportunities, states were formed without an integrated national base. This produced nations whose governments exalted the maintenance of order to the detriment of social and political integration.

The state adopted an oligarchical form responsive to the interests of landowners and the business capital linked with international trade. Oligarchical man represents a backward bourgeoisie personified by large property holdings, but with incomplete control over capital. His power is derived from the control over people's lives that land ownership provides. But along with the development of the means of production, the social relations of production always involve force and permanent violence that goes beyond economic power.

State protection of this type of political order always generates despotic forms of authority that deploy permanent violence. The reasons why this was not the case in Costa Rica but was clearly prevalent in El Salvador and Guatemala have been examined elsewhere.[1] Certainly violence is related to the existence and consolidation of the state in Central America. It was through violence that the power of economic interests shaped the reconstruction of agrarian landholding through the seizing of peasant and Indian lands. Exclusion from society was also political; the real citizenry was comprised of landowners and the literate. The subordinate position of the peasantry was intensified by ethnic differentiation. In the three countries being analyzed, racist elements complete the seigneurial ideology under which the political system functioned even before the first half of the twentieth century. In the last decade, because of this system, the people's protest became a politically disastrous life-or-death challenge because it questioned societal order and its cultural and political bases.

The political–social syndrome is more complex and deals with the consolidation of private property in an environment that sanctioned its physical defence through *private* means. The direct use of terrorism by landowners preceded and later accompanied the creation of national armies that were part of the liberal reform in Guatemala, El Salvador and Nicaragua. For example, since about 1885 in El Salvador, a new "police force" was created to "control the rural population . . . to confront . . . the social unrest caused by the redistribution of land".[2] More than a dozen peasant uprisings in the years following the Zaldivar reform in El Salvador in 1886 have been recorded, as well as a peasant war in the Barrios period in Guatemala in 1873. In El Salvador in 1912, the National Guard was created as a rural police force supplemental to the army. Neighbourhood and cantonal patrols of a semi-voluntary nature were also established.

The Indian massacre of 1932 in El Salvador changed many things, among them the mood of the propertied classes in the region. Distrust turned to panic and contempt for the lower classes was institutionalized through the creation of armed forces – for example, the Civil Guard – with clearly paramilitary duties. The Civil Guard and other groups that functioned without interruption were the antecedents of ORDEN (the acronym means "order"), created in 1960 to keep watch over the peasants from within their own territories.[3]

Guatemala has a long tradition of Indian genocide; the Indian is not dealt with fairly, but is treated in a manner reminiscent of the dawn of the industrial society. Martin Luther's biblical wrath against idleness demanded that it be so.[4] The punishment of vagrancy has often served as an occasion to employ violence against, and arbitrary abuse of, the peasants. In 1934 all landowners and their employees were authorized to bear arms and shoot "anyone found stealing on another's property".[5] Méndez Montenegro revived this murderous practice in 1967.

A central aspect of this panorama relates to the way in which the government, in fulfilling its function of maintaining order, was propelled by the landholders' nightmarish fear of the peasantry. The following pages contain brief references to the paramilitary experience in El Salvador, Guatemala and Nicaragua. In fact the counter-insurgency tactics that the state employs today are the outgrowth of the long experience of horror and violence perpetrated against the rural population under the pretext of combating vagrancy since the last part of the nineteenth century – or of the exaggerated repression against the defenders of communal lands, or of punishment in connection with control of clandestine production of liquor and tobacco (in defence of the state monopoly), or of levying taxes, or military recruitment, etc. In the decades that preceded the real emergence of the guerrillas, military forces were not the only ones in charge of maintaining order and keeping watch over peasant unrest. There was also a paramilitary network operating under various names that grew threateningly and without restriction.

The doctrine of "national security" only served to reinforce the tradition of state violence, although the government defined it in such a way as to mean technical and political modernization, to broaden their justification of the menacing military police force which the state had been assembling. Technological and ideological innovation aside, the plain truth is that the state forces exercised their duties of maintaining order while catering to the private interests that even today participate in financing and enforcing order.

Since the beginning of the cold war, the doctrine of national security has been popularized, emphasizing the imminence of an undeclared war that would be fought in the universities, factories, neighbourhoods, and city streets, etc., while society was technically at peace. To confront this threat, that is, to stage an "internal defence", the goals of *development* (to eliminate the causes of unrest) and of *coercion* (to eliminate the impending danger of civil disorder) were established. The positivist inspiration for order with progress was translated into a new language, and in a time of crisis, the goals of development and of nation-building were postponed indefinitely while resources and technical assistance were dedicated to the creation of paramilitary forces, counter-intelligence and terrorism.

In the mid 1950s, the Central American countries had already

signed the Mutual Defense Assistance Agreement that established
a virtual monopoly over weapons sales for the USA. Such was
also the case of the InterAmerican Defense Treaty that tied the
commitment to national defence to eventual Soviet aggression. The
installation of material structures of the counter-revolution with a
clearly preventive character occurred at the beginning of the 1970s.

In Guatemala this was facilitated by the multiple effects of Jacobo
Arbenz's fall from power in 1954 and the defeat of a people's
movement that was becoming more and more radical. For example,
72 hours after the entry of Castillo Armas into Guatemala as
part of a CIA conspiracy,[6] the Committee for Defense Against
Communism was founded and easily recovered more than 600 000
documents with complete lists of members of political parties, labour
unions and organizations of the Arbenz period. Everyone was
surprised by the committee's efficiency and order and by its arbitrary
and bloody use of the information. Based on this information there
was compiled the first "black list" of 70 000 citizens many of whom
became victims of the ensuing repression.[7] Today it is common
knowledge that this material was compiled by special agents from
the USA. The security and intelligence system had been organized
earlier in Guatemala and at the beginning of the 1960s, years before
the first guerrilla outbreaks, the entire system was practically
modernized.

The *coup d'état* of March 1963 against President Ydigoras, that
was in fact an act of veto against constitutional power, was a clear
indication of openly political action by the Armed Forces and was
the first example in Guatemala's history of a Bonapartist institutional
takeover calling itself "a government by the armed forces". According
to Adams,[8] this was a preventive operation – in fact, the first step
in the huge forthcoming operation of counter-insurgency.[9]

El Salvador experienced similar developments at about the same
time. On the occasion of the widespread civil strikes against General
Lemus's military regime in 1961, the US Embassy alarmedly
reported an outbreak of civil disorder in the city of San Salvador.
From this time on, the establishment of a security system was
superimposed on the army – an effective intelligence system with
national operational capacity.

Through the then-existent ICA (later named AID), the Defense
Department and the CIA created training programmes for technical
assistance, and supplied equipment for the police forces in Central
American countries. Assistance for friendly governments at that
time emphasized the modernization of police functions over military
functions which meant that the armies of those countries, having

been away from the war fronts for more than 100 years (except for a brief interruption during the Honduras–El Salvador conflict) forgot their historic pretext of defending national sovereignty and, under foreign counsel, made internal security their mission. The doctrine of national security, with its technical counter-insurgency component, made it easier for the military to add a new dimension to its role in society. Traditional guarantor of internal order, the military had an exaggerated perception of internal danger in the face of obvious social malaise that had not been resolved in the post-war years. Counter-insurgency endowed the army with an amply supplied modern war arsenal, facilitated the "discovery" of an internal enemy and created an awareness of new responsibilities.

At various times in the 1960s the Central American governments requested the USA to prepare contingency plans in the event of outbreaks of civil disorder. The response went far beyond training in tactics to control strikers and street riots. The USA rapidly established large-scale cooperation by supplying equipment suitable for war operations.[10]

It is necessary to point out that *paramilitary* is defined as *a special type of action* and is not defined by the nature of its organization, which is always military. Its internal structure, commands and codes are the same as those of the army, but its actions are "unconventional", though not necessarily secret. Such forces have the advantage of being an organization with a grassroots component, allowing the incorporation of the military into society. This approach confuses the public and private spheres and projects the state to the pinnacle in a system of domination that is deeply rooted in society, especially in the countryside. One must not forget that the paramilitary in Central America has always had a peasant base. This is the origin of the feared *jueces de mesta* (cattlemen judges) in Nicaragua that from the time of Zelaya (1889) exercised powers of espionage, arraignment and arrest within their small rural sphere. The initial character of the struggle against Somoza prevented him from redefining the role of this traditional paramilitary structure.

The "military commissioners" in Guatemala also originated from the liberal revolution during the 1870s. Until 1960, they were typically military reserve officers appointed in each municipality, village or rural estate whose chief function was to facilitate the forced recruitment of soldiers and occasionally to give information to their bosses who were local officials.[11] After the military uprising on 13 November 1960, the army took measures to ensure that more information was forthcoming from the countryside. The innovation, Adams indicates, was to convert the commissioner system from a simple tool of local control to a widespread active spy network.[12] With the rise of the doctrine of counter-insurgency in that decade the number of commissioners and their helpers increased considerably, becoming more like a police and counter-intelligence agency. After the military *coup d'état* in 1963 the paramilitary network in the countryside was complete, having been equipped with weaponry and a nationwide system of communications.[13]

Although organized later, the Salvadoran army's system of control was without a doubt more efficient, involving the creation of a military structure that served multiple support purposes. The National Democratic Organization (whose acronym ORDEN translates as "order") was an immense network of irregular forces whose function was to collect information for the army's intelligence service, to serve as a force for conducting "shady" counter-insurgency operations, and to provide the social base for local military recruitment. After 1967, it went public and served as an electoral support base for the National Reconciliation Party (PCN)[14] that won every election in the country from 1962 until the young officers' coup of 1979.

ORDEN was an organization of peasants which created its base by recruiting middle peasants and agricultural labourers, who were responsible for the bloody repression of their own social-class brethren. To give an idea of the magnitude of the development of this irregular force created by the state under army control, in 1967 it succeeded in mobilizing 100 000 people.[15] With the election of General Fidel Sánchez its hierarchy became more obvious – the president became the commander-in-chief of ORDEN. The peasant revolution in El Salvador was confronted with violence from ORDEN members backed by the National Guard, the police force, and the army – iron bands through which the people's organization was filtered. The first civil–military junta in 1979 "dissolved" ORDEN making it into a civil defence organization.

In Guatemala as well as in El Salvador, the counter-revolutionary structure was complete after 1965 when all the military forces, various types of paramilitary forces, customs, immigration and treasury police, and other related services were joined together in one central intelligence system. In El Salvador, this was the National Security Agency (its acronym ANSESAL): a 1983 report indicates that one in every fifty Salvadorans was an ANSESAL informant.[16] Its hierarchy was composed of high-ranking military officials directly responsible to the president. "It functions as the brain of a vast security network that reaches into each town and neighborhood of the country, supplies information and gives orders to the death squads."[17] In Guatemala a similar structure named the Centre for Regional Communications was organized and functioned under various names from 1966, the last year of Peralta Azurdia's military government. This is a modern complex system of communication among all police forces, military quarters and local army commandos that is also headed by the president's office.[18]

Insurgency was already defined by the Joint Chiefs of Staff of the US Armed Forces in 1958 as "the illegal opposition against a government, that can range from passive resistance, illegal strikes, public demonstrations to open guerrilla operations".[19] Using these criteria, various paramilitary groups were formed, the most extreme of which – the death squads – first took responsibility for selective political crimes, then later resorted to open indiscriminate terrorism against the masses. The last three years of General Lucas's government in Guatemala (1978–82), the years of General Romero's government and the first and second juntas in El Salvador (1977–81) were periods during which government terrorist tactics multiplied. Hundreds of members of political groups, labour unions and students' groups were assassinated or disappeared. It was also during this time that the armed struggle increased to the point of open warfare.

References to Nicaragua so far in this chapter have been minor because of the way in which the government reacted to (or anticipated) social unrest and because the people's armed struggle was of a different nature. The Somoza regime prolonged its exercise of power far longer than expected in the midst of a critical situation. The Somozas perceived power as hereditary and exercised power as a family matter. The National Guard was not a national army, in spite of the later efforts of its creator – the USA. Originally, the USA called Nicaragua's national guard a "constabulary" which means "an armed body that functions as a police force", but the modernization of the National Guard was intense. Between 1950 and 1979, 5673 officials underwent military training on foreign soil,[20] representing 37 per cent of all Central American military so trained. A modern system of security and counter-intelligence was formed and there was a special brigade dedicated to the counter-insurgency struggle, the Infantry Basic Training School, directed by Anastasio Somoza III.

Because of the origins of the Somoza dictatorship and of the praetorian duties of the National Guard, the phenomenon that has been analysed in reference to the other countries did not appear in Nicaragua. Counter-insurgency did not contribute to the moderniza- tion of a repressive state system and although it did reinforce the tradition of repression, it did not give the National Guard the political possibilities that it afforded other countries. Their bonds and loyalties to the Somoza group prevented it.

Democracy: A Circular Transition?

A retrospective view of this whole period suggests that the phenomenon of counter-insurgency, military modernization, the quickening of civil discontent, government terrorism,[21] and war, created a change in the structure of the political regimes in Guatemala and in El Salvador. At the beginning of the 1960s political regimes appeared whose characterization, based on classifications in use at the time, seem contradictory. Military governments that resulted from *coups d'état* reworked the same legal constitutional institutions using different language and played at alternating the office of the presidency through elections. The "government by the armed forces" headed by Colonel Peralta in Guatemala was followed by a phase from 1966 to 1982 during which four presidents were chosen in four electoral processes. In El Salvador, after successive *coups d'état* and after an intense period of intramilitary crisis (1960–2) four presidents were elected in a perioid of sixteen years – 1962 to 1979.

How does one assess military governments elected through an electoral game limited by its ideological options and predetermined by high-level army decisions? Depending upon one's ideological viewpoint, these political regimes were classified either as counter-revolutionary dictatorships or as the potential pre-democratic cocoon containing all the attributes of the age of representative government.

The mass sectors grew at an uneven rate in their organizational capacities and it was not until the 1970s that they were able to establish mass movements seeking to reclaim lost rights, which later gave rise to, or were linked to, the revolutionary struggle. As indicated before, the crisis deepens when civil discontent transcends the limits of this political system that never intended democracy for subordinate groups.

The Central American bourgeoisie experienced important growth because it benefited directly from economic expansion without precedent in the 1960s, because it solidified itself politically through powerful trade associations, and because it associated itself with foreign capital. The so-called "private sector" became an unpredict-able ally of the military but with no possibility of seeking and organizing public support. Its anti-democratic tendencies came to be accented during the crisis of the 1980s.

These regimes can be defined by what they lack – true political pluralism and truly competitive elections. On many occasions fraud was a handy mechanism available to resolve the difficulties caused by choice. This happened in three strategic electoral events; opportunities to introduce democracy were miserably wasted. In 1972 in El Salvador, Duarte, a Christian Democrat with a broad-based political alliance won the elections but the National Reconciliation Party put Colonel Molina in power through a scandalous voting fraud; in 1973 Anastasio Somoza II established himself as the sole candidate after the earthquake in Managua; in 1974 in Guatemala a candidate from a coalition headed by the Christian Democrats won the elections but lost the vote count to General Laugerud. These three opportunities for the initiation of democratic transition that arose in the moment of gestation of the crisis were lost.

The electoral process becomes a meaningless ritual because it is not the occasion of a real confrontation but only the ratification of a pre-planned outcome. There are opportunities to organize and freedom to participate only for the centre-to-right-wing parties. In Central American electoral history, a civil candidate from the opposition party has never won when a military candidate has also participated in the elections. There is no tolerance when it comes to the presidency.

These were not one-party regimes: the loyal opposition parties won important positions such as the governorship of capital cities, the most important elections next to the presidency. But competition and freedom are minimized not only in the vertical hierarchical sense, but also horizontally in which democracy is almost an urban attribute: violence and abuses increase in the most isolated rural zones. The political arena of competition is reduced to a monotonic pluralism. State control over who participates and how, smothers ideological and policy debate on platforms and ideology and dulls the joy of democratic participation.

The superiority of a well-armed, centralized organization that is built on discipline and hierarchies that are implicitly accepted provides the army with a clear advantage over political parties and social class organizations and especially over the poorly organized masses. But the military's dealings with such forces are handled differentially. These politico–military regimes always have the collaboration of some of the most important bourgeois factions so that they do not have to depend upon popular support, or to resort to support from coalition parties. On the contrary, there is a constant move to depoliticize public life and an intense repressive effort to demobilize the people. The trade union, student, and peasant movements are savagely repressed.

Without doubt, these are authoritarian regimes that have resolved the problem of legitimacy by the route of previous selection of candidates (from higher up) and electoral sanction of such decisions (from below). They have solved the problem of succession by changing the government cast of characters every four years in Guatemala and every five years in El Salvador.

This political structure that justified itself as part of the initial democratic experience – as a transition – did not satisfy anyone with the implicit farce of elections because they provide no competition. The political climate was increasingly marked by state terrorism. The state functioned as a political Janus: deploying extreme violence against the public sectors and at the same time convoking elections at set intervals. A chastened citizenry vacillated between being repressed for political organizing and the obligation of organizing to get out the vote. In Central America voting is mandatory except for illiterate women.

The lives of these "store front democracies" (*democracias de fachada*)[22] were brief and bloody. During their sixteen years of existence in Guatemala and El Salvador they further aggravated the polarization that the political crisis had precipitated, pushed the masses toward armed struggle and proved themselves incapable of administering the economic crisis. Exalting violence as a mechanism of control, they created further disorder within society. This experience will not be seen as the beginning of a democratic tradition in Guatemala, El Salvador, and Nicaragua. It did not help to modernize political life or create a climate of tolerance. During the last years of this experience of "stunted democracy" the people's armed criticism became established in this region.

The development of the revolutionary struggle has elements peculiar to each of the countries under analysis. It is not possible within the framework of the chapter to explore the most relevant of these local developments. In Nicaragua's experience, it is enough to say that the fight against Somoza acquired a national character only after the general strike of January and February 1978 and that the crisis was resolved in July 1979,[23] when the masses, led by the Sandinista National Liberation Front (FSLN) successfully combined different methods of mobilization and forced the dictator to resign his position. Somoza's fall was much more than the defeat of a government clique. The magnitude of the changes produced by the triumph of armed masses even with a programme of conventional reform was accentuated in Nicaragua's case becasue Somoza's flight revealed the weakness of the bourgeoisie. The political change became a social revolution because of the force of circumstance.[24] The defeat of the political regime meant the erosion of the state because of the total disintegration of the National Guard, the flight of the governing cohort, the absence of a similar force to replace it, and above all the existence of a many-faceted mobilized populace.

In El Salvador the political crisis of the sixteen years of "store front" democracy occurred as the result of an internal fracture in the army on 15 October 1979, at the same time in which the organization and actions of the masses had reached a dimension unknown until that time. The military coup against the president, General Romero, opened the way for the first civil–military junta that represented the sum of contrasting forces within Salvadoran society. At that time representatives of the People's Forum, of the businessmen and the two factions of the army consented to sharing power. Between the first and fourth juntas, the crisis became more profound because of the popular revolutionary movement's increasing capacity for mobilization and because of the nature of the reforms that satisfied neither of the two groups into which society had become polarized. During fourteen months of junta rule, the government drifted toward Christian Democracy with an ever-growing US presence in the country. The Farabundo Martí National Liberation Front (FMLN) launched its final offensive in January 1981 without success, but extended the territory under its control.

In Guatemala the collapse was precipitated in a less dramatic way and with controlled effects, but without a doubt also provoked by the upswing of the organization of the masses and of guerrilla warfare. If in El Salvador, the peak of these demonstrations was reached during the marches of 22 January and 24 March 1980 (the latter at the funeral of Archbishop Romero), in Guatemala it occurred with the Ixtahuacan miners' march which reached Guatemala City in November 1977 and the "red carnation" incident at the burial of the two student-leaders in August that year. The revolutionary struggle spread throughout the whole north-west part of the country between 1978 and 1980. Finally the internal crisis occurred with a military coup against the president, General Romeo Lucas in March 1982 and later against General Ríos Montt in August 1983.[25]

In El Salvador as well as in Guatemala, the period between the internal military crisis referred to earlier and the convocation of elections was a bloody interval during which there was an attempt to reconstruct the government cohort and military strategy radically. As a result of these efforts, the Guatemalan army crowned its struggle against the Indian peasantry in the north-west with success, destroying 400 villages, murdering more than 14000 people and instigating the movement of more than 50000 peasants to Mexico.

In summary, war and crisis are signs of the times in Central American life. Nothing could be more unfavourable for an attempted transition to democracy. Crisis and war mutually reinforce their combined effects of disorder, poverty and violence. Regional experience shows that in a social climate of this nature (polarization, terrorism, hate and intolerance) authoritarian values of forced discipline, compulsive order and appointed hierarchies tend to become intensified. However, at the mid-point of the 1980s there are civil governments in all of Central America that have resulted from electoral processes in which parties and candidates have confronted each other in formal competition. In Guatemala, El Salvador and Honduras civil candidates from the opposition parties won.

What has happened in Central America, particularly in Nicaragua, Guatemala and El Salvador? The economic crisis has reinforced underlying tendencies in the existing economic structure, resulting in an absolute and relative increase in the number of poor people, reinforcing a decline in real salaries through growing inflation, and severely limiting people's access to services because of the fiscal crisis. In a word, the scope of poverty has expanded both horizontally and vertically, especially among the peasantry and the salaried middle class. National differences are important even when countries share similar patterns of economic crisis. The political crisis that arose because of the active participation of the masses led to the collapse of military regimes in the three countries, and at about the same time. It is well-known that counter-insurgency politics – which shaped a special type of political regime – and democratic politics – still seeking to be established – are contradictory and irreconcilable doctrines. The first established a pathological definition of contenders, within a definition of politics which does not involve the free play of the opposition in a civil electoral framework. It is also both tragic and hypocritical that US foreign policy that fosters war in Nicaragua and directs it from El Salvador has included in its repertoire of activities for Central America – for the first time – the theme of democracy.

All except the ingenuous know that elections are not synonymous with democracy. In Central America, given the counter-insurgent character of the political regimes in Guatemala and in El Salvador, the construction of democracy does not necessarily happen through a foreign-inspired electoral process. Notwithstanding, the elections that have taken place in these two countries (two of the Constitutional Assembly and two presidential) have been technically free except for a few fundamental reservations: the vote has been allowed to "float" in the sense that the voter appears to be free within the limited framework of options. At the same time the climate of terror (with its statistics of deaths and disappearances) has remained unchanged as the fundamental method of maintaining order. Since voting is obligatory, electoral participation increases and as abstention decreases the transition to democracy appears to gain strength.

The victories of the Christian Democrats in El Salvador and Guatemala hold different meanings even though in both cases they express a break from what Baloyra calls "reactionary despotism".[26] A desperate attempt is being made to reconstruct the political centre lost during the years of the "store front" democracies. Counter-insurgency also punished the alternative bourgeois reformers and those bearers of a platform of gradual transition to democracy.

The existence of a prolonged unstable peoples' war in El Salvador with a rebel army – a unique case in history – that operates and supplies itself within its own territory,[27] as well as the existence of an army that has been reconstructed twice through massive US assistance, makes Duarte's civil government precarious. The internal factors that influence control are not as powerful as those that originate with the US government.

The coming-to-power of Christian Democracy in Guatemala also had distinctive characteristics. Its electoral triumph appears to be backed by masses who have experienced voting as a democratic opportunity to show contempt for military government. It also occurs in conjunction with severe losses for the revolutionary struggle, with an army that has had long counter-revolutionary experience. It is possible that this may be the Central American way of initiating a transition to democracy. Both experiences reveal in their own ways the weakness of civil power: the day-to-day ambiguity of the civil government that is reduced to public administration, and the realm of power decisions over which the army retains control.

In Nicaragua there were elections on 4 November 1984. Because of the way in which elections were called, they can be considered in two ways: as one more mechanism of political legitimization, an event common to liberal democracy; or as an act of consultation and establishment of popular support. Elections are always pre-planned mechanisms with foreseeable results. To ensure the continuity of an electoral democracy, the continual creation of rival factions is necessary – as long as their actions are pre-planned and foreseeable.[28] In other words, they are not competing for control of the state, but for control of the government. It is not even the structure of the political regime that is at stake but something less fundamental. In any case, political pluralism (that is, the existence of various discrepant but similar alternatives) in Western democracy occurs with the limits of continuity of the system. In the context of such profound change as occurred in Nicaragua, elections were more popular consultation than they were a recourse to legitimization. Revolutionary processes only resort to this process after the fact, because the roots of their legality are derived elsewhere.

Nicaragua's history during this century records numerous elections. Only two of these have been technically free. The one that took place on 4 November 1928 (colloquially described as *supervigiladas* – extremely closely supervised) was handled according to the Dodds Act and was won by the Liberal Party. The other one, that occurred on 4 November 1984, was won by the Sandinista National Liberation Front and confirmed the real existence of considerable popular support.[29] Fifty-six years passed between the two. Then, as well as now, Nicaragua is in a state of war, provoked by US intervention. So war between Nicaraguans remains the constant in Nicaragua's history.

The brutal harassment to which the Sandinista regime is subjected makes prognosis for democracy difficult. Under present conditions, it is impossible to exercise democratic liberties. Transition to democracy is also incompatible with a state of civil war in El Salvador, and, in Guatemala, with government control in the hands of those who cater to counter-insurgency interests and who employ counter-revolutionary practices. At any rate, elections and war are by definition incompatible. Electoral democracy is based upon the triumph of a numerical majority and it works as a competitive game to strengthen consensus, while war is the trimph of force. It is based upon a zero-sum game that presupposes the death of the opponent.

The people are called upon to correct the errors of the past. In search of a new society and in the organization and development of the armed struggle, democratic objectives have been overwhelmed by revolutionary necessities, as if they referred to contradictory ends and means. It seems that old political convictions were forgotten in the midst of this terrible, bloody conflict. But it is important to reiterate time and again that the struggle for a more just social order is tied to the daily practice of and the permanent conviction in support of political democracy. Without peace there can be no truly civilized life in Central America.

Notes

1. Jan L. Flora and Edelberto Torres-Rivas, "Sociology of Developing Societies: Historical Bases of Insurgency in Central America," in this volume.
2. Legislative decree passed on 9 February 1884, cited by David Browning, *El Salvador: Landscape and Society* (Oxford: Clarendon Press, 1971) p. 331.
3. This theme is developed in Michael McClintock, *The American Connection*, vol. I, pp. 117–34. It is also cited in R. Armstrong and J. Shenk, *El Salvador: The Face of Revolution*, J. Pearce, *Promised Land; Transition* (The University of North Carolina Press, 1982); Arnon Hadar, *The United States and El Salvador: Political and Military Involvement* (Berkeley: US–ES Research and Information Center, 1981); Liisa North, *Bitter Grounds, Roots of Revolt in El Salvador*; T. S. Montgomery, *Revolution in El Salvador: Origins and Revolution*.
4. Cited in F. Engels, *Las Guerras Campesinas en Alemania* (Mexico: Colección Grijalbo, 1971) p. 62.
5. Code of laws, Revista de la Facultad de Ciencias Jurídicas y Sociales, p. 207.
6. Two exceptional books that have utilized unclassified documents are: R. H. Immerman, *The CIA in Guatemala: The Foreign Policy of Intervention*, p. 192; and Stephen Schlesinger and Stephen Kinzer, *Bitter Fruit: The Untold Story of the American Coup in Guatemala*.
7. David Atlee Phillips, *The Night Watch* London: Robert Hale, 1978, p. 52, cited in Michael McClintock, *The American Connection*, vol. II, p. 33. "Black list" information appears in Norman La Charite "Political Violence in Guatemala 1963–67," American University, Ph.D. dissertation, p. 80.
8. Richard Adams, *Crucifixion by Power*, pp. 242 and 244.
9. In 1959 the US Congress modified the Mutual Security Act to intensify internal security in Latin American countries. Later plans for the organization of national armies were drawn up in view of the danger of subversion. See W. Barber and N. Ronning, *Internal Security and Military Power: Counterinsurgency and Civic Action in Latin America* (Columbus: Ohio State University Press, 1966) p. 45.
10. M. T. Klare and C. Arnson, *Supplying Repression, US Support for Authoritarian Regimes Abroad* (Washington: IPS, 1981); A. Hadar, The United States and El Salvador; M. McClintock *The American Connection: El Salvador*, vol. I and *Guatemala*, vol. II.
11. For information about the military structure of the commissioners group, see G. A. Moore, "Social and Ritual Change in a Guatemalan Town," Ph.D. Dissertation, Columbia University, 1966, p. 359, cited by R. Adams, *Crucifixion by Power*, p. 271.
12. Ibid.
13. John Durston, "Power Structure in a Rural Region of Guatemala,"

thesis, University of Texas, 1966, p. 46. Jerry Weaver, "Aportes", no. 12, April 1969, pp. 143–5.

14. McClintock, *The American Connection*, vol. I, p. 206.
15. For an exhaustive analysis of the peasant rebellion, see Jenny Pearce, *Promised Land*, p. 90. Also see Carlos Rafael Cabarrus, *Génesis de una Revolución*, (Mexico: ed. de la Casa Chata, 1983), that analyses the political transformation of the peasantry through a theological vision involved with the problems of the poor.
16. McClintock, vol. I, p. 219, specifically note number 282.
17. Ibid.
18. The details of the workings and organization of this network are related by CIA agent, Alfred W. Nauricki, who held the position of Regional Communications Advisor for Public Safety for all of Central America and the Caribbean in End of Tour Report, cited by M. McClintock, *The American Connection*, vol. II, p. 73.
19. Dictionary of US Military Terms for Joint Usage, Joint Chief of Staff, Washington, DC, 1 February 1962, p. 114, cited by McClintock, *The American Connection*, vol. I, pp. 30 and 78.
20. Michael Klare and Cynthia Arnson, *Supplying Repression*, p. 48, Table VII.
21. George A. López, "A Scheme for the Analysis of Government as Terrorist", in Michael Stohl and George López (eds), *The State as Terrorist*, (Westport, Connecticut: Greenwood Press, 1983) p. 38.
22. The term is used by Mario Solórzano in an article by the same name soon to be published by FLACSO, 1986.
23. There are many works that analyze this period. The most complete analysis without a doubt is found in Lucrecia Lozano, *De Sandino al Triunfo de la Revolución*. López, Núñez, Chamorro and Seres, *La Caída de Somocismo y la Lucha Sandinista* (EDUCA, San José, 1979), and Equipo Interdisciplinario Latinoamericano, *Teoría y Práctica Revolucionarias en Nicaragua* (Ed. Contemporaneas, Nicaragua, 1983).
24. Theda Skocpol, *State and Social Revolutions* (Cambridge University Press, 1979), p. 33.
25. Analysis of the military crisis is found in G. Aguilera, *Las Fases del Conflicto Bélico en Guatemala* and in *La Guerra Oculta: La Estrategia Contrainsurgente en Guatemala* (both ICADIS, Costa Rica, 1985 and 1986, respectively). Also of interest is the series of analyses found in *Polémica* magazine, no. 7–8, 12, 14–15 and 19; SAIS Papers, *Report on Guatemala*, no. 7, (SAIS–The John Hopkins University, Washington, 1985). James Painter, "Guatemala in Civilian Garb", *The Third World Quarterly* (July 1986) p. 818.
26. E. Baloyra, *El Salvador*, chap. V. An important article by the same author is "Negotiating War in El Salvador: The Politics of Endgame", *Journal of Interamerican Studies and World Affairs*, vol. 7, p. 123.
27. R. Benítez Manaut, *La Teoría Militar y La Guerra Civil en El Salvador*, thesis, Facultad de Ciencias Políticas y Sociales, UNAM, Mexico, 1986. This work is the most complete analysis of classical theory of war

applied imaginatively to the Salvadoran situation. It has been used frequently in this work.

28. Giovanni Sartori, *Theorie de la Democracie* (Paris: Armand Colin, 1973) p. 107. Also important in reference to this theme is C. B. McPherson, *La Democracia Liberal y su Época* (Madrid, Alianza Editorial, 1982).

29. "Report of the LASA Delegation to Observe the Nicaraguan General Elections of Nov. 4, 1984", LASA Forum vol. XV, no. 4, Winter 1985, pp. 9–44. W. A. Cornelius, "The 1984 Nicaraguan Elections Revisited", *LASA Forum*, vol. XVI, no. 4, Winter, 1986, pp. 22–9. By the same author: "The Nicaraguan Elections of 1984: A Reassessment of Its Significance", in P. Drake and E. Silva (eds), *Elections and Democratization in Latin America 1980–85*, (San Diego; Center for US–Mexican Studies, University of California, 1986) p. 61, and in the same book, J. Booth, "Election amid War and Revolution", pp. 37–59.

Bibliography

Abbreviations

EDUCA   Editorial Universitaria Centroamericana
LAP   Latin American Perspectives
NACLA   Nacla Report on the Empire

Central America

Anderson, Thomas P. 1981. *The War of the Dispossessed: Honduras and El Salvador, 1969.* Lincoln and London: University of Nebraska Press.
———. 1982. *Politics in Central America: Guatemala, El Salvador, Honduras, and Nicaragua.* New York: Praeger Publishers.
Berryman, Phillip. 1984. *The Religious Roots of Rebellion: Christians in Central American Revolutions.* Maryknoll, NY: Orbis Books.
Camacho, Daniel and Menjivar, Rafael, eds. 1985. *Movimientos Populares en Centroamerica.* San José: EDUCA.
Central America: The Process of Revolution. 1983. *LAP* 10, 1 (Winter).
Central America: The Strongmen are Shaking. 1980. *LAP* 7, 2 and 3 (Spring and Summer).
Coleman, Kenneth M. and Herring, George C. 1985. *The Central American Crisis: Sources of Conflict and the Failure of US Policy.* Wilmington, Delaware: Scholarly Resources, Inc.
del Cid V., Rafael. 1977. "Las clases sociales y su dinámica en el agro hondureño", *Estudios Sociales Centroamericanos* no. 18: 119–55.
Diskin, Martin, ed. 1983. *Trouble in Our Backyard: Central America and the United States in the Eighties.* New York: Pantheon Books.
Domínguez, Enrique and Huntington, Deborah. 1984. "The Salvation Brokers: Conservative Evangelicals in Central America". *NACLA* 17, 1 (January–February) pp. 2–36.
Ellis, Frank. 1978. *The Banana Export Activity in Central America in 1947–1976: A Case Study of Plantation Exports by Vertically-Integrated Transnational Corporations.* D. Phil. thesis, Sussex University.
Feinberg, Richard E. 1982. *Central America: International Dimensions of the Crisis.* New York and London: Holmes & Meier Publishers, Inc.
—— and Bagley, Bruce M. 1986. *Development Postponed: The Political Economy*

of Central America in the 1980s. Boulder and London: Westview Press.

Grabendorff, Wolf; Krumwiede, Heinrich-W. and Todt, Jorg. 1984. *Political Change in Central America: Internal and External Dimensions*. Boulder and London: Westview Press.

Helms, Mary W. 1975. *Middle America: a Cultural History of Heartland and Frontiers*. Englewood Cliffs, New Jersey: Prentice Hall.

LaFeber, Walter. 1984. *Inevitable Revolutions: The United States in Central America*. New York and London: W. W. Norton & Co. Miles, Sara. 1986. "The Real War: Low Intensity Conflict in Central America". *NACLA* 20, 2 (April–May): pp. 17–48.

Pearce, Jenny. 1981. *Under the Eagle: US Intervention in Central America and the Caribbean*. London: Latin America Bureau (published in the USA by South End Press, Boston).

Torres-Rivas, Edelberto. 1975. "La integración económica centroamericana: resumen crítico", *Cuadernos de Ciencias Sociales*. San José, Costa Rica: CSUCA.

— —. 1981. *Interpretación Del Desarrollo Social Centroamericano*. San José: EDUCA. (Originally published in Chile by Editorial PLA, 1971.)

— —. 1983. *Crisis Del Poder En Centroamerica*. San José: EDUCA.

— — and Pinto, Julio César. 1983. *Problemas En La Formación Del Estado Nacional En Centroamerica*. San José: Instituto Centroamericano de Administración Pública.

US President. 1984. *Report of the National Bipartisan Commission on Central America:* Washington, DC: US Government Printing Office. Weeks, John. 1985. *The Economies of Central America*. New York and London: Holmes & Meier.

Willems, Emilio. 1975. *Latin American Culture: An Anthropological Synthesis*. New York: Harper & Row.

Woodward, Ralph Lee. 1985. *Central America: A Nation Divided*, 2nd edn New York and London: Oxford University Press.

Wortman, Miles L. 1982. *Government and Society in Central America, 1680–1840*. New York: Columbia University Press.

Costa Rica

Bartlett, Peggy F. 1982. *Agricultural Choice and Change: Decision Making in a Costa Rican Community*. New Brunswick, New Jersey: Rutgers University Press.

Bell, John Patrick. 1971. *Crisis in Costa Rica: The 1948 Revolution*. Austin and London: University of Texas Press for the Institute of Latin America Studies.

Churnside, Roger. 1985. *Formación De La Fuerza Laboral Costarricense* San José: Editorial Costa Rica.

Rovira Mas, Jorge. 1982. *Estado Y Política Económica En Costa Rica 1948–1970*. San José: Editorial Porvenir, SA.

Rowles, James P. 1985. *Law and Agrarian Reform in Costa Rica*. Boulder, Colorado: Westview Press.

Seligson, Mitchell A. 1980. *Peasants of Costa Rica and the Development of Agrarian Capitalism*. Madison; University of Wisconsin Press.

Sojo, Ana. 1984. *Estado Empresario y Lucha Política en Costa Rica*. San José: EDUCA.

El Salvador

Anderson, Thomas P. 1971. *Matanza: El Salvador's Communist Revolt of 1932*. University of Nebraska Press.

Armstrong, Robert and Shenk, Janet. 1982. *El Savador: The Face of Revolution*. Boston: South End Press.

Burns, E. Bradford. 1975. "The Modernization of Underdevelopment: El Salvador, 1858–1931", *The Journal of Developing Areas*, 18, 3 (April) p. 298.

Clements, Charles. 1984. *Witness to War: An American Doctor in El Salvador*. New York: Bantam Books.

Erdozaín, Plácido. 1981. *Archbishop Romero*. New York: Orbis Books.

McClintock, Michael. 1985. *The American Connection: State Terror and Popular Resistance in El Salvador*, vol. 1. London: Zed Books.

Montgomery, Tommie Sue. 1982. *Revolution in El Salvador: Origins and Evolution*. Boulder, Colorado: Westview Press.

North, Liisa. 1981. *Bitter Grounds: Roots of Revolt in El Salvador*. Toronto: Between the Lines.

Pearce, Jenny. 1986. *Promised Land: Peasant Rebellion in Chalatenango El Salvador*. London: Latin America Bureau.

Simon, Laurence R.; Stephens, James C. Jr. and Diskin, Martin. 1981. "El Salvador Land Reform 1980–1981." Boston: OXFAM America, Inc.

Thomson, Marilyn. 1986. *Women in El Salvador: The Price of Freedom*. Philadelphia: Institute for the Study of Human Issues.

Webre, Stephen. 1979. *José Napoleón Duarte and the Christian Democratic Party in Salvadoran Politics 1960–1972*. Baton Rouge, Louisiana: Louisiana State University Press.

White, Alistair. 1973. *El Salvador*. New York: Praeger Publishers.

Guatemala

Adams, Richard. 1970. *Crucifixion by Power*. Austin: University of Texas Press.

Black, George, with Jamail, Milton and Chinchilla, Norma Stoltz. 1983. "Garrison Guatemala", *NACLA* 17, 1 (January–February) pp. 2–35.

— —. 1983. "Guatemala – the War is Not Over", *NACLA* 17, 2 (March–April) pp. 2–38.

Brintnall, Douglas E. 1979. *Revolt Against the Dead: the Modernization of a Mayan Community in the Highlands of Guatemala.* New York: Gordon & Breach.

Cambranes, J. C. 1985. *Coffee and Peasants in Guatemala.* South Woodstock, Vermont: CIRMA: Plumsock Mesoamerican Studies.

Civil Patrols in Guatemala: An Americas Watch Report. 1986. New York: The Americas Watch Committee.

Davis, Shelton H. and Hodson, Julie. 1982. "Witness to Political Violence in Guatemala: the Suppression of a Rural Development Movement". Boston, OXFAM America, Inc.

Fried, Jonathan L.; Gettleman, Marvin E.; Levenson, Deborah T. and Peckenham, Nancy. 1983. *Guatemala in Rebellion: Unfinished History.* New York: Grove Press.

Handy, Jim. 1984. *Gift of the Devil; A History of Guatemala.* Boston: South End Press.

Immerman, R. H. 1982. *The CIA in Guatemala: The Foreign Policy of Intervention.* Austin: University of Texas Press.

Krueger, Chris and Enge, Kjell. 1985. *Security and Development Conditions in the Guatemalan Highlands.* Washington: Office on Latin America.

McClintock, Michael. 1985. *The American Connection: State Terror and Popular Resistance in Guatemala,* vol. II. London: Zed Books.

Payeras, Mario. 1983. *Days of the Jungle: The Testimony of a Guatemalan Guerrillero 1972–1976.* New York: Monthly Review Press.

Report on Guatemala: Findings of the Study Group on United States–Guatemalan Relations. 1985. Boulder, Colorado: Westview Press, Inc.

Schlesinger, Stephen and Kinzer, Stephen. 1983. *Bitter Fruit: The Untold Story of the American Coup in Guatemala.* New York: Anchor Books.

We Continue Forever: Sorrow and Strength of Guatemalan Women. 1983. New York: Women's International Resource Exchange.

Wolf, Eric. 1959. *Sons of the Shaking Earth.* Chicago: The University of Chicago Press.

Honduras

Boyer, Jefferson C. 1982. *Agrarian Capitalism and Peasant Praxis in Southern Honduras.* Ph.D. thesis, University of North Carolina at Chapel Hill.

Danby, Colin, and Swedberg, Richard. 1984. *Honduras: Bibliography and Research Guide.* Massachusetts: Central American Information Office.

Durham, William H. 1979. *Scarcity and Survival in Central America: Ecological Origins of the Soccer War.* Stanford, California: Stanford University Press.

Honduras: Realidad Nacional y Crisis Regional. 1986. Honduras; Centro de Documentación de Honduras.

Lapper, Richard and Painter, James. 1985. *Honduras: State for Sale.* London: Latin America Bureau.

MacCameroin, Robert. 1983. *Bananas, Labor, and Politics in Honduras: 1954–1963.* New York: Maxwell School of Citizenship and Public Affairs.

Meza, Victor. 1982. *Honduras: la Evolución de la Crisis.* Tegucigalpa: Editorial Universitaria.

Morris, James A. 1984. *Honduras: Caudillo Politics and Military Rulers.* Boulder, Colorado: Westview Press.

Parsons, Kenneth. 1978. "Key Policy Issues for the Reconstruction and Development of Honduran Agriculture Through Agrarian Reform." Madison, Wisconsin: Land Tenure Center, 22pp.

Peckenham, Nancy, and Street, Annie. 1985. *Honduras: Portrait of a Captive Nation.* New York: Praeger.

Posas, Mario. 1979. "Política estatal y estructura agraria en Honduras (1950–1978)", *Estudios Sociales Centroamericanos* 8, 24 (September–December) pp. 37–116.

— —. 1981. *El movimiento campesino hondureño: una perspectiva general.* Tegucigalpa: Editorial Guaymuras.

— —. 1981. *Luchas Del Movimiento Obrero Hondureño.* San José: Editorial Universitaria.

— —, and del Cid, Rafael. 1983. *La Construcción Del Sector Público y Del Estado Nacional En Honduras 1876–1979.* San José: EDUCA.

Rosenberg, Mark B. 1983. "The Current Situation in Honduras and US Policy", *Two Approaches to an Understanding of US–Honduran Relations.* Miami: Latin America and Caribbean Center, Florida International University.

Santos de Morais, Clodomir. 1975. *Estrategia de desarrollo y reforma agraria: la opción hondureña.* Tegucigalpa.

Salomon, Leticia. 1982. *Militarismo y reformismo en Honduras.* Tegucigalpa: Editorial Guaymuras.

Tendler, Judith. 1976. *Inter-Country Evaluation of Small Farmer Organizations: AID and Small Farmer Organizations – Lessons from the Honduras Experience.* Washington, D.C.: Agency for International Development (Latin American Bureau, Office of Development Programs).

Volk, Steven. 1981. "Honduras: On the Border of War", *NACLA Report on the Americas* 15, 6 (November–December) pp. 2–37.

White, Robert. 1977. *Structural Factors in Rural Development: The Church and the Peasant in Honduras.* Ph.D. dissertation, Cornell University (reprinted in two volumes by University Microfilms International, Ann Arbor, Michigan).

Nicaragua

Armstrong, Robert; Edelman, Marc and Matthews, Robert. 1985. "Sandinista Foreign Policy: Strategies for Survival", *NACLA* 19, 3 (May–June) pp. 13–56.

Black, George. 1981. *Triumph of the People: The Sandinista Revolution in Nicaragua*. London: Zed Press.

Booth, John A. 1982. *The End and the Beginning: The Nicaraguan Revolution*. Boulder, Colorado: Westview Press.

Cabezas, Omar. 1985. *Fire From the Mountain*. New York: Crown Publishers, Inc.

Colburn, Forrest D. 1986. *Post-Revolutionary Nicaragua: State, Class, and the Dilemmas of Agrarian Policy*. Berkeley, California: University of California Press.

Collins, Joseph. 1985. *Nicaragua: What Difference Could A Revolution Make?* 2nd edn. San Francisco, California: Institute for Food and Development Policy.

Crawley, Eduardo. 1979. *Dictators Never Die: A Portrait of Nicaragua and the Somozas*. New York: St Martin's Press.

Diederich, Bernard. 1982. *Somoza and the Legacy of US Involvement in Central America*. London: Junction Books.

Donahue, John M. 1986. *The Nicaraguan Revolution in Health*. South Hadley, Bergin & Garvey, Publishers, Inc.

Harris, Richard L. 1986. "Economic Development and Revolutionary Transformation in Nicaragua", *Latin American Issues*. 3 Meadeville, Pennsylvania: Allegheny College.

Human Rights in Nicaragua 1986. 1987. An Americas Watch Report. New York: The Americas Watch Committee

Lozano, Lucrecia. 1985. *De Sandino al Triunfo de la Revolución*. Mexico: Siglo XXI Editores.

Matthews, Robert. 1986. "Sowing Dragon's Teeth: The US War Against Nicaragua", *NACLA* 20, 4 (July–August) pp. 13–40.

Miller, Valerie. 1985. *Between Struggle and Hope: The Nicaraguan Literacy Crusade*. Boulder, Colorado: Westview Press.

Nicaragua: Democracy and Revolution. 1985. *LAP* 12, 2 (Spring).

On the Revolutionary Transformation of Nicaragua. 1987. *LAP* 14, 1 (Winter 1987).

O'Shaughnessy, Laura Nuzzi, and Serra, Luís H. 1986. "The Church and Revolution in Nicaragua". Ohio: Ohio University Center for International Studies.

Randall, Margaret, 1981. *Sandino's Daughters: Testimonies of Nicaraguan Women in Struggle*. Toronto, Canada: New Star Books.

— —, 1983. *Christians in the Nicaraguan Revolution*. Toronto, Canada: New Star Books.

Report of the Latin American Studies Association Delegation to Observe the Nicaraguan General Elections. 1984. Austin, Texas: Latin American Studies Association.

Selser, Gregorio. 1981. *Sandino*. New York: Monthly Review Press. *The Miskitos in Nicaragua*. 1984. An Americas Watch Report. New York: The Americas Watch Committee.

Torres, Rosa Maria. 1985. *Nicaragua: Revolución Popular, Educación Popular*. Mexico: Editorial Linea.

Vilas, Carlos M. 1986. *The Sandinista Revolution: National Liberation and Social*

Transformation in Central America. New York; Monthly Review Press.
Walker, Thomas W. 1986. *Nicaragua: The Land of Sandino.* Boulder, Colorado:
Westview Press.

Periodicals

Boletin Informativo Honduras

Centro de Documentación de Honduras (CEDOH)
PO Box 1882
Tegucigalpa, Honduras

Central America Writers Bulletin: an Annotated Bibliography of Articles on Central America and *Central America News Pak*

Central America Resource Center
PO Box 2327
Austin 78768

Envío (Spanish and English)

Instituto Histórico Centroamericano
Apartado A–194
Managua, Nicaragua

Central American Historical Institute
Intercultural Center
Georgetown University
Washington, DC 20057

Estudios Centroamericanos

Apartado 668
Universidad Centroamericana José Simeon Canas
San Salvador, El Salvador

Estudios Sociales Centroamericanos

Apartado 37
Cuidad Universitaria
San José, Costa Rica

Honduras Update

Honduras Information Center
One Summer St
Somerville, Massachusetts 02143

Inforpress Centroamericana and *Central America Report*
9a Calle "A" 3–56, Zona 1
Guatemala, Guatemala

LADOC, Bimonthly Publication of Latin American Documentation
Apartado 5594
Lima 100, Peru

Latin American Perspectives
Sage Publications, Inc.
275 South Beverly Drive
Beverly Hills, California 90212

Latin American Research Review
Latin American Institute
801 Yale NE
University of New Mexico
Albuquerque, New Mexico 87131

Latin American Weekly Report and *Latin American Regional Report/Mexico and Central America*
Latin American Newsletters, Ltd.
61 Old Street
London EC1V 9HX England

Mesoamerica
Institute for Central American Studies
Apt 300
1002 San José
Costa Rica

NACLA Report in the Americas
North American Congress on Latin America, Inc.
151 West 19th St, 9th Fl.
New York, New York 10011

Nicaraguan Perspectives
Nicaragua Information Center
PO Box 1004
Berkeley, California 94701

Pensamiento Propio

Apartado Postal no. C–16
Managua, Nicaragua

Polemica

Instituto Centroamericano de Documentación e Investigaciones Sociales
(ICADIS)
Apartado Postal 174
Sabanilla, Montes de Oca 2070
San José, Costa Rica

Index

Nicaragua – *continued*
74, 172, 185, 187 (*see also*
Nicaragua—rural proletariat,
agrarian reform, land reform,
and reform, ATC); petty
bourgeoisie 169, 187, 192n47
(*see also* Nicaragua—middle
class); popular classes 167–9,
171 (*see also* Nicaragua—social
class); popular participation
38, 43, 167, 170, 173, 202, 203,
205, 206 (*see also* Nicaragua—
guerrilla movement,
insurrection, working class);
primitive communism 168;
private sector 182, 184, 185
(*see also* Nicaragua—export
agriculture, industrial
bourgeoisie, capitalism,
economic policy); proletariat
see Nicaragua—working class;
public sector *see* Nicaragua—
state sector; repression 38,
175, 191n35, 200 (*see also*
Nicaragua—National Guard;
US—Central American policy,
security assistance);
revolutionary transition 165,
168, 169, 172, 178, 181, 182,
183, 188, 206; rural
proletariat 43, 167–72, 175,
181, 184–7, 192n44 (*see also*
Nicaragua—ATC, agrarian
reform, peasantry, land
invasions, economic policy,
social class): landless 168, 170;
Sandinista Defense
Committees (CDS) 169, 173;
Sandinista Front for National
Liberation (FSLN) 43, 84, 87,
88, 98, 154, 167, 171, 175–7,
180, 185–7, 200, 206 (*see also*
Nicaragua—national
sovereignty); Sandinista
Workers' Federation (CST)
43, 175–7, 179, 188 (*see also*
Nicaragua—labour unions,

working class, popular
participation); seasonal
employment 166, 168, 181,
184; social class 76, 165–77,
183, 186–8n1; social security
174, 175, 180, 181; social
services 169, 174, 179 (*see also*
Nicaragua—payment in kind,
wages, economic policy):
"social wage" 179;
socialism 165, 176,
182, 183, 187;
speculation 177 (*see also*
Nicaragua—economic policy,
black market, informal sector);
state of economic emergency
176 (*see also* Nicaragua—
economic crisis, economic
policy); state sector 171, 182,
185 (*see also* People's Property
Area); subsidies 170, 180 (*see
also* Nicaragua—economic
policy); transisthmian canal
xv, 13, 42 (*see also* Bryan–
Chamorro treaty, Zelaya,
Nicaragua—national
sovereignty); unemployment
177, 178, 183, 188 (*see also*
Nicaragua—working class);
urban informal sector *see*
Nicaragua—informal sector;
urbanization 166–70; US
military intervention xv, xvi,
13, 42 (*see also* US—Marines);
wages 77, 169, 171, 175–86,
188 (*see also* Nicaragua—
economic policy, working class,
payment in kind, social
services); white collar fraction
169; women's labour force
participation 184; working
class 43, 77, 165–8, 170, 171,
175–7, 179–88: worker
discpline 171, 177, 180, 182,
188; worker participation 167,
168, 175; productivity 175,
177, 181–3, 191n35